Environment and Sustainability for ESG and SDGs

Toshiyuki Sueyoshi · Mika Goto

Environment and Sustainability for ESG and SDGs

Measured by Data Envelopment Analysis in Time Horizon

Springer

Toshiyuki Sueyoshi
The Center for Economic Research, School of Shandong Development
Shandong University
Jinan, China

School of Environment and Society
Institute of Science Tokyo
Tokyo, Japan

Mika Goto
School of Environment and Society
Institute of Science Tokyo
Tokyo, Japan

ISBN 978-981-96-2466-9 ISBN 978-981-96-2464-5 (eBook)
https://doi.org/10.1007/978-981-96-2464-5

This Springer imprint is published by the registered company Springer Nature Singapore Pte Ltd.
The registered company address is: 152 Beach Road, #21-01/04 Gateway East, Singapore 189721, Singapore

Preface

The global warming and climate change are recently referred to as "burning" by UN (United Nations). The climate change is now a very serious problem all over the world. The climate issue, due to the global warming (burning), implies an increase in average global temperature on air, sea and land on the earth. Natural events and economic activities, including industrial developments and business activities, contribute to an increase in average global temperature. Such a climate change is primarily caused by an increase in greenhouse gases such as carbon dioxide (CO_2). We are now facing various environmental difficulties, such as how to handle nuclear and industrial wastes, all of which are by-products of our economic and industrial developments.

To combat the environmental issues in the world, we discuss the importance of both economic success and environmental protection to attain a high level of global sustainability. Our underlying philosophy in this book is that we need to develop a methodology to measure a progress of eco-technology innovations and its related managerial challenges. These developments support a progress for reducing an amount of greenhouse gas emissions. In challenging toward such a research direction, we propose a new use of "Data Envelopment Analysis (DEA)", as a holistic approach, to assess various aspects on sustainability development. In this sense, the new methodology proposed in this book is referred to as "DEA Environmental Assessment (DEA-EA)".

This book has three major concerns to be addressed here. First, this book is an extension of the previous book:

Sueyoshi, T. Goto, M. (2018) Environmental Assessment on Energy and Sustainability by Data Envelopment Analysis, John Wily & Sons, NJ, USA and West Sussex, UK.

Second, this book considers "a time horizon" because the environmental sustainability needs the measurement over time. This book is not interested in a standard use of DEA-based performance assessment, rather discussing the new approach for assessing a level of sustainability development.

Finally, we need to describe the following important concerns to discuss the proposed approach for environmental assessment:

(a) *Undesirable outputs*: Standard DEA incorporates multiple components of an input vector and those of an output vector in measuring the performance of many entities in private and public sectors. The previous DEA approaches have only the two types of production factors. Meanwhile, this study additionally incorporates multiple components of an undesirable (bad) output vector, so having the three types of production factors (inputs, desirable outputs and undesirable outputs).
(b) *Disposability concepts*: The proposed environmental assessment utilizes two disposability concepts. One of the two concepts is "natural disposability". This concept implies that operational performance is the first priority and environmental performance is the second priority. The other disposability concept is "managerial disposability". The concept has an opposite priority (the first priority: environmental and the second priority: operational) on operational and environmental performance measures. Here, the disposability concepts indicate the elimination of inefficiency sources by measuring distances from two efficiency frontiers.
(c) *Input direction*: The proposed environmental assessment incorporates an analytical capability to increase or to decrease the components of an input vector. The input increase implies an "economic or corporate growth" under managerial disposability, while the input decrease implies these "utilization enhancement" under natural disposability. The input increase has an upper limit on an efficiency frontier on undesirable outputs, while the input decrease has a lower limit in an efficiency frontier on desirable outputs. The analytical feature is very different from the standard DEA that incorporates only a decrease of an input vector along with an increase of a desirable output vector. The direction of an input vector becomes important in examining and developing social or corporate sustainability.
(d) *Environmental, social and governance (ESG) and sustainable development goals (SDGs)*: This book attempts to convey a message to our audience that we can fully utilize DEA-EA over time to discuss ESG and SDGs in which all entities need to satisfy for their investments for sustainability enhancement. We consider two unique features of DEA-EA as a methodology. One of the two features is that the method incorporates undesirable outputs into its production process. The other feature is that it measures ESG investment opportunities by which we allocate funds and resources to enhance the level of sustainability. Moreover, DEA-EA incorporates a time horizon so that ESG leads to an aspect of SDGs, so indicating the sustainability enhancement in a long run.

Here, we clearly acknowledge that it is very difficult for us to solve all issues related to ESG and SDGs. Rather, using DEA-EA, we attempt to discuss that DEA-EA may deal with part of various issues regarding ESG and SDGs. The UN has discussed these sustainability concepts due to a drastically change of our climates.

It is true that the UN has a long qualitative discussion on the importance and implementation of ESG and SDGs, but not these "quantitative" explorations. Such a policy limitation is a major problem of UN. This book attempts to open up a new quantitative approach to handle ESG and SDGs although our effort is not perfect and very limited in the research scopes.

In the end of this preface, we must mention that comments and constructive criticisms should be directed to the first author of this book. After spending 2.5 years, he can finally escape from a painful effort to produce this book. Currently, he will be able to reply to positive inquiries, not negative ones, about the book. All errors and mistakes related to this book belong to only his responsibility.

Chiba, Japan Toshiyuki Sueyoshi
Tokyo, Japan Mika Goto

Acknowledgements The SDU Chair Professorship (SDU: Shandong University, No.: 12120082463247) has financially supported this research in China. The Japan Society for the Promotion of Science (JSPS) has also funded this research under a Grant-in-Aid for Scientific Research (KAKENHI) 20KK0106 and 24H00441. We really appreciate for the three financial supports on this research project. We cannot complete this book without these supports.

Contents

Chapter 1
General Description

Abstract This chapter describes the structure of this book. Our description focuses upon the analytical structure and practicality of Data Envelopment Analysis-Environment Assessment (DEA-EA) which may be useful for sustainability enhancement. The method, originated from the unique features of DEA, has extended it by incorporating undesirable (bad) outputs, such as CO_2 emission, into its analytical feature. The DEA does not require any specification of a functional form, rather measuring weights (multipliers) among inputs and outputs (desirable and undesirable). Thus, the method is non-parametric and distribution-free estimation. In this book, we discuss the strengths and drawbacks of DEA-EA from the perspective of several sustainability developments. Our discussion in this book will focus upon energy and its consumption, along with environmental issues, because many energy issues are closely related to various environmental difficulties. Acknowledging the importance of combatting various energy and environmental issues, we pay attention to the importance of not only pollution reduction but all economic prosperity for sustainability enhancement. Many individuals, including policy makers, business leaders and researchers, believe that we must solve various environmental issues even with or without capital accumulation. It may be true that an effective resource allocation from capital accumulation is indeed important for future eco-technology developments as found in the concept of Environmental, Social and Governance (ESG). Our underlying philosophy discussed in this book is that we need to develop green innovation and managerial challenges to support technology progress and economic policy to reduce an amount of Greenhouse Gas (GHG) emission so that we can reduce a temperature change and other climate changes in the world. However, we know that our research scope is, however, limited within the boundary of quantitative methods such as DEA, DEA-EA and other statistical approaches. Toward such a research direction, this book methodologically discusses three concerns. First, we propose the use of DEA-EA, as an approach, to assess various aspects concerning ESG developments along with Sustainable Development Goals (SDGs). Second, we consider the formulations of DEA-EA in a time horizon because many environment difficulties occur over time. Finally, we are not interested in a standard use of DEA for conventional performance assessment, rather discussing a new use for sustainability developments which are closely related to ESG and SDGs.

T. Sueyoshi and M. Goto, *Environment and Sustainability for ESG and SDGs*,
https://doi.org/10.1007/978-981-96-2464-5_1

Keywords Sustainability · DEA · Environmental Assessment (EA) · ESG · SDGs

1.1 Introduction

It is important for readers to keep it in their minds that the purpose and interest of this book are not the standard formulations and their applications of Data Envelopment Analysis (DEA) for conventional efficiency measurement and performance analysis. Rather, this book is interested in a new use of DEA-EA (Environmental Assessment) which we can apply for environment assessment and sustainability development in a time horizon.

As mentioned in the preface, this book is an extension of the previous work:

Sueyoshi, T. and Goto, M. (2018), Environmental Assessment on Energy and Sustainability by Data Envelopment Analysis, John Wily & Sons.

The methodology used in this book is "DEA-EA", starting from DEA, but the analytical structure and applicability are different from the original ones. Besides the environment concerns and sustainability enhancements, this book often pays attention to "energy sectors" whose data sets are usually structured in a time horizon and they are closely related to various industrial pollutions and climate changes. The energy industries (e.g., electricity) provide us with fundamental sources for our lives and industrial developments. The energy sectors need qualitative analysis for their industrial policy developments.

Environmental issues to be discussed in this book become major difficulties in making our modern societies. These social issues ask us a challenging question such as how to challenge the "global warming (boiling) and climate change" in the world. Acknowledging our research limit on many environment concerns, we will attempt to investigate the global issues from not only methodology but also business, policy and economics perspectives so that we can methodologically assist our technology developments to avoid serious consequences such as heat waves, droughts, floods, food crisis as well as other damages to human, social and economic systems.

At the end of this chapter, we need to note that this book will challenge the climate changes by fully utilizing the analytical capabilities of DEA-EA. This book will attempt to change a profit (efficiency)-driven business logic, previously incorporated in a standard use of DEA, in such a manner that it can fit within a global trend for the development of our sustainability. The remainder of this chapter has the following structure: Sect. 1.2 discusses the structure of this chapter. Section 1.3 summarizes abbreviations used in this book.

1.2 Structure

This section describes the structure of this book. We specify abbreviations used in this book. Each chapter has a list of nomenclatures to enhance the readability on mathematical formulations.

First of all, this book needs to mention that DEA is not a perfect methodology, rather being a useful approximation approach, for performance assessment on many organizations in public and private sectors. It may be true that DEA has historically made academic contributions by providing corporate leaders and policy makers with empirical guidelines to assist their decision makings. See Sueyoshi et al. (2017) and Sueyoshi and Goto (2018) that have summarized previous 693 DEA contributions applied to energy and sustainability enhancement.

To extend the previous contributions further, this book will summarize many new uses of DEA-EA by which we may discuss various environmental issues and sustainability developments. In such a research direction, this book contains the following eight chapters:

Chapter 1 (General Description): This starting chapter provides a general description on the research need for DEA-EA that may analytically express concepts regarding modern business and policy issues such as Environmental, Social and Governance (ESG) and Sustainable Development Goals (SDGs). It is indeed true that ESG and SDGs are very popular among us including corporate leaders and policy makers. However, so far, none clearly specifies these concepts and discusses how these concepts can reduce various environment pollutions.

Chapter 2 (ESG and SDGs): Chap. 2 discusses what ESG and SDGs are along with a rationale on why we need to conduct research on them by using DEA-EA. The chapter will serve as a conceptual base for preparing various DEA-EA approaches and its related mathematical formulations. To proceed our description, we start from a description on sustainable development of economy and environment, often referred to as the practice of ESG principles. Many countries around the world continue to promote their coordination among them, in accordance with the ESG principles and funding along with SDGs over time.

Chapter 3 (Standard DEA Models from Energy Economics): This chapter discusses "DEA standard models" which we measure the level of Operational Efficiency *(OE)*. These models, starting from the Debreu-Farrell type of efficiency measurement, have many formulations for performance analysis. The standard models are usually classified into two categories under variable or constant Returns to Scale (RTS). See Sueyoshi and Goto (2018). We attempt to provide analytical linkages between the two groups of radial models from the perspective of their analytical and practical differences in "energy economics". This chapter also discusses the theoretical development from radial to non-radial measurement. It is necessary for a DEA user(s) to examine which model(s) should be used for their research works on ESG and SDGs. The examination provides a guideline for the model selection from perspectives of sustainability measurement, as well. The retreat on the standard models will provide us with a start to understand the practicality of DEA-EA in Energy Economics.

Chapter 4 (Three DEA-EA Models for ESG): This chapter theoretically compares the three (radial, non-radial and intermediate) approaches for DEA-EA which examine the level of simultaneous achievement on economic prosperity and environmental protection. The proposed DEA-EA measures the sustainability performance of many entities which utilize inputs to produce not only desirable outputs (e.g., electricity) but also undesirable outputs (e.g., CO_2). The two types of outputs produce a newly combined measure, referred to as "unified efficiency", in the chapter. The DEA-EA was methodologically classified into radial or non-radial category in the previous studies (e.g., Sueyoshi & Goto, 2018). This chapter newly proposes an "intermediate" model, analytically locating between the radial and non-radial measures as the third alternative. We discuss their analytical features by theoretically comparing among the three alternatives.

Chapter 5 (Intermediate Model for SDGs): This chapter discusses a use of DEA-EA in a time horizon. Chapter 4 discusses the three approaches but it does not discuss them in time series. The data sets on Environmental Assessment (EA) are often structured by time series. In applying DEA to environment assessment, we need to examine efficiency changes among different periods because they indicate a technology progress on desirable and/or undesirable outputs. We focus upon the intermediate approach among the three alternatives as an example. An important feature of the proposed EA approach is that it incorporates the concept of "natural disposability" and "managerial disposability" into the computational framework of DEA-EA. The chapter extends the two disposability concepts into a time horizon. In this chapter, we utilize "window efficiency analysis" and "window index analysis" to measure the change of efficiency frontiers over time. As an illustrative example, we apply the proposed three approaches (e.g., cross-sectional, window efficiency and window index) to a data set on US coal-fired power plants during 1995–2007. We find that the coal-fired power plants have gradually paid attention to environmental protections under US CAA (Clean Air Act).

Chapter 6 (Malmquist Index Measurement for SDGs): This chapter reorganizes the use of DEA-EA by a Malmquist index approach that decomposes the frontier shift into its subcomponents. The index measurement incorporates a framework of Malmquist index decomposition into DEA-EA to examine the frontier shift among multiple periods from its subcomponents. The frontier shift indicates a technology progress and/or managerial improvement during observed periods so that we can measure the change of SDGs. The computational process of Chap. 5 discusses a change of unified efficiency measures. Meanwhile, Chap. 6 measures the change of frontier shifts and their subcomponents, not efficiency changes, over different periods.

Chapter 7 (Club Convergence): This chapter discusses the club convergence of unified efficiency and unified index measures. For preparing business strategy and/or policy development to combat the climate change, we must consider a change of sustainable development and green growth economy in a long run convergence. The approach assesses a technological progress over time, focusing upon CO_2 reduction.

We apply the proposed approach to 37 nations in Organization for Economic Co-operation and Development (OECD) countries during 1995–2014, examine performance differences among country groups and discuss these convergences over the observed periods. The proposed empirical study has compared between OECD and Non-OECD nations. It concludes that the former group has outperformed the latter group in their environmental measures and club convergence. We expect that the OECD provides member nations with an opportunity to improve the status of green technology for economic growth. However, we cannot find their overall convergence. Rather, they are classified into two member groups. The results indicate that there are uneven economic and technological progresses between the two (higher and lower) groups. The disparity implies that OECD membership does not guarantee uniform green growth and sustainable development among member countries. We also find that "renewable and nuclear" energy shares are important in maintaining the higher group within OECD because both are zero-carbon emission energy sources.

Chapter 8 (A Time Lag Model for Technology Shift): This chapter pays attention to a time lag in DEA applications. While there is a plethora of literature on technology transfer (or spin-out), there is a paucity of studies on technology transition. We try to fill a gap in the existing literature by assessing the technology transition from small firms to a large governmental organization such as the US Department of Defense (DoD). This chapter proposes a new use of DEA with a time lag which incorporates two-stage production processes. The new DEA model compares the technology transfer within the US military industry with that of environmental protection. This chapter considers their formulations and implications in terms of technology transfer. Implications obtained in this chapter on the military application have important implications for international sustainability development of Chap. 7.

1.3 Remarks

Many researchers and practitioners often believe that DEA is a very useful method in the manner that they can apply it to any real data sets. They often think that all computer codes are available for DEA operation. Unfortunately, such believes are not correct. It is indeed true that DEA is useful as an evaluation method whose practicality is documented in many previous applications. However, the truth is by far different from the reality. All formulations included in DEA computer codes are old and useless, being unable to use for the measurement of ESG and SDGs. It is better for DEA users to develop mathematical programming (mainly liner programming) codes used for DEA and DEA-EA in this book.

The following concerns are important to keep in our minds before applying DEA and DEA-EA to many performance assessments (Sueyoshi & Goto, 2018) on ESG and SDGs:

(a) *Data independence*: All DMUs operate independently each other so that their input and desirable output vectors have independence among them. Thus, no rank deficit occurs in a data domain for inputs and outputs (desirable and undesirable).
(b) *Zero and negative values in data*: DEA usually treats a data set under the condition that it does not contain any zero and negative values. Such negative data (e.g., negative growth and net income) can be easily found in many financial and economic analyses. In such a case, DEA needs an additional treatment to handle the zero in a data set. The previous book (i.e., Sueyoshi & Goto, 2018) has discussed how to deal with zero or negative values in a data set within the computational framework of DEA environmental assessment. It is often observed that a data set, containing zero in the observations, does not disturb DEA computation. However, such a case is just a lucky accident. Most of DEA users, in particular students, misunderstand the computational limitation of DEA and DEA-EA.
(c) *Selection of inputs and desirable outputs*: It is not easy for us to determine which inputs and outputs are used for DEA-based performance analysis. The best strategy is to ask a decision maker(s) (e.g., a director in a public agency and a president in a firm) about the selection of their production factors. However, the selection of production factors depends upon his subjective decision of a user(s). The subjectivity may not reflect the operational reality of DUMs in many cases. Furthermore, we need to keep it in our minds that the less input and generally produces the better performance in standard DEA. An opposite case is found in the output selection. The selection logic on inputs and outputs works on only a conventional use of DEA, but it does not work on DEA-EA because outputs are classified into two categories (i.e., desirable and undesirable outputs). Many users believe that they can treat both inputs and undesirable outputs in the same manner, but such a treatment is not correct from a theoretical perspective. See Sueyoshi et al. (2017) and Sueyoshi and Goto (2018).
(d) *Outlier in data*: If an outlier exists in a data examined by DEA, it is often necessary to drop it from the data because the outlier may destroy the shape of an efficiency frontier so that DEA does not produce a reliable result. We may drop the outlier in such a case, but the decision is subjective.
(e) *Data adjustment*: When an input(s) or an output(s) is much larger than the remaining other production factors, the large factor often dominates the whole DEA computational process. In the case, it is necessary for us to adjust the data set by dividing all observations on each production factor by the factor average. Such a data adjustment produces more reliable DEA results than the one without the adjustment. Here, it is important to note that the data adjustment should not produce any zero and negative values because DEA cannot directly handle them. Therefore, the normalization [i.e., (an observed value - an average value)/ a standard deviation], widely used in statistics and econometrics, does not work because it produces zero and negative values. See Sueyoshi and Goto (2018) for a description on the property of "unit invariance". The property indicates that the unit of inputs and outputs should not influence an efficiency measure. The

property originates from a mathematical rationale on DEA results. However, our suggestion is due to a computational perspective on a computer code.

Abbreviations used in this book are summarized as follows:

Abbreviations

AEc	Allocative and Scale Efficiency
AEv	Allocative Efficiency
AI	Artificial Intelligence
AM	Additive Model
AR	Assurance Region
AR5	Fifth Assessment Report
°C	Celsius (Degree)
CAA	Clean Air Act
CDTR	Constant Damages to Return
CE	Cost Efficiency
CEc	Cost and Scale Efficiency under CRTS
CEv	Cost Efficiency under VRTS
CH_4	Methane
CO_2	Carbon Dioxide
COVID-19	Coronavirus Disease 2019
COP	Conference of the Parties
COP 27	The 27th COP
CR	Cone Ratio
CRTD	Constant Returns to Damage
CRTS	Constant Returns to Scale
CSCs	Complementary Slackness Conditions
CSE	Cost-based Scale Efficiency
CSM	Cross-Sectional and Managerial Disposability
CSN	Cross-Sectional and Natural Disposability
CSR	Corporate Social Responsibility
DDTR	Decreasing Damages to Return
DEA	Data Envelopment Analysis
DEA-EA	Data Envelopment Analysis-Environmental Assessment
DC	Desirable Congestion
DMU	Decision Making Unit
DoC	Degree of Change
DoD	Department of Defense
DSDG	Division for Sustainable Development Goals
DTR	Damages to Return
DTS	Damages to Scale

EA	Environmental Assessment
EBA	European Banking Authority
EC	Eigenvector Centrality
EE	Energy Efficiency
EF	Efficiency Frontier
EI	Energy Intensity
EPA	Environmental Protection Agency
ESG	Environmental, Social and Governance
EU	European Union
EV	Electrical Vehicle
ES	East South
EW	East West
FERC	Federal Energy Regulatory Commission
FIT	Feed-in Tariff
GDP	Gross Domestic Product
GHG	Greenhouse Gas
GSDR	Global Sustainable Development Report
GW	Gigawatt
I	Intermediate
IAEA	International Atomic Energy Agency
IPCC	Intergovernmental Panel on Climate Change
IDTR	Increasing Damages to Return, Inter-temporal Unified Efficiency
IM	Malmquist Index under Managerial disposability with no cross-over
IMC	Malmquist Index under Managerial disposability with Crossover
IN	Malmquist Index under Natural disposability without Crossover
INC	Malmquist Index under Natural disposability with Crossover
IPCC	Intergovernmental Panel on Climate Change
IRTS	Increasing Returns to Scale
IT	Information Technology
IUEN	Inter-temporal Unified Efficiency under Natural disposability
IUEM	Inter-temporal Unified Efficiency under Managerial disposability
IUIN	Inter-temporal Unified Index under Natural disposability
IUIM	Inter-temporal Unified Index under Managerial disposability
I-WAM	Unified Indexes: Window Analysis and Managerial Disposability
I-WAN	Unified Indexes: Window Analysis and Natural Disposability
KW	Kilowatt
K-W	Kruskal-Wallis
KWh	Kilowatt hour
LNG	Liquefied Natural Gas
M&A	Merger and Acquisition
MCP	Market Clearing Price
MDGs	Millennium Development Goals
MRT	Marginal Rate of Transformation
mmBtu	Million British thermal unit
MWh	Megawatt hour

NATO	North Atlantic Treaty Organization
NE	North-East
NR	Non-Radial
NOx	Nitrogen Oxides
NW	North-West
OE	Operational Efficiency
OE_v	Operational Efficiency under VRTS
OE_c	Operational and Scale Efficiency under CRTS
OECD	Organization for Economic Co-operation and Development
O&M	Operating & Maintenance
PB	Period Block
PEV	Plug-in EV
PoPS	Pollution Possibility Set
Pr&PoPS	Production and Pollution Possibility Set
PrPS	Production Possibility Set
PRI	Principles for Responsible Investment
PSE	Production-based Scale Efficiency
PT	Production Technology
Q.E.D	Quod Erat Demonstrandum
R	Radial
RAM	Range-Adjusted Measure
R&D	Research & Development
RM	Radial Measure
RTD	Returns to Damage
RSU	Rate of Substitution
RTO	Regional Transmission Organization
RTS	Returns to Scale
SBM	Sustainability Business Model
SCI	Science Citation Index
S.D	Standard Deviation
SDGs	Sustainable Development Goals
SE	Scale Efficiency
SEC	Scale Economies
SEM	Scale Efficiency under Managerial Disposability
SEN	Scale Efficiency under Natural Disposability
SCSCs	Strong Complementary Slackness Conditions
SO_2	Sulfur Dioxide
SOCP	Second-Order Cone Programming
SRI	Socially Responsible Investment
SSCI	Social Science Citation Index
s.t.	Subject to
SW	South West
TWh	Terawatt hour
UE	Unified Efficiency
UEM	Unified Efficiency under Managerial Disposability

UEN	Unified Efficiency under Natural Disposability
UIM	Unified Index under Managerial Disposability
UIN	Unified Index under Natural Disposability
UK	United Kingdom
UN	United Nations
UNFCCC	United Nations Framework Convention on Climate Change
UNDESA	United Nations Department of Economic and Social Affairs
UNEP	(United Nations Environment Program)
URS	Unrestricted
US	United States
USA	United States of America
VRTS	Variable Returns to Scale
WAM	Window Analysis and Managerial disposability
WAN	Window Analysis and Natural disposability

References

Sueyoshi, T., & Goto, M. (2018). *Environment Assessment an energy and sustainability by data envelopment analysis*. Wiley.

Sueyoshi, T., Yuan, Y., & Goto, M. (2017). A literature study for DEA applied to energy and environment. *EneRgy Econ., 62*, 104–124.

Chapter 2
Environmental, Social and Governance (ESG) and Sustainable Development Goals (SDGs)

Abstract This chapter discusses a rationale regarding why we need to conduct environmental assessment by Data Envelopment Analysis-Enviromental Assessment (DEA-EA). Our description will serve as a conceptual basis for preparing various DEA and DEA-EA formulations and applications for environmental protection and sustainability enhancement. Such underlying concerns will be analytically explored in the remaining chapters of this book. To precede our discussion, this chapter starts with concepts on sustainable development for economy and environmental protection, often referred to as the practice of Environmental, Social and Governance (ESG) and Sustainable Development Goals (SDGs). The United Nations (UN) has gradually developed these principles. Many countries around the world continue to promote its coordinated developments in accordance with the principles of ESG and SDGs under the UN leadership. This chapter considers that ESG indicates "investment" opportunities at all levels of entities (e.g., counties and firms) and SDGs focus upon 17 sustainability goals, including environment protection, over time. Both are closely related each other in conducting environmental protection and sustainability enhancement. We also consider that both need a long run perspective (so, time series). The use of DEA-EA methodologically serves as an analytical tool to measure the level of ESG and SDGs enhancements. This chapter starts with reviewing what ESG and SDGs practically imply for our current and future life. The review on the two concepts provides us with the methodological importance (along with strengths and drawbacks) of DEA and DEA-EA in applying them for the measurement of global sustainability development.

Keywords ESG · SDGs · Environment · Energy · Sustainability

T. Sueyoshi and M. Goto, *Environment and Sustainability for ESG and SDGs*,
https://doi.org/10.1007/978-981-96-2464-5_2

2.1 Introduction

This chapter starts with a description of ESG[1] and that of SDGs[2]. We will explore them from various perspectives on environmental protection and energy consumption as well as these policy and business implications. The proceeding chapters will describe a methodological linkage between these concepts and DEA-EA so that we can document these economic and social benefits for sustainability measurements.

In discussing ESG and SDGs, we must first describe Intergovernmental Panel on Climate Change (IPCC)[3], which United Nations (UN) has established within its environmental program. The organization has discussed our necessity to reduce the amount of Greenhouse Gas (GHG) emissions, in particular the emission of CO_2, by 40–70% compared with those of 2010 by 2050 in "Climate Change 2014: Synthesis Report". The report has discussed the amount of CO_2 emission at the level that it becomes almost zero or below in 2100 by transforming the current industrial systems to energy-efficient ones. The IPCC has warned that global warming and climate change are destroying our natural and socioeconomic systems with a rapid speed. Consequently, we will face various risks, including heat waves, droughts, floods, food crises as well as damages to human, social and economic systems, on the earth. As an extension of the international agreement, the new IPCC AR5 (Fifth Assessment Report)[4] has claimed that industrial sectors have contributed about 19% of the total energy use and 30% of the total GHG emissions. It may be easily imagined that the identification of better ways to reduce our energy uses and carbon emissions in public and private sectors will be critical in achieving a low-carbon society.

This book will attempt to convey our message that the use of DEA-EA is a practical approach to measure the level of such changes as requested by ESG and SDGs. It may be true that there are other quantitative methods (e.g., statistics and econometrics), not DEA, to measure the level of ESG and SDGs. However, we consider that DEA-EA can serve as a practical (but not the best) non-parametric approach for ESG and SDGs assessment because of its non-parametric nature (e.g., no functional form as requested in statistics and econometrics). Moreover, DEA-EA can incorporate multiple desirable (good) outputs and multiple undesirable (bad) outputs in its computational framework. This chapter will gradually discuss such

---

[1] Environmental, social and corporate governance, also known as ESG is a framework designed to be embedded into an organization's strategy that considers the needs and ways to generate value for all organizational stakeholders (such as employees, customers, suppliers, and financiers). See https://en.wikipedia.org/wiki/Environmental,_social,_and_corporate_governance. See also Sect. 2.2.1 of this chapter.

[2] The 2030 Agenda for Sustainable Development, adopted by all UN members in 2015, created 17 world SDGs. They were created with the aim of peace and prosperity for people and the planet while tackling climate change and working to preserve oceans and forests. The SDGs highlight the connections between the environmental, social and economic aspects of sustainable development. Sustainability is at the center of the SDGs. See https://sdgs.un.org/. See also Sect. 2.2.2 of this chapter.

[3] https://www.ipcc.ch/

[4] https://www.ipcc.ch/assessment-report/ar5.

unique features of DEA-EA as a methodology of sustainability assessment so that we can discuss and measure the level of ESG and SDGs.

The remainder of this chapter has the following structure: Sect. 2.2 describes the historical trend of ESG and SDGs. Section 2.3 discusses the international efforts on ESG and SDGs. Section 2.4 considers possible opportunities for sustainable investment related to ESG and SDGs. Section 2.5 visually summarizes organizational rationales (processes) concerning why and how we may use DEA-EA to enhance the level of ESG and SDGs. Section 2.6 summarizes this chapter.

2.2 ESG and SDGs: Historical Progress

2.2.1 Environmental, Social and Governance (ESG)

Today, with the sustainable development of economy and society, the world faces not only many opportunities but also various challenges for our future such as a global spread of the pandemic (e.g., COVID-19: Coronavirus disease 2019). The COVID-19, originated from China, has widely spread out all over the world[5]. We consider that the pandemic accidentally occurred, not intentionally and not its military purpose to attack other nations. Sueyoshi et al. (2021) have discussed a rationale concerning why COVID-19 has widely spread among industrial nations in the world. They have examined the relationship between their healthcare systems and the number of deaths[6] by applying DEA-EA. This may be considered as a global (S and G) issue of ESG. The Chinese government had not paid serious attention on the initial occurrence of COVID-19. However, we know that there is no nation in the world which can make a perfect policy decision.

Since 2020, there has been accelerating pressure from UN to disclose ESG data, along with SDGs. The term "ESG" was first introduced in a 2004 UN whitepaper[7], "Who Cares Wins". The white paper was a joint initiative of financial institutions at the invitation of UN. During about 20 years, the ESG movement has grown from a corporate social responsibility initiative launched by UN into a global phenomenon. According to the report of the Global Sustainable Investment Alliance (GSIA) in 2021[8], global sustainable investing assets represent more than US$35 trillion in 2020.

[5] See L. O. Gostin and G. K. Gronvall, "the origins of COVID-19 - why it matters (and why it doesn't)" on New England Journal of Medicine. Published June 7, 2023. See also https://www.ncbi.nlm.nih.gov/pmc/articles/PMC9874793/ on the origin of COVID-19.

[6] The accumulated number of deaths was 7,010,681 on April 13, 2024 according to COVID - Coronavirus Statistics - Worldometer (worldometers.info).

[7] https://www.unepfi.org/fileadmin/events/2004/stocks/who_cares_wins_global_compact_2004.pdf.

[8] https://www.gsi-alliance.org.

The concept of ESG is a framework that designs to be incorporated into organization's investment strategy. The concept may generate a financial value for all stakeholders such as employees, customers, suppliers and financiers. For example, a corporate report on ESG may be useful for stakeholders to assess materiality or sustainability-related important risks and opportunities, relevant to an organization. ESG implies that investors need to incorporate it into the evaluation of their corporate values.

Table 2.1 lists the three types of ESG components. First, Environmental (E) aspect is related to a climate change due to many components such as Greenhouse Gas (GHG), biodiversity loss, deforestation, pollution, energy inefficiency and inappropriate water management.

Second, Social (S) aspect is related to employee safety and health, working conditions, diversity, equality, inclusion and conflicts and humanitarian crises that are relevant in risk and return assessments. To respond to the request for global sustainability enhancement, we need to consider not only managerial efforts of a company but also those including a large supply chain connection over the world. In this study, we also include the war in the category. The war is very serious violation of global sustainability and environment protection. The war has been producing a large amount of carbon dioxide (CO_2) emission and various pollutions, so being environmental violations and destroying international ESG agreements[9]. Recently, the war implies that a large military nation (e.g., Russia) demonstrates the violation of all international agreements, international laws and environmental protection efforts so that the nation destroys the worldwide "global sustainability".

Finally, Governance (G) aspect is related to corporate governance such as preventing bribery and corruption, executive compensation, cybersecurity and privacy practices, and management structure. The ESG issues presented here need to be discussed from global and sustainable aspects in our business world. The theme of sustainable and comprehensive development, from investment opportunities, has become the main topic of worldwide concern.

The rule of ESG is a standard and strategy used by investors to evaluate corporate behavior and future financial performance. The Principles for Responsible Investment (PRI), which has been proposed by former UN Secretary-General Kofi Annan in 2006, defines the investment as "a strategy and practice to incorporate ESG factors in investment decisions and active ownership". The ESG factors help us in measuring the sustainability and social impact of business activities (EBA: European Banking Authority, 2020). The EBA states that "the ESG may have a positive or negative impact on the financial performance or solvency of an entity, sovereign or individual" (EBA, 2020). As a value of sustainable and coordinated development that takes into account-economic, environmental, social and governance, the ESG is an investment philosophy that pursues a long-term value growth. It is also a comprehensive, concrete and down-to-earth governance method.

[9] See G. Rannard, "COP27: War causing huge release of climate warming gas, claims Ukraine" Published on 15 November 2022. https://www.bbc.com/news/science-environment-63625693.

Table 2.1 Environmental, social and governance (ESG)

Dimension	Factors
Environmental (E)	GHG emissions, energy consumption and efficiency, air pollutants, water usage and recycling, waste production and management (water, solid, hazardous), impact and dependence on biodiversity, impact and dependence on ecosystems, innovation in environmentally friendly products and services, and climate change
Social (S)	Work force freedom of association, child labor, forced and compulsory labor, workplace health and safety, customer health and safety, discrimination, diversity, equal opportunity, poverty and community impact, supply chain management, training and education, customer privacy, community impacts, military invasion, infectious disease (e.g., COVID-19) and regulation, and power balance
Governance (G)	Codes of conduct and business principles, accountability and responsibility, transparency and disclosure, executive pay, board diversity and structure, bribery and corruption, stakeholder engagement, shareholder rights, performance measurement, generation gap on information technology, and energy mix

Note (a) This table is originally prepared by T-T Li, K. Wang, T. Sueyoshi, D. Wang (2021), ESG: research progress and future prospects. Sustainability, 13, 11,663, 1–28. This study modifies the original table by adding important ESG components and reorganizes the table for our description. The classification belongs to our responsibility. (b) Sustainability is multidimensional concept (E, S and G) which are further separated into many components as exhibited in the table. Such components are important, but we cannot cover all components of ESG. (c) For a component of the society (S), we need to consider an occurrence of "war". A large country may invade a small nation and violate many international agreements and laws. The war decreases the level of global ESG in the world. This chapter cannot handle such a difficulty due to the war occurrence, unfortunately. (d) The successful invasion (war) should be completed within a very short period (e.g., within few days). The military of a large country (e.g., Russia) should be accepted by people of a small country (e.g., Ukraine). If not accepted, such an invasion is useless and is completely a strategic mistake to produce hatred among people in a small country. The war consumes money, resources and international reputation for nothing. It invites high inflation, as well. It increases the death of military and common people, so just indicating "no sustainability" (no EGS) for its future existence. (e) The best military strategy is to obtain "win" without any invasion (war). Any war should be done within international agreements and laws (e.g., no murder of comment people and no rape on women in a small county). The violation decreases the reputation of such an evil nation such as Russia. See Chap. 8 for a description on technology development of the US military industry by the use of DEA with a time lag. (f) Threaten, but no invasion (no war), may be the best strategy. For example, it is very difficult for a large nation (e.g., Russia) to use the tactical nuclear weapon because it invites a counter-nuclear attack, implying the end of the world. "Balance of Power", implying that all nations should have a similar level of military strengths, may be the best strategy for them in the world. All efforts for ESG discussed here will be useless and meaningless with the military invasion (war). An excellent leader is the person who is able to consider his country, sustainability and economy for future. (g) Recent military invasion of Israel to Gaza may indicate no future sustainability of Israel. The invasion will not obtain any international support from the world because of "too much military reaction" to Gaza. It is very clear that the USA has showed its "double standards" on military supports for both Israel and Ukraine. The USA should control Israel on military reaction. That is a major mistake of US international politics.

The ESG concepts, formally proposed in the UN (2004), have actively practiced in Europe, the USA, Japan and other developed countries. A series of the achievements promote the development and maturity of these factors as a whole such as the establishment of an evaluation system and disclosure standards. These factors are constantly building a new trend of sustainable development. Along with the trend, ESG has gradually become a mainstream of business and policy making. The concept of ESG has been widely examined, practiced and popularized in the practical economic field, and it has aroused the interest of scholars from all over the world (EBA, 2021).

At the current moment, there are many research works on ESG research. They have mainly focused upon ESG investment (Daugaard, 2020), the importance of ESG metrics in SRI (Socially Responsible Investment: Widyawati, 2020), the influence of the ESG score on measuring corporate sustainability performance (Drempetic et al., 2020), the origin and significance of the name of ESG in investment (Eccles & Viviers, 2011) and the importance and role of ESG factors in the financial decision-making process (Ziolo et al., 2019). Furthermore, there are literature reviews on the role and performance of corporate governance (G) in ESG (Yoshikawa et al., 2021) and discussions of the relationship between corporate governance and corporate social responsibility (Aluchna, 2019). See also Broken et al. (2014) and Friede et al. (2015) for a literature review on sustainable business.

As specified in Table 2.1, ESG mainly focuses upon the three groups of factors (E, S and G). However, we find that ESG, as an integrated framework and concept among environmental, social and governance factors, displays an interactive relationship between these dimensions. Practically, ESG is an important driving force to trigger the sustainable development in enterprises, and the interactive relationship between these dimensions is also a major concern to which we pay attention. From a research perspective of ESG practice, we need to mention that previous research efforts have not yet developed any practical and commonly used quantitative method at the level that we can apply it to the measurement of ESG enhancement. Therefore, we recommend the use of DEA-EA to analytically measure the level of ESG, focusing upon environmental and energy issues, which are major components of the global sustainability in the world.

Requirement for Quantitative Assessment: Environment protection activities and these related investments are the main concerns of ESG enhancement. Any quantitative assessment, including DEA and DEA-EA, needs to incorporate both desirable (positive) outputs such as the amount of sales and undesirable (negative) outputs such as CO_2 emissions. The ESG assessment needs to incorporate an analytical process to identify "investment" opportunities in the methodological framework of both increasing desirable outputs and decreasing undesirable outputs. See Chap. 4 in which we discuss how to measure the level of ESG by applying a new type of DEA.

2.2.2 *Sustainable Development Goals (SDGs)*

The 2030 Agenda for Sustainable Development was adopted by all UN Member States in 2015. According to UN, the agenda provides a shared blueprint for peace and prosperity for people and the planet for now and the future[10]. There are 17 SDGs, on which UN requests an urgent call for action to all countries.

The short titles of the 17 SDGs are "no poverty" (SDG 1), "zero hunger" (SDG 2), "good health and wellbeing" (SDG 3), "quality education" (SDG 4), "gender equality" (SDG 5), "clean water and sanitation" (SDG 6), "affordable and clean energy" (SDG 7), "decent work and economic growth" (SDG 8), "industry, innovation and infrastructure" (SDG 9), "reduced inequalities" (SDG 10), "sustainable cities and communities" (SDG 11), "responsible consumption and production" (SDG 12), "climate action" (SDG 13), "life below water" (SDG 14), "life on land" (SDG 15), "peace, justice, and strong institutions" (SDG 16) and "partnerships for the goals" (SDG 17).

The SDGs build on decades of work by UN including Department of Economic and Social Affairs. In June 1992, at the Earth Summit in Rio de Janeiro, Brazil[11], more than 178 countries adopted Agenda 21, a comprehensive plan of action to build global partnership for sustainable development to improve human lives and to protect the environment. Member States unanimously adopted the Millennium Declaration at the Millennium Summit in September 2000 at the UN Headquarters. The Summit led to the elaboration of eight Millennium Development Goals (MDGs) to reduce extreme poverty by 2015. See the UN website[12] for the history of SDGs.

The Johannesburg Declaration on Sustainable Development[13] and the Plan of Implementation, adopted at the World Summit on Sustainable Development in South Africa in 2002, reaffirmed the global community's commitments to poverty eradication and the environment. It built on Agenda 21 and the Millennium Declaration by including more emphasis on multilateral partnerships.

At the UN Conference on Sustainable Development in Rio de Janeiro, Brazil, in June 2012, Member States adopted the outcome document "The Future We Want" in which they decided to launch a process to develop a set of SDGs to build upon the Millennium Development Goals (MDGs) and to establish the UN High-level Political Forum on Sustainable Development[14].

In 2013, the General Assembly set up a 30-member Open Working Group to develop a proposal on the SDGs. In January 2015, the General Assembly began a negotiation process on the post-2015 development agenda. The process culminated in the subsequent adoption of the 2030 Agenda for Sustainable Development, along

[10] https://sdgs.un.org/goals

[11] https://www.un.org/en/conferences/environment/rio1992.

[12] https://en.wikipedia.org/wiki/united_nations_millennium_declaration

[13] https://www.un.org/en/conferences/environment/johannesburg2002.

[14] https://www.un.org/en/conferences/environment/rio2012.

with 17 SDGs at the core at UN Sustainable Development Summit in September 2015[15].

The year 2015 was a landmark year for multilateralism and international policy shaping, along with the adoption of several major agreements: Sendai Framework for Disaster Risk Reduction (March 2015) and Addis Ababa Action Agenda on Financing for Development (July 2015). Transforming our world: the 2030 Agenda for Sustainable Development with its 17 SDGs was adopted at the UN Sustainable Development Summit in New York in September 2015. Currently, the annual High-level Political Forum on Sustainable Development serves as the central UN platform for the follow-up and review of the SDGs[16].

Today, the Division for Sustainable Development Goals (DSDG) in the UN Department of Economic and Social Affairs (UNDESA) provides substantive support and capacity-building for SDGs and their related thematic issues including water, energy, climate, oceans, urbanization, transport, science and technology, the Global Sustainable Development Report (GSDR), partnerships and Small Island Developing States. The DSDG plays a key role in the evaluation of UN system-wide implementation of the 2030 Agenda and on advocacy and outreach activities relating to the SDGs. To make the 2030 Agenda to be practical, broad ownership of the SDGs must translate into a strong commitment by all stakeholders to implementation. Although the origin of the ESG framework may be traced back to the 70 s, the SDGs, established by the United Nations General Assembly in 2015, set forth 17 critical areas to address economic, social and environmental challenges by 2030[17].

The SDGs are generally recognized as a macro-level policy guidance, while ESG may be viewed as a corporate perspective that encourages companies to highlight their investment efforts to be socially and environmentally responsible under effective governance. The ESG framework also encourages companies to adopt internal and external policies that change their operations and improve communication with stakeholders including investors, customers and governmental agencies. The business sector accounts for 72% of GDP in the 38 member countries of OECD[18]. With ESG goals, strategies and policies that are effective and timely, businesses can assure that we can all eventually live on a healthy planet within a safe and equitable society.

Requirement for Quantitative Assessment: The UN has discussed the 17 SDGs principles for our future sustainability goals, each of which has a very wide scope of its implication range. To implement the SDGs, we need a long assessment process in which we specify the "priority" among 17 goals in discussing our try-and-error approach. Goal among the 17 SDGs, energy (SDG 7), economic growth (SDG 8), industrial innovation (SDG 9), sustainability (SDG 12) and climate action (SDG13) may be important research targets to start our quantitative assessments. The sustainability in SDGs implies the strategies and policies in a long range planning so that any assessment, including DEA-EA, should incorporate a long time horizon. Thus,

---

[15] A detailed description on SDG's 17 goals are listed in https://sdgs.un.org/goals.

[16] https://sustainabledevelopment.un.org/post2015/summit.

[17] https://www.un.org/en/desa

[18] https://www.oecd.org/tax/tax-policy/revenue-statistics-highlights-brochure.pdf.

the quantitative approaches need to incorporate a "goal specification/priority setting process" and a "long time horizon' in the computation processes. See Chap. 4 in which we discuss how to handle the goal specification. See also Chaps. 5, 6 and 7 in which we discuss how to handle a time series data.

2.3 International Efforts on ESG and SDGs

We consider that SDGs are a set of specific concepts for ESG which has broad implications in its policy implementations. Before analytically discussing ESG and SDGs in the proceeding chapters, we need to review international efforts to implement their policy implication. Such a description will be an analytical base to shift these fuzzy concepts to corresponding mathematical formulations.

In this book, the uniqueness of ESG and SDGs is characterized by two concerns from the use of DEA-EA. One of the two concerns is that they are very fuzzy so that we have a difficulty in analytically specifying them. We must describe part of ESG (i.e., green investment) and SDGs 7, 8, 12, 13 (i.e., energy, sustainability, innovation, climate change) from the analytical capability of DEA-EA. The other concern is that both ESG and SDGs need international efforts and coordination among all nations under the UN leadership. Chaps. 3, 4, 5, 6 and 7 discuss how to utilize DEA-EA for the enhancement of ESG and SDGs as an analytical method.

The international efforts on ESG and SDGs are summarized in Fig. 2.1. The figure visually describes the major international efforts on global sustainability enhancement and climate change protection. At the beginning of the new millennium, world leaders gathered at UN to shape a broad vision to fight poverty from its many dimensions. The vision was translated into eight Millennium Development Goals (MDGs). The MDGs report (2015) specified these MDGs for development. The report included an overarching development framework for the world for the proceeding 15 years[19].

The second major step was Kyoto Protocol adopted on December 11, 1997. Due to a complex ratification process, it entered into force on February 16, 2005. The Kyoto Protocol operationalized the UN Framework Convention on Climate Change by committing industrial counties and economies in transition to limit and reduce GHG emissions in accordance with agreed individual targets. It asked the developed counties to adopt policies and measures on mitigation and to report periodically[20].

The Kyoto Protocol was based upon the principles and provisions of the convention and followed its annex-based structure. It banded only developed counties and placed a heavier burden on them under the principle of common but differential responsibility and respective capabilities because it recognized that they were largely responsible to the current high level of GHG emissions.

The third step was United Nations Environment Program (UNEP) in 2011. The program proved a landmark in which many of the transformational reforms, launched

---

[19] https://www.who.int/news-room/fact-sheets/detail/millennium-development-goals-(mdgs).

[20] https://unfccc.int/kyoto_protocol

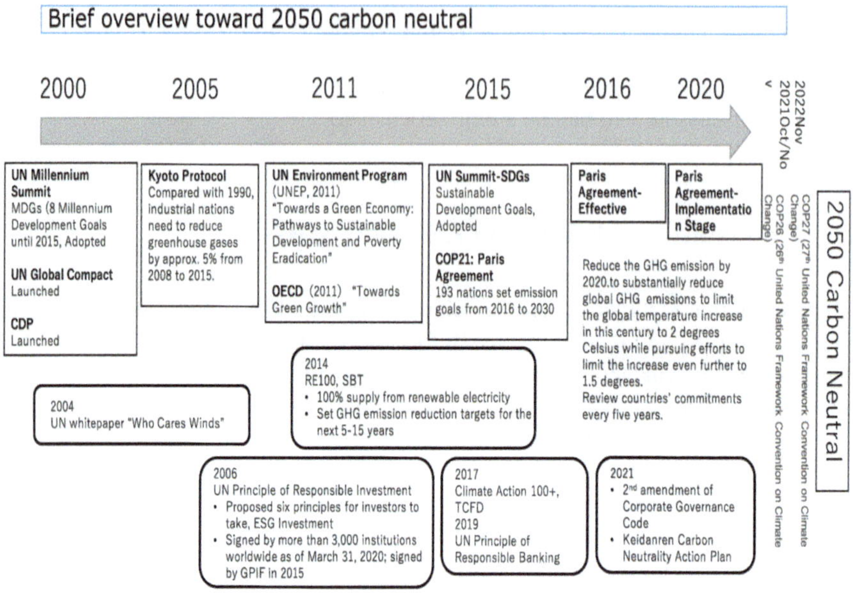

Fig. 2.1 Global sustainability and climate change. *Note* Fig. 2.1 does not list COP 27 and COP 28. We add our description and concern on COP 27 and COP 28 in the context of this chapter

in 2008, really began to bear fruit in terms of a transition to a results-based, more effective and more responsive UNEP. The program had implemented with "OECD's Green Growth Strategy". It has provided concrete recommendations and measurement tools to support countries to achieve economic growth, while at the same time, ensuring that natural assets to prove ecosystem services on which our wellbeing relies. The strategy proposes a flexible policy framework that can be tailored to different country's circumstances and stages of development[21].

The fourth step was the UN summit for adoption of the post-2015 development agenda. That was held from September 25 to 27, 2015, in New York and convened to a high-level plenary meeting of the General Assembly. From September 24 to 25, 2019, heads of government gathered at the UN headquarters in New York to follow up and comprehensively review progress in the implementation of the 2030 agenda for sustainable development and the 17 SDGs. The event was the first UN summit on the SDGs since the adoption of the 2030 Agenda in September 2015. The SDGs summit resulted in the adoption of the Political Declaration, "Gearing up for a decade of action and delivery for sustainable development". World leaders called for a decade of action to deliver the SDGs by 2030 and announced actions they are taking to advance the agenda. The General Assembly endorsed the Political Declaration on October 15, 2019[22].

---

21 https://www.oecd.org/greengrowth/

22 https://sustainabledevelopment.un.org/sdgsummit

The fifth step was the recognition that the climate change was global emergency beyond national borders. It required international cooperation and coordinated solutions at all levels of sustainability and industrial developments. To handle the climate change and its negative impacts on environment, world leaders at the UN COP21 at Paris reached a breakthrough on December 12, 2015 and attained the historic Paris Agreement[23]. The agreement sets long-term goals so that they guide all nations to follow the three agreements. First, we need to substantially reduce global GHG emissions to limit the global temperature increase in this century to 2°C while pursuing efforts to limit the increase even further to 1.5 degrees. Second, we review countries' commitments every five years. Third, we provide financial supports to developing countries to mitigate climate change, strengthen resilience and enhance abilities to adapt to climate impacts.

The agreement was a legally binding international treaty. It entered into force on November 4, 2016. The agreement included commitments from all nations to reduce their emissions and worked together to adapt to the impacts of climate change and called on countries to strengthen their commitments over time. The agreement provided a pathway for developed nations to assist developing nations in their climate mitigation and adaptation efforts while creating a framework for the transparent monitoring and reporting of countries' climate goals. It provided a durable framework for guiding the global effort for decades to come. It marked the beginning of a shift toward a net-zero emissions world. Implementation of the agreement is essential for the achievement of the SDGs.

In addition to the visual description in Fig. 2.1, we need to discuss recent two conference efforts of UN. One of the two is that the COP 27 (27th session of the conference) of the Parties to the UN Framework Convention on Climate Change opened from November 6 to 20, 2022 at Sharm el-Sheikh, Arab Republic of Egypt. The important outcome of COP27 is that industrial nations will financially assist other (i.e., developing) nations which have suffered from the negative impacts of climate changes[24]. Admitting the conference effort, we need to mention that all developed nations have recently suffered from a huge deficit. There are many homeless people and less income people even if in the USA, Japan and European nations.

The other conference of UN is that on Dec 12, 2023, COP 28 has taken place from November 30 to December 12, 2023, in Dubai, United Arab Emirates. The contribution of COP 28 was that it explicitly mentioned the technology shift from all kinds of fossil fuels to renewable energy sources. There are two issues related to COP 28. One of the two issues is that it recommends the use on nuclear power generation to attain zero carbon emission. The recommended shift includes various risks related to nuclear power generation such as nuclear wastes and operational difficulties[25]. See Goto and Sueyoshi (2016) that explained Japanese policy making changes after the disaster of Fukushima Daiichi power plant.

---

[23] https://www.un.org/en/climatechange/paris-agreement.

[24] https://www.un.org/en/climatechange/cop27.

[25] https://unfccc.int/cop28.

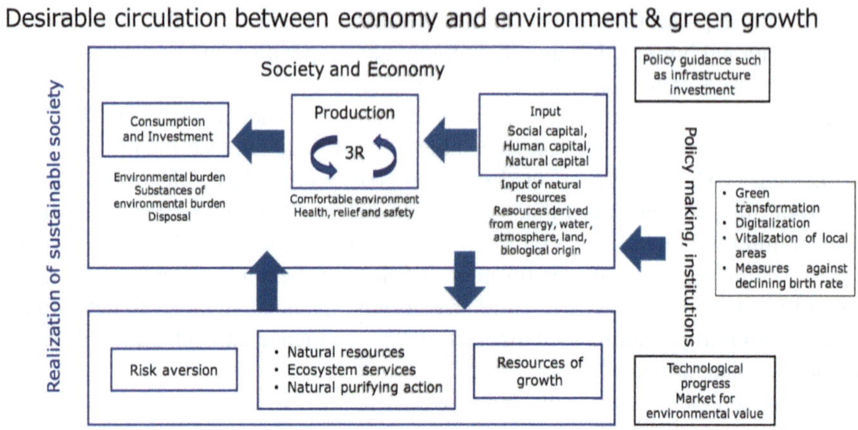

Fig. 2.2 Cycle for sustainable society. *Note* 3R stands for Reduce, Reuse and Recycle

At the end of this section, we need to add a flow of economic activities from various capitals as inputs. Figure 2.2 depicts such a flow from consumption and investment through production of values under 3R activities where the 3R stands for "Reduce, Reuse and Recycle". Meanwhile, conventional economic framework has not considered the lower panel; natural resources, ecosystem services, natural purifying action, but all of which have supported the upper panel social and economic activities as fundamental factors. Such fundamental factors imply to (a) reduce the level of various risk, (b) reduce the need of natural resources, (c) enhance the capability of the ecological system and (d) purify the level of nature. They provide resources for economic growth.

2.4 Sustainability Investment

This section first pays attention to "green investment", requested by ESG, because we are interested in discussing on how the proposed DEA-EA can fit within the scope of ESG. To visually describe our concern, this section first prepares Fig. 2.3 which depicts its business implication from corporate strategy.

The business strategy, as depicted in Fig. 2.3, is usually separated into "upstream" and "downstream", where the upstream specifies the supply side of corporate activity and the downstream specifies its demand side. Conventionally, business entities need to pay attention to "corporate value" enhancement for customers by (a) increasing the amount of sales and profits, (b) making a benefit for shareholders, (c) allocating a part of profit to employees and (d) considering the whole management system including group companies. As a result, they can establish "environment-conscious management", "sustainable management" and "carbon neutral management".

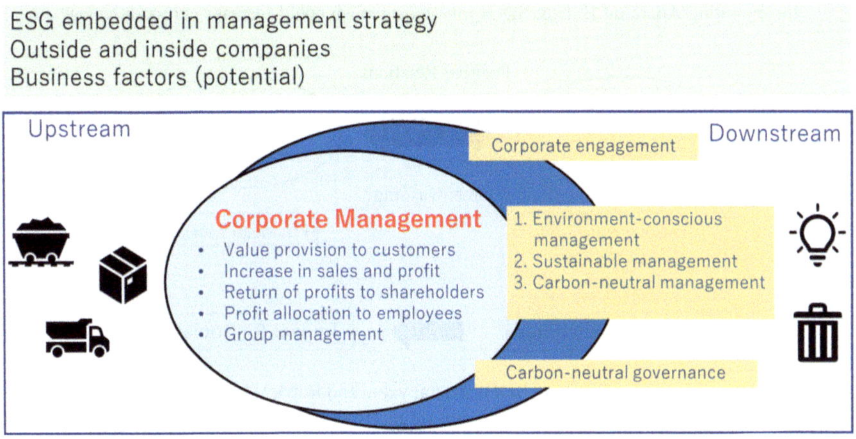

Fig. 2.3 Corporate governance for ESG enhancement

In modern business, sustainability is a corporate driver rather than a cost center. Companies create social and economic values by addressing social needs and challenges, leading to the next round of innovation and productivity improvements (Porter & Kramer, 2011).

Figure 2.4 depicts the implications of ESG and SDGs in terms of enhancing the corporate value. Before the current focus on ESG, research efforts on Corporate Social Responsibility (CSR) accumulated from the early 2000s. For example, Bansal and Roth (2000) conducted a qualitative study of motivations and contextual factors which induced corporate ecological responsiveness. Analytic induction used in their study was applied to data collected from 53 firms in the UK and Japan and it revealed three motivations: competitiveness, legitimation and ecological responsibility. Their research motivations were influenced by three contextual conditions: field cohesion, issue salience and individual concern. Furthermore, McWiliams and Siegel (2001) outlined a supply and demand model of CSR. Based upon their framework, the study hypothesized that a corporate level of CSR depended on the size, the diversification level, R&D, advertising, government scales, consumer income, labor market condition and stage of industrial life cycle. Moreover, Stubbs and Cocklin (2008) seeked to develop a "Sustainability Business Model (SBM)", where sustainability concepts shaped the driving force of the firm and its decision making. The SBM was drawn from two case studies of organizations both of which were for leaders in operationalizing sustainability and were informed by ecological modernization perspective of sustainability. The analysis revealed that organizations adopting SBM had to develop internal structural and cultural capabilities to achieve firm-level sustainability and collaborate with key stakeholders to achieve sustainability.

Figure 2.4 visually notes our additional concerns. In the figure, "Outputs" are products or services produced from inputs while "Outcomes" are resulting effects and achievements from our economic activities. The outputs may include positive (e.g., profit) and/or negative (e.g., GHG) results. The outcomes usually indicate

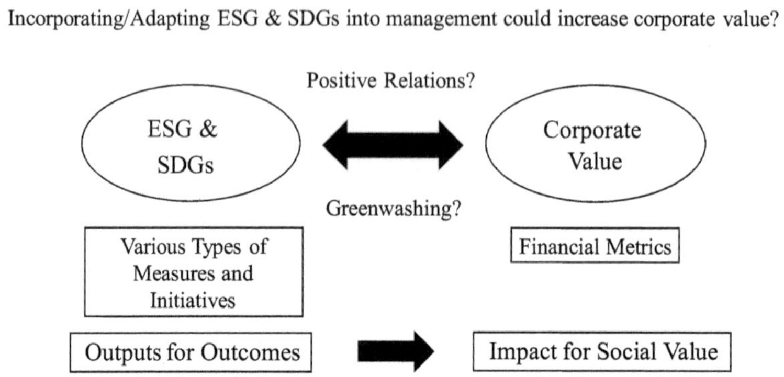

Fig. 2.4 Economic value to ESG and SDGs, social value and impact. *Note* (a) The enhancement of ESG and SDGs leads to an increase in corporate value. (b) ESG was previously considered as CSR (Corporate Social Responsibility). (c) "Outputs" are products or services produced from inputs while "outcomes" are resulting effects and achievements. The outputs may have positive and/or negative results. The outcomes indicate positive results. (d) "Greenwashing" implies the practice of companies or some other entities that may take advantage of advertising, investment or tax benefits by appearing to be committed to environmental or sustainability issues. There is a high possibility that the advertising is not effective on real environmental protection

positive (desirable) results. In the figure, "Greenwashing" indicates the practice of companies or some other types of organizations that may take advantage of advertising, investment or tax benefits by appearing to be committed to environmental or sustainability issues. There is a high possibility that their efforts on environment protection are not effective in reality.

An example of "greenwashing" at a nation level is the production of Electrical Vehicle (EV) that China, the USA and other industrial nations financially support the car productions and sales. The production of EVs may be indeed "promising" as a new industry because the car operation does not produce any engine sound noise and may be equipped with advanced Information Technology (IT) and Artificial Intelligence (AI) systems. However, it does not guarantee that EVs can substantially reduce the amount of global GHG emissions because the reduction depends upon the type of electric power generations. For example, if electricity is generated by fossil fuel power plants, then the operation of EVs does not reduce the amount of CO_2 emission. The price of electricity may also influence EV popularity among consumers. Besides, we know that the battery is a main element of EV and it is large and heavy, often becoming a huge problem in carrying such a heavy battery. So, EVs may be energy (environmentally) inefficient. The recycle is very limited on the battery, as well. One of the answers may be to produce "small (mini) EVs" which are much smaller than current EVs, "hybrid cars", or more promisingly to produce "hydrogen vehicles" which may produce only water after their operations.

In the EV market, China wants to dominate the new car industry as its national strategy (i.e., dominate the global market), just declaring that Chinese EVs are for environment protection. Such an industrial strategy is nothing wrong, rather encouraging. But, the production of Chinese EVs may neglect a production balance between supply and demand in the world EV consumption. It is trivial that China sells its EVs because they are less expensive than the ones produced by the other nations. Nothing is wrong, just working on an economic rule. The rule is that the fittest is a survival in the global international market.

Figure 2.5 visually summarizes that the sustainability investment has a "positive correlation" to increase corporate financial or market performance based on the research of Lee and Suh (2022). As depicted in Fig. 2.5, they have mentioned that previous research findings on ESG remain inconclusive for an increase of financial performance. Their research has not identified nor explained the "underlying mechanisms" behind the relationship. To encourage future research efforts, their study has discussed the mechanisms by identifying the first-order, mediating and moderating variables. They have synthesized recent studies for emerging themes and implications; argued for a process; and integrated approach for modeling causality between ESG and financial performance variables. Their models have advocated for researchers to explore the idea that balances corporate conduct among ESG components which have provided relations with financial performance. Their study has also discussed how to identify "greenwashing" in the process and the integrated model may explain the ESG conduct and financial performance link.

At the end of this section, it is necessary for us to clearly specify differences between ESG and SDGs. Table 2.2 focuses upon differences and similarities between them from four research concerns. The first concern is that ESG discusses various environmental, social and governance issues mainly in private sectors, while SDGs discuss sustainability goals in private and public sectors. The corporate investment is

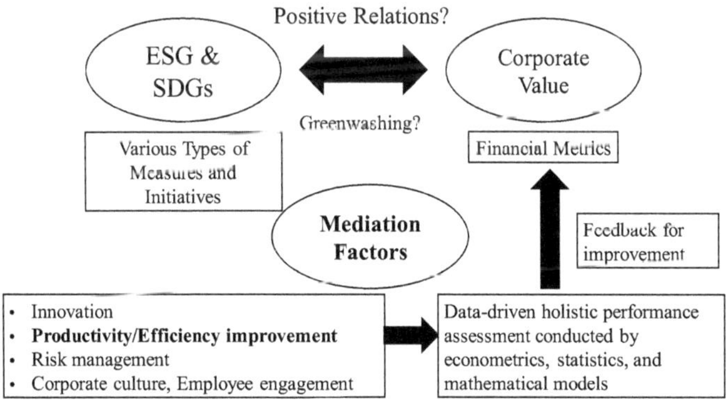

Fig. 2.5 Investment on ESG and SDGs to increase financial performance. *Note* (a) In statistics, a mediation model seeks to explain a process that underlies an observed relationship between an independent variables and a dependent variable via the inclusion of a mediator variable (also known intermediary variable or intervening variable). Rather than a direct causal relationship between independent variables and a dependent variable, a mediation model proposes that the independent variable may influence the mediator variable, which in turn influences the dependent variable. Thus, the mediator variable serves to clarify the nature of relationship between the independent and dependent variables. (b) We use DEA-EA to measure the level of productivity or efficiency improvement as a mediation factor

Table 2.2 Differences and similarities between ESG and SDGs from DEA perspectives

Features	ESG: Environmental, social and governance	SDGs: Sustainable development goals
Target	Mainly private sectors by "investment" on environment protection. General sustainability	Public and private sectors. Specific on 17 social goals (no priority among goals)
Concern from DEA-EA	Environment protection from various pollutions	Energy (SDG 7), Economic Growth (SDG 8), Industrial Innovation (SDG 9), Sustainability (SDG 12) and Climate Action (SDG 13)
Strategy	Investment as a governance strategy	Investment is not considered as a sustainability goal
Time horizon	A time horizon is not clearly incorporated into sustainability framework	A time horizon is clearly incorporated into sustainability development

an important governance strategy of ESG, while SDGs do not directly incorporate the investment strategy. Second, ESG is concerned with remedying various pollutions from the perspectives of society and corporate governance, while SDGs pay attentions to 17 specific sustainability goals. The proposed DEA-EA approach may explore only the quantitative aspect of 17 SDGs in this study. We will focus upon considering only how to combat the climate change and environment protection by the use of DEA-EA. This type of study is limited on the other research issues. Third, the investment is a governance strategy of ESG, but it is not clearly specified in SDGs. Finally, ESG does not incorporate a time horizon in the sustainability framework, but SDGs discuss the goals from a long run perspective. This requests us that the proposed DEA-EA must incorporate various formulations over time.

2.5 DEA-EA for Sustainability Enhancement

It is indeed true that many nations have been working on the reduction of various pollutions and the climate change. However, most of their efforts were not necessarily successful as they expected. One of such rationales was that the previous efforts did not have enough empirical evidences from analytical approaches. For the development of ESG and SDGs, such efforts need to evaluate multifactor activities of many entities under both economic prosperity and environmental protection.

To overcome the methodological problems related to ESG and SDGs, we recommend the use of DEA-EA as a "mediation measure" as specified in Fig. 2.5. Figure 2.6 depicts such an organizational process of DEA-EA as part of "social intelligence" for both mitigating the level of environmental pollutions and enhancing the status of economic prosperity.

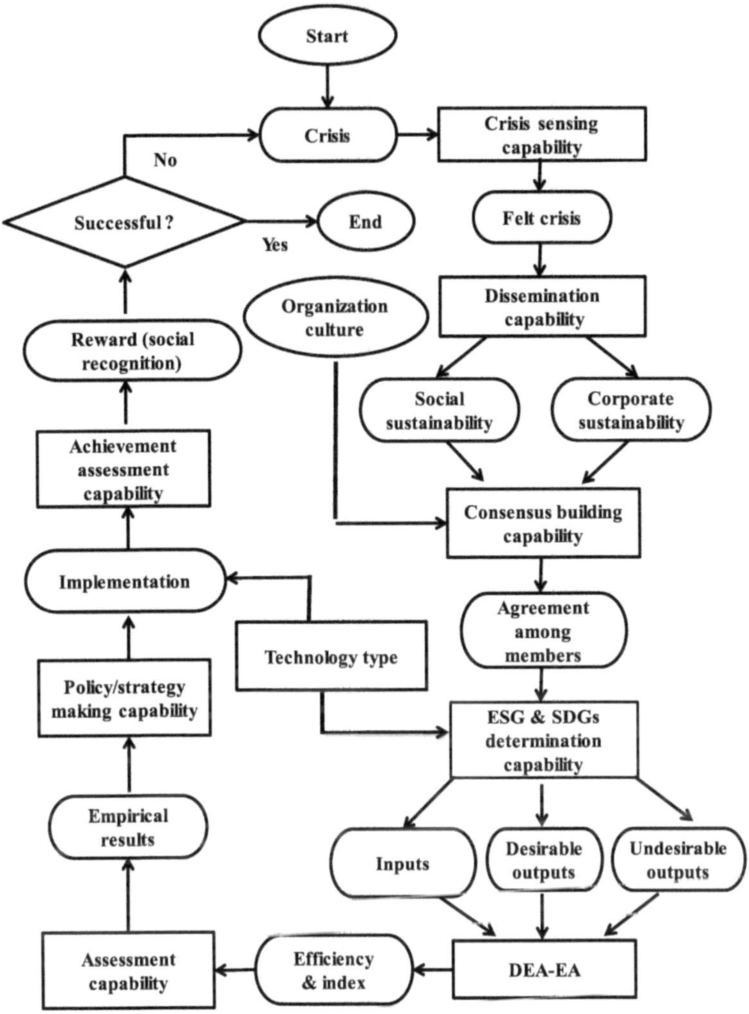

Fig. 2.6 DEA-EA process for ESG and SDGs enhancement

A methodology selection starts from our intelligence capability, where "intelligence" implies a social capability by which an organization can handle various issues related to ESG and SDGs through corporation among members. The social capability may function for systematic adjustment to various changes (e.g., regulation changes on industrial pollutions), so not directly linking to any conventional engineering context (e.g., AI: artificial intelligence in computer science). Such a social capability depends upon the utilization of a data processing capability equipped in a modern computer and other types of Information Technology (IT) devices that can simultaneously deal with a large database, often called "big data and/or data mining" related to economy and environment. Both factors regularly exist in our modern business and society.

As an initial step in Fig. 2.6, a DMU (e.g., a firm or a public agency) needs to find that it faces a serious crisis due to various types of pollution (e.g., air, soil, or water pollution). As a result of such recognition on the existence of pollution, consumers do not want to purchase products from any dirty-imaged entity in a case of private sector. They purchase products from green-imaged companies even if their prices are much higher than those of dirty-imaged companies. More seriously, a very large opportunity cost may often occur along with industrial pollution, which can make a huge damage on each firm.

For example, the disaster of Fukushima Daiichi nuclear power plant, caused by the Great East Japan Earthquake occurred on March 11, 2011, was such an example of the huge opportunity cost. To avoid the problem, each organization needs to incorporate "a sensing capability" by which the organization can identify an existence of such a serious crisis due to industrial pollution. The sensing capability may be often found in an individual member from the top to the bottom or a group of members within the organization.

The felt crisis leads to "social sustainability" in a public sector or "corporate sustainability" in a private sector. The concept of "social sustainability", supported by many international organizations such as UN, is related to global social responsibility and "accountability" for preventing the global warming (boiling) and climate change that have been gradually changing our ecological systems. The concept of social sustainability contains worldwide implications in a long-term horizon. In contrast, the concept of corporate sustainability has another type of implications, so being different from the social sustainability, all of which are related to modern business concerns. That is, the corporate sustainability is closely related to business survivability via a public image as a "good corporate citizen".

Moreover, it is important to note that the opportunity cost (e.g., a damage due to industrial pollution), which is much larger than any other production-related cost components, may terminate an existence of a firm as a going concern. Thus, we need to clearly distinguish between the two sustainability concepts in discussing worldwide policy issues (e.g., global warming/boiling and climate change) and modern corporate behaviors for preventing industrial pollutions.

After identifying an organizational objective (e.g., social or corporate sustainability), each organization needs to make "consensus building" among members. In the consensus building process, the necessity of sustainability is "disseminated" among all the members. The consensus building process functions under "organization culture" that provides members with free speech and an opportunity to express member's opinion under a democratic environment. Contrarily, under a non-democratic environment, the dictatorship organization will not utilize any constructive concern.

In a public section, the UN conferences (e.g., a series of COP) were such examples of a consensus building process at the Paris Agreement[26]. They represented the conscientiousness of 196 parties who attended the conference. The agreement was supposed to become effective when it was supported by at least 55 countries which together represent at least 55% of global GHG emissions. According to the organizing committee, the expected result was an agreement to set a goal of limiting the temperature increase to avoid global warming in the manner that it should be less than 2 degrees Celsius (°C), compared to the pre-industrial level. The agreement called for net-zero GHG emissions to be reached during the second half of the twenty-first century. The conference can be considered as an example of such a consensus building process that shares the necessity of social sustainability in the world.

After making the consensus building among members, an organization needs to determine what consists of ESG factors for corporate sustainability assessment. This type of social intelligence is referred to as "a production factor determination capability". The DEA-EA, as a holistic approach, is used in the stage as one of many methodological alternatives for assessing the level of sustainability. Some member(s) should have an analytical capability for operating DEA-EA assessment in this stage. This type of social intelligence is referred to as "a measurement capability".

After applying DEA-EA for assessment, the organization obtains empirical results, indicating the level of sustainability, which we identify by relatively comparing its performance with the others. This is referred to as "an assessment capability". Based upon the empirical results, the organization needs to prepare policy or corporate strategy for pollution prevention. The type of intelligence is referred to as "a policy/strategy making capability". The organization needs to implement the policy or strategy for sustainability enhancement. The type of intelligence is referred to as "an achievement assessment capability".

In the implementation stage, we need to pay attention to the type and origin of technology. For example, the technology may originate from a public sector (e.g., US DoD: Department of Defense) for military development. The US Environmental Protection Agency (EPA) promotes for the development of environment protection technology. Such public sector-oriented technology is different from private sector-oriented technology in the implementation process of ESG. A technology shift is a key component of this stage. Chap. 7 will discuss OECD's development for sustainability where many industrial nations have to coordinate their engineering capability. It is not easily to attain such international coordination. Chap. 8 for the US DoD's technology development within the USA where US DoD can make coordination among military forms. The comparison between the two chapters will provide us with the implication and limitation of technology development and international cooperation.

In the use of DEA-EA, if the implementation is successful, then a reward or a social recognition should be given to the organization. In contrast, if it is not successful, the result implies a necessity of felt crisis for the organization by returning to the initial stage of the proposed social intelligence. Thus, a gradual improvement process is

[26] https://unfccc.int/process-and-meetings/the-paris-agreement.

necessary and repeated many times until each organization can attain eliminating the crisis-related environmental pollution. Consequently, we must use DEA-EA in a long time horizon for our applications. So, it may serve as a cycle for SDGs principle.

Finally, it is important to note that if one of such intelligence capacities, depicted in Fig. 2.6, may not exist in an organization, then it will be unable to survive as a going concern entity in our modern business and society, so indicating “no sustainability” in future.

2.6 Discussion

This chapter discussed a rationale concerning why we need to study the assessment on sustainability and environment by DEA-EA. We first reviewed the historical perspectives of ESG and SDGs and then we discussed a conceptual base for preparing various DEA-based environmental applications. Such applications of DEA-EA will be explored in the remaining chapters of this book.

The sustainable developments of economic prosperity and environment concerns are often referred to as the practice of ESG and SDGs principles. The ESG factors have been developed for many years, starting from its formal proposal in 2004 as mentioned in Sect. 2.2.1. Countries around the world have continued to promote its coordinated development in accordance with ESG and SDGs principles. The concepts were indeed important but they belonged to just as qualitative discussions. Previously, there was no practical method to empirically assess the level of both ESG and SDGs. This book proposes a new use of DEA-EA for quantitative analysis of ESG assessment. Moreover, it also focuses upon time series perspectives because SDGs need many repeating processes for gradual improvement as depicted in Fig. 2.6.

At the end of this chapter, we address that UN agreements do not have any legal force to control each member nation. This international concern is applicable to various environmental issues (e.g., zero CO_2 emission). It is a high likelihood that many nations do not follow the UN agreements even if they promise the implementation. Why? It has two rationales on the implementation difficulties. One of the two difficulties is that many developing nations have limited financial capabilities to combat various environmental issues. The other, explored in this remaining chapter, is that we do not have appropriate methodologies to evaluate the progress of ESG and that of SDGs which include both economic and environmental achievements. In this book, we document some uses of DEA-EA to partly handle the second difficulty.

References

Aluchna, M., & Roszkowska-Menkes, M. (2019). Integrating corporate social responsibility and corporate governance at the company level. *Towards a Conceptual Model. Engineering Economics, 30*, 349–361.

Bansal, P., & Roth, K. (2000). Why companies go green: A model of ecological responsiveness. *Academy of Management Journal, 43*, 717–736.
Bocken, N. M. P., Short, S. W., Rana, P., & Evans, S. (2014). A literature and practice review to develop sustainable business model archetypes. *Journal of Cleaner Production, 65*, 42–56.
Daugaard, D. (2020). Emerging new themes in environmental, social and governance investing: A systematic literature review. *Accounting. Finance., 60*, 1501–1530.
Drempetic, S., lein, C., Zwergel, B. (2020) The influence of firm size on the ESG score: Corporate sustainability ratings. *J. Bus. Ethics 167*, 333–360.
Eccles, N. S., & Viviers, S. (2011). The origins and meanings of names describing investment practices that integrate a consideration of ESG issues in the academic literature. *Journal of Business Ethics, 104*, 389–402.
EBA (2020) EBA report on ESG risks management and supervision. 2020–10–15 BoS—ESG Report MASTER FILEcl.docx (europa.eu). https://www.unpri.org/an-introduction-to-responsible-investment/what-is-responsible-investment/4780
EBA (2021) Environmental social and governance disclosures. Factsheet on ESG Disclosures (europa.eu).
Friede, G., Busch, T., & Bassen, A. (2015). ESG and financial performance: Aggregated evidence from more than 2000 empirical studies. *J. Sustain. Financ. Invest., 5*, 210–233.
Goto, M., & Sueyoshi, T. (2016). Electricity market reform in japan after Fukushima: Implications for climate change policy and energy market developments. *Economics of Energy & Environmental Policy, 5*(1), 15–30.
International finance corporation. (2004) Who cares wins: Connecting financial markets to a changing world. https://documents1.worldbank.org/curated/en/280911488968799581/pdf/113237-WP-WhoCaresWins-2004.pdf
Lee, M. T., & Suh, I. (2022). Understanding the effects of environment, social, and governance conduct on financial performance: Arguments for a process and integrated modelling approach. *Sustain. Technol. Entrep., 100004*, 1–12.
Li, T.-T., Wang, K., Sueyoshi, T., & Wang, D. (2021). ESG: Research progress and future prospects. *Sustainability, 13*(11663), 1–28.
McWilliams, A., & Siegel, D. (2001). Corporate social responsibility: A theory of the firm perspective. *Academy of Management Review, 26*(1), 117–127.
MDGs (2015) https://www.un.org/millenniumgoals/2015_MDGReport/pdf/MDG%202015%20rev%20(July%201).pdf.
Porter, M.E., Kramer, M.R. (2011) Creating shared value. Harvard Business Review, 1–17
Stubbs, W., & Cocklin, C. (2008). Conceptualizing a sustainability business model. *Organ. Environment., 21*, 103–127.
Sueyoshi, T., Ryu, Y., & Yun, J.-Y. (2021). Coronavirus-19 response and prospects of clean/sustainable energy transition in industrial nations: New environmental assessment. *Energies, 14*(1174), 1–27.
Widyawati, L. (2020). A systematic literature review of socially responsible investment and environmental social governance metrics. *Bus. Strat. Environ., 29*, 619–637.
Yoshikawa, T., Nippa, M., & Chua, G. (2021). Global shift towards stakeholder-oriented corporate governance? Evidence from the scholarly literature and future research opportunities. *Multinational Business Review, 29*, 321–347.
Ziolo, M., Filipiak, B. Z., Bak, I., & Cheba, K. (2019). How to design more sustainable financial systems: The roles of environmental, social, and governance factors in the decision-making process. *Sustainability, 11*, 5604.

Chapter 3
Standard DEA Models for Efficiency Measures: Perspectives from Energy Economics

Abstract Chap. 2 has discussed the principles of ESG and SDGs. In the chapter, we propose the use of DEA-EA as a method to discuss and examine the level of ESG and SDGs achievements within the scope of sustainability development. Prior to our description on its applicability, this chapter needs to explain the standard use of DEA. Chap. 4 extends the standard model to DEA-EA after incorporating undesirable outputs (e.g., CO_2), so incorporating ESG into an analytical framework of DEA-EA. We admit that DEA has many different formulations. This chapter starts from a description on "radial models" used for measurement of "energy" and "sustainability". The DEA description considers the concept of Operational Efficiency (*OE*) and then extends its applicability from "Energy Economics" because the energy consumption is closely linked to ESG and SDGs. "Energy Intensity" and "Energy Efficiency" serve as very important concepts in energy economics, further for sustainability enhancement. This chapter discusses the two measures from the framework of standard DEA and *OE* measurement. The DEA standard models, discussed in this chapter, belong to the Debreu-Farrell type of efficiency measurement. They are usually classified into two categories under variable or constant Returns to Scale (RTS) from conceptual extensions. This chapter provides us with analytical linkages between two radial models and sustainability enhancement for ESG and SDGs.

Keywords Radial measurement · Operational efficiency · Multiplier restriction · Cost analysis · Energy economics · Energy intensity · Energy efficiency

3.1 Introduction

As an extension of Sueyoshi and Goto (2018), this book first discusses standard radial models for efficiency measurement and then describes them from "energy economics" because energy consumption is closely related to ESG and SDGs.

T. Sueyoshi and M. Goto, *Environment and Sustainability for ESG and SDGs*,
https://doi.org/10.1007/978-981-96-2464-5_3

The DEA-based efficiency to be discussed in this chapter is a methodology which we can extend it to the measurement of a level of ESG and that of SDGs. The efficiency measured by DEA was conventionally referred to as "technical efficiency[1]" in production economics. Meanwhile, we use "Operational Efficiency *(OE)*" because the conventional term does not imply any "technology" and/or "engineering" implications. This book is interested in discussing "technology shift" or engineering development among different organizations and different periods so that we must distinguish between the two terms (conventional: technical efficiency and this book: operational efficiency)[2] in this book.

Sueyoshi and Goto (2018, Chap. 4) have discussed a historical rationale on the two different terms. Chap. 8 of this book will discuss a technology shift in the US military industry which may be considered as the most advanced technology. The technology shift is also compared with the one for environmental protection of Chap. 7. Such a comparison provides us with useful implications for developing the principles of ESG and SDGs.

Generally speaking, the previous DEA research proposed the two types of formulations. One of the two types was referred to as "radial measures", while the other was "non-radial measures". This chapter focuses upon the former (radial) measures for economic and environmental assessments. The two radial models were first proposed by Charnes et al. (1978) and Banker et al. (1984), respectively, depending upon the type of Returns to Scale (RTS): constant RTS or variable RTS. The radial measure proposed by Charnes et al. (1978) had a linear programming formulation under constant RTS and the other model proposed by Banker et al. (1984) had another formulation under variable RTS. Both radial models belong to the "Debreu-Farrell measures"[3] in production economics and we can solve them by linear programming, so computationally tractable in most of DEA applications.

The two radial models have a unique feature in measuring a degree of *OE*. They directly measure an efficiency score in the objective function of their linear programming formulations. In addition to the radial models, the conventional DEA studies have the non-radial measures (e.g., an additive model: Charnes et al, 1985) that

[1] The concept of technical efficiency, which we temporally use it here, was first axiomatically proposed by Debreu (1951, 1959). Following the work of Debreu (1951), Farrell (1954, 1957) used a well-known "activity analysis approach" with matrix inversions. Based upon the advice of Alan Hoffman (an OR researcher), who was one of the commentators on his article of Farrell (1957), Farrell and Fieldhouse (1962) proposed a linear programming formulation for measuring a level of so-called technical efficiency, or operational efficiency in this study. Unfortunately, almost no attention had been given to their works on efficiency measurement for a long time (Sueyoshi and Goto, 2018).

[2] The DEA-based efficiency measurement has been extensively investigated after Charnes et al. (1978) proposed DEA. See Glover and Sueyoshi (2009) and Ijiri and Sueyoshi (2010) for a history of DEA. It is easily thought that methodologies for environmental assessment, which this book attempts to contribute, can be considered as extensions from a conventional (standard) use of DEA.

[3] We clearly understand that DEA has other variations on the radial models, but they do not have practicality at the level of the two types of radial models. Since the non-radial models have a limited practicality in environmental assessment. Chapter 4 will compare between radial and non-radial models along with intermediate model locating between them.

determine a level of *OE* by examining a total amount of slacks on optimality, not by an efficiency score. This is because each non-radial measure does not have any efficiency score in the objective function. An important feature is that the non-radial models can directly deal with negative and zero in a data set. This feature indicates the practicality of non-radial models. In conventional DEA studies, this type of efficiency measures belongs to "Pareto–Koopmans measure" (Koopmans, 1951).

Here, it is necessary to describe that we have another type of DEA model, referred to as "intermediate measure", first proposed by Russell (1985, 1990). This type of efficiency measure is referred to as "Russell measure" in conventional DEA studies. A unique feature of this measure is that it combines between inputs and outputs in efficiency measurement so that it produces an efficiency score, locating between radial and non-radial measures. A problem is that we must solve the conventional Russell measure by" nonlinear" programming (not linear programming), so that it has a computational difficulty. Chap. 4 of this book will overcome the computational difficulty by a reformulation that changes the original model from nonlinear to linear programing. The intermediate formulation measures unified (operational and environmental) efficiency by linear programming. See the research of Sueyoshi and Yuan (2017) that has discussed how to solve the intermediate formulation by linear programming.

At the end of this section, we must mention that DEA-EA is a non-parametric method because it does not measure parameter estimates of a functional model, but rather measures weights among multiple production factors (multiple inputs and multiple desirable outputs as well as multiple undesirable outputs). The relationship among them does not assume any functional form which is required in econometrics and statistics. The productivity/efficiency in Fig. 2.5 corresponds to *OE* so that its measurement is a practical method for ESG and SDGs enhancements.

The remainder of Chap. 3 has the following structure: Sect. 3.2 describes input-oriented radial models (for EI: Energy Intensity). Section 3.3 discusses output-oriented radial models (for EE: Energy Efficiency). The outputs in this chapter are desirable outputs, not considering the existence of undesirable outputs. Section 3.4 compares between these radial models from the perspective of energy economics. Section 3.5 describes multiplier restriction and cross reference approaches that are useful for SDGs. Section 3.6 describes cost models that are conceptually linked to the input-oriented radial models. Section 3.7 summarizes various efficiency measures, along with three illustrative examples, within the proposed radial measurement. Section 3.8 summarizes this chapter. Finally, note that this book uses an "italic" expression for "variables" such as *OE*, hereafter.

3.2 Input-Oriented Radial Models (for Energy Intensity)

This section starts with a standard DEA model which is an original structure of DEA. We will reorganize DEA to be fit within environmental assessment, later. In this chapter, we classify DEA into the two types (input oriented or output oriented) of formulations, both of which can measure the level of "energy intensity" or "energy economics". The previous studies have not discussed the two concepts in DEA because they are specific for energy economics. But they are very important in terms of discussing ESG and SDGs. Chaps. 4 and 5 extend the standard model into DEA-EA which we can use for the measurement of ESG and SDGs.

As mentioned previously, among DEA models, Radial Model (RM) is widely accepted by many users who apply DEA for performance assessment. The model produces an efficiency score by which DEA can express the performance of each DMU by a percentage expression. Previous DEA studies visually specified the RM by a L2 norm expression because it appealed to us more intuitively than a L1 norm. Such a use for projection from the status of inefficiency to an efficiency frontier is only our visual convenience. Mathematically, such a claim is "incorrect" because DEA belongs to L1 norm. See Sueyoshi and Goto (2018) for a historical description on the L1 norm. Hereafter, following the conventional description on RM, we describe an input-oriented RM(v) where the (v) stands for variable Returns to Scale (RTS).[4]

Input-oriented RM(v) under *variable RTS (for Energy Intensity)*: We use the model to measure "energy intensity (EI)" that serves as a key concept in energy economics. The measurement on EI is important for assessing the level of ESG. We measure the degree of EI under an economic condition where a single output is Gross Domestic Product (GDP) and multiple inputs are energy factors such as oil, natural gas and renewable energy.

By duplicating the standard RM and adding a constraint of $\sum_{j=1}^{n}\lambda_j = 1$ into the formulation (Sueyoshi & Goto, 2018), the input-oriented RM(v) has the following mathematical structure to measure an efficiency score (θ_k) of the specific k th DMU:

$$
\begin{aligned}
& Minimize \ \theta_k - \varepsilon_n\left(\sum_{i=1}^{m} d_i^x + \sum_{r=1}^{s} d_r^g\right) \\
& s.t. \quad -\sum_{j=1}^{n} x_{ij}\lambda_j - d_i^x + \theta_k x_{ik} = 0 \quad (i = 1,\ldots,m), \\
& \qquad \sum_{j=1}^{n} g_{rj}\lambda_j - d_r^g = g_{rk} \quad (r = 1,\ldots,s), \\
& \qquad \sum_{j=1}^{n} \lambda_j = 1, \\
& \qquad \theta_k : URS,\ \lambda_j \geq 0\,(j = 1,\ldots,n), \\
& \qquad d_i^x \geq 0\,(i = 1,\ldots,m)\ \&\ d_r^g \geq 0\,(r = 1,\ldots,s).
\end{aligned}
\tag{3.1}
$$

Here, x_{ij} is an observed value of the i th input on the j th DMU, x_{ik} is an observed value of the i th input on the specific k th DMU, g_{rj} is an observed value of the r th output on the j th DMU, g_{rk} is an observed value of the r th output on the specific k th DMU, λ_j is an intensity or structural variable related to the j th DMU, d_i^x is a slack of the i th input, d_r^g is a slack of the r th desirable output, θ_k (URS: unrestricted)

[4] In economics, the concept of Returns to Scale (RTS) explains a long-run linkage of increase in outputs (production) relative to associated increases in inputs (factors of production). Sueyoshi and Goto (2018) provided a detailed mathematical description on RTS.

is an unknown efficiency score measured by an input-oriented RM and ε_n is a non-Archimedean small number which a DMU user need to prescribe for mathematical convenience. In fact, none knows what it is, but we use a very small number (e.g., $\varepsilon_n = 0.0001$).

Since Model (3.1) incorporates the side constraint ($\sum_{j=1}^{n} \lambda_j = 1$), the surface of a production possibility set for Model (3.1) consists of a convex polyhedral cone under variable RTS. As an alternative, we may drop the side constraint from Model (3.1) where a production possibility set is under constant RTS. In the case, Model (3.1) becomes input-oriented "RM(c)" where c indicates the status of constant RTS.

*Energy Intensity (*EI*)*: We need to discuss two analytical concerns on Model (3.1). One of the two concerns is that Model (3.1) minimizes inputs along with a given input vector and a given output vector. As discussed previously, if we measure the inputs by "energy components" (e.g., oil, natural gas and nuclear) and a single output (e.g., GDP), then the input reduction implies EI that examines the level of each energy consumption over a total amount of economies (i.e., GDP). The EI measure becomes an empirical basis for preparing energy policy. See Sueyoshi and Goto (2023) on the EI measurement by using the Radial Model (RM).

Operational Efficiency (*OE*): The other concern to be noted is that the term $-\varepsilon_n\left(\sum_{i=1}^{m} d_i^x + \sum_{r=1}^{s} d_r^g\right)$ may become zero (on a full level of efficiency) or negative (on some level of inefficiency) on the optimality of Model (3.1). The objective value consists of an efficiency score (θ) and a total sum of slacks, where the latter may adjust the level of each production factor in measuring the level of efficiency (*OE*). Here, if the slack adjustment term represents a level of inefficiency, then the sign before the term should be negative in the objective function of Model (3.1) so that it can maintain the required efficiency range between zero and unity.

Strengths and Drawbacks: To describe methodological strengths and drawbacks of Model (3.1), we formulate the following dual model:

$$
\begin{aligned}
& Maximize \ \sum_{r=1}^{s} u_r g_{rk} + \sigma \\
& s.t. \quad -\sum_{i=1}^{m} v_i x_{ij} + \sum_{r=1}^{s} u_r g_{rj} + \sigma \leq 0 \quad (j = 1, \ldots, n), \\
& \qquad \sum_{i=1}^{m} v_i x_{ik} = 1, \\
& \qquad v_i \geq \varepsilon_n (i = 1,\ldots, m),\ u_r \geq \varepsilon_n \quad (r = 1, \ldots, s)\ \& \\
& \qquad \sigma: URS.
\end{aligned}
\tag{3.2}
$$

Here, $V = (v_1, \ldots, v_m)$ and $U = (u_1, \ldots, u_s)$ are two row vectors of dual variables related to the first (inputs) and second (outputs) sets of constraints in Model (3.1). An unrestricted dual variable (σ) is derived from the third constraint of Model (3.1). In transforming from Model (3.1) to its dual formulation (3.2), we implicitly treat that $-v_i \leq -\varepsilon_n$ and $-u_r \leq -\varepsilon_n$ are changed to $v_i \geq \varepsilon_n$ for all i and $u_r \geq \varepsilon_n$ for all r in Model (3.2). The dual variable (σ: URS, implying "unrestricted") indicates the intercept of a supporting hyperplane on Model (3.2). The intercept determines the type ($\sigma > 0$: decreasing, $\sigma = 0$: constant or $\sigma < 0$: increasing) of RTS. See Sueyoshi and Goto (2018) for the classification of RTS under an occurrence of multiple solutions on the intercept.

The objective function of Model (3.1) equals that of Model (3.2) on optimality. Thus, the level of OE regarding the k th DMU under variable (v) RTS is determined by on the optimality of Models (3.1) and (3.2). Equation (3.3) implies how much the increase of each g_{rk} (the r th output) may increase the level of OE.

$$OE^*_{kv} = \theta^* - \varepsilon_n\left(\sum_{i=1}^{m} d_i^{x*} + \sum_{r=1}^{s} d_r^{g*}\right) = \sum_{r=1}^{s} u_r^* g_{rk} + \sigma^* \tag{3.3}$$

In Model (3.2), all dual variables ($v_i \geq \varepsilon_n$ for all i and $u_r \geq \varepsilon_n$ for all r) are strictly positive in their signs, so being able to function as multipliers, expressing weights for production factors. As a result, the inputs and the desirable outputs are fully utilized in input-based performance evaluation although some dual variables may become very small as multipliers in such a manner that $v_i \geq \varepsilon_n$ for all i and $u_r \geq \varepsilon_n$ for all r. This feature is very important in measuring a type of RTS, Marginal Rate of Transformation (MRT), Rate of Substitution (RSU) between production factors and other scale-related measures. In these measurements, multipliers (dual variables) should be strictly positive. Otherwise, we cannot measure the degree of these scale-related measures. See Sueyoshi and Yuan (2016) for a detailed description on MRT and RSU.

Underlying Concept: This book conveys a message that we can use DEA to measure not only an efficiency score but also other important measures (e.g., RTS). Consequently, DEA may become a holistic approach for performance assessment. However, DEA needs to satisfy various conditions on the solutions. One of such conditions, for example, is that all dual variables should be strictly positive.

A drawback of Model (3.1) is that ε_n is a prescribed small number, often referred to as a non-Archimedean small number, in previous DEA studies. The specification of ε_n incorporates a subjective decision by a user(s). In reality, none knows what the small number is. Many users often drop the non-Archimedean small number in their efficiency assessments. Model (3.1) without the very small number becomes as follows:

$$\begin{aligned}
&\textit{Minimize}\ \ \theta_k \\
&s.t.\quad -\sum_{j=1}^{n} x_{ij}\lambda_j - d_i^x + \theta_k x_{ik} = 0 \quad (i = 1, \ldots, m), \\
&\qquad\ \ \sum_{j=1}^{n} g_{rj}\lambda_j - d_r^g = g_{rk} \quad (r = 1, \ldots, s), \\
&\qquad\ \ \sum_{j=1}^{n} \lambda_j = 1, \\
&\qquad\ \ \theta_k : URS,\ \lambda_j \geq 0 \quad (j = 1, \ldots, n), \\
&\qquad\ \ d_i^x \geq 0 (i = 1, \ldots, m)\ \&\ d_r^g \geq 0 \quad (r = 1, \ldots, s).
\end{aligned} \tag{3.4}$$

As mentioned previously, when we measure the level of *OE* concerning the k th DMU, Models (3.1) and (3.4) may not produce any major difference between them because ε_n is the very small number. The elimination may be seemingly acceptable in economic perspective. Mathematically, however, such a difference may produce an inconvenience to us. To discuss it, we need to return to a dual formulation of Model (3.4).

The dual formulation has the following structure:

$$\begin{aligned} & Maximize \sum_{r=1}^{s} u_r g_{rk} + \sigma \\ & s.t. \quad -\sum_{i=1}^{m} v_i x_{ij} + \sum_{r=1}^{s} u_r g_{rj} + \sigma \leq 0 \quad (j = 1, \ldots, n), \\ & \qquad \sum_{i=1}^{m} v_i x_{ik} = 1, \\ & \qquad v_i \geq 0 \, (i = 1, \ldots, m), \; u_r \geq 0 \quad (r = 1, \ldots, s) \; \& \\ & \qquad \sigma : URS. \end{aligned} \tag{3.5}$$

Here, all mathematical descriptions on Model (3.2) are applicable to Model (3.5).

The objective value of Model (3.4) equals that of Model (3.5) on optimality. Thus, we measure the level of *OE* regarding the kth DMU under constant (c) RTS by on the optimality of Models (3.4) and (3.5).

$$OE_{kc}^{*} = \theta_k^{*} = \sum_{r=1}^{s} u_r^{*} g_{rk} + \sigma^{*} \tag{3.6}$$

Models (3.4) and (3.5) have the three important features. First, Model (3.5) has $\sum_{i=1}^{m} v_i x_{ik} = 1$ because θ is URS (unrestricted) in Model (3.4). In other words, the upper bound of θ^* is unity in Model (3.4), indicating the status of full efficiency, because the first constraint indicates $\sum_{r=1}^{s} u_r g_{rk} + \sigma \leq \sum_{i=1}^{m} v_i x_{ik} = 1$ in Model (3.5) for the k th DMU. The left hand side of the equation is the objective value of Model (3.5). Hence, both Models (3.4) and (3.5) indicate $\theta_k^* = \sum_{r=1}^{s} u_r^* g_{rk} + \sigma^* \leq \sum_{i=1}^{m} v_i^* x_{ik} = 1$ on the optimality of the k th DMU. There is no lower bound on θ_k^* because the efficiency score is expected to be unrestricted in Model (3.4). However, a standard use of the efficiency score, applied to a cross-sectional data set, becomes non-negative because Model (3.5) is structured by a maximization problem within an efficiency frontier.

Second, $v_i \geq 0$ ($i = 1, \ldots, m$) and $u_r \geq 0$ ($r = 1, \ldots, s$) in Model (3.5) may have a possible occurrence of $v_i = 0$ for some i and/or $u_r = 0$ for some r. This clearly indicates that DEA may not fully utilize some production factors in the efficiency assessment, so being problematic in this type of empirical assessment. Therefore, standard DEA studies (e.g., Charnes et al., 1978) have incorporated $\varepsilon_n\left(\sum_{i=1}^{m} d_i^x + \sum_{r=1}^{s} d_r^g\right)$ into the objective function as formulated in Model (3.1). As a result of such incorporation, Model (3.2) has $v_i \geq \varepsilon_n$ ($i = 1, \ldots, m$) and $u_r \geq \varepsilon_n$ ($r = 1, \ldots, s$) so that all dual variables, or multipliers (weights), are strictly positive in their signs.

Finally, a problem of the non-Archimedean small number (ε_n) is that none knows what it is in reality. Consequently, a subjective decision is included in the selection process of ε_n. We do not use ε_n to avoid the selection subjectivity in this book.

Input-oriented RM(c) under Constant RTS: We formulate Models (3.1) and (3.2) under variable RTS. If Model (3.1) drops $\sum_{j=1}^{n} \lambda_j = 1$, then the dual variable (σ) becomes zero in Model (3.2). The input-oriented RM(c) under constant RTS has the following primal and dual formulations:

$$
\begin{aligned}
&\textit{Minimize} \ \ \theta_k - \varepsilon_n\left(\sum_{i=1}^{m} d_i^x + \sum_{r=1}^{s} d_r^g\right) \\
&\text{s.t.} \quad -\sum_{j=1}^{n} x_{ij}\lambda_j - d_i^x + \theta_k x_{ik} = 0 \quad (i = 1,.., m), \\
&\qquad\ \ \sum_{j=1}^{n} g_{rj}\lambda_j - d_r^g = g_{rk} \quad (r = 1, \ldots, s), \\
&\qquad\ \ \theta_k : URS,\ \lambda_j \geq 0 \quad (j = 1, \ldots, n), \\
&\qquad\ \ d_i^x \geq 0\,(i = 1, \ldots, m)\ \&\ d_r^g \geq 0 \quad (r = 1, \ldots, s),
\end{aligned}
\tag{3.7}
$$

and

$$
\begin{aligned}
&\textit{Maximize} \ \ \sum_{r=1}^{s} u_r g_{rk} \\
&\text{s.t.} \quad -\sum_{i=1}^{m} v_i x_{ij} + \sum_{r=1}^{s} u_r g_{rj} \leq 0 \quad (j = 1, \ldots, n), \\
&\qquad\ \ \sum_{i=1}^{m} v_i x_{ik} = 1, \\
&\qquad\ \ v_i \geq \varepsilon_n\ (i = 1, \ldots, m) \& u_r \geq \varepsilon_n (r = 1, \ldots, s).
\end{aligned}
\tag{3.8}
$$

Here, all mathematical descriptions on dual variables in Model (3.2) are applicable to Model (3.8).

3.3 Output-Oriented Radial Models (for Energy Efficiency)

Output-oriented RM(v) under Variable RTS: As an alternative to input-oriented RM(v) and RM(c), previous DEA studies have paid attention to the following output-oriented model, or RM(v), to estimate an efficiency score (θ_k) regarding the k th DMU:

$$
\begin{aligned}
& \textit{Maximize} \quad \tau_k + \varepsilon_n\left(\sum_{i=1}^{m} d_i^x + \sum_{r=1}^{s} d_r^g\right) \\
& s.t. \quad \sum_{j=1}^{n} x_{ij}\lambda_j + d_i^x = x_{ik} \quad (i = 1, \ldots, m), \\
& \qquad -\sum_{j=1}^{n} g_{rj}\lambda_j + d_r^g + \tau_k g_{rk} = 0 \quad (r = 1, \ldots, s), \\
& \qquad \sum_{j=1}^{n} \lambda_j = 1, \\
& \qquad \lambda_j \geq 0 (j = 1, \ldots, n), d_i^x \geq 0\,(i = 1, \ldots, m), \\
& \qquad d_r^g \geq 0 (r = 1, \ldots, s)\ \&\ \tau_k : URS.
\end{aligned} \tag{3.9}
$$

We measure the level of *OE* (θ_k^*) by an unrestricted measure (τ_k^*), implying inefficiency, along with slacks on the optimality of Model (3.9):

$$
OE_{kv}^* = 1/\left[\tau_k^* + \varepsilon_n\left(\sum_{i=1}^{m} d_i^{x*} + \sum_{r=1}^{s} d_r^{g*}\right)\right] \tag{3.10}
$$

Energy Efficiency (EE): Model (3.9) has the three important concerns as follows. First, the model can measure the level of EE where inputs are energy-related sources (e.g., oil, coal and natural gas) and a single output is GDP. Second, the model becomes more than unity ($\tau_k^* \geq 1$) on optimality. We determine the *OE* measure of desirable output-oriented RM(v) by Eq. (3.10). Finally, the objective function of Model (3.9) incorporates a positive sign before the term regarding the total sum of slacks as $+\varepsilon_n\left(\sum_{i=1}^{m} d_i^{x*} + \sum_{r=1}^{s} d_r^{g*}\right)$, not $-\varepsilon_n\left(\sum_{i=1}^{m} d_i^{x*} + \sum_{r=1}^{s} d_r^{g*}\right)$ as found in Model (3.7), because τ_k^* does not directly indicate the level of *OE*. Rather, we measure the level of *OE* (θ_k^*) by a reciprocal of the inefficiency score via Eq. (3.10).

Model (3.9) has the following dual formulation:

$$
\begin{aligned}
& \textit{Minimize} \quad \sum_{i=1}^{m} v_i x_{ik} + \sigma \\
& s.t. \quad \sum_{i=1}^{m} v_i x_{ij} - \sum_{r=1}^{s} u_r g_{rj} + \sigma \geq 0 \quad (j = 1, \ldots, n), \\
& \qquad \sum_{r=1}^{s} u_r g_{rk} = 1, \\
& \qquad v_i \geq \varepsilon_n (i = 1, \ldots, m),\ u_r \geq \varepsilon_n\,(r = 1, \ldots, s)\ \& \\
& \qquad \sigma : URS.
\end{aligned} \tag{3.11}
$$

Here, all mathematical descriptions on dual variables in Model (3.2) are applicable to Model (3.11) by changing inputs to outputs.

As mentioned previously, we may drop the non-Archimedean small number (ε_n) from Model (3.9) and Eq. (3.10). In the case for our mathematical tractability, the output-oriented RM(v) becomes

$$
\begin{aligned}
& \mathit{Maximize} \ \ \tau_k \\
& s.t. \quad \sum_{j=1}^{n} x_{ij}\lambda_j + d_i^x = x_{ik} \quad (i = 1, \ldots, m), \\
& \qquad -\sum_{j=1}^{n} g_{rj}\lambda_j + d_r^g + \tau_k g_{rk} = 0 \quad (r = 1, \ldots, s), \\
& \qquad \sum_{j=1}^{n} \lambda_j = 1, \\
& \qquad \lambda_j \geq 0 (j = 1, \ldots, n), d_i^x \geq 0 \quad (i = 1, \ldots, m), \\
& \qquad d_r^g \geq 0 (r = 1, \ldots, s) \ \& \ \tau_k : URS.
\end{aligned}
\tag{3.12}
$$

We measure the level of OE_{kv}^* (θ_k^*) by an unrestricted measure (τ_k^*) by

$$\theta_k^* = 1/\tau_k^* \tag{3.13}$$

The input-oriented OE (minimization) is a reciprocal of the output-oriented OE (maximization). In the proceeding chapters, we will fully utilize the property of output-oriented approach.

Model (3.12) has the following dual formulation:

$$
\begin{aligned}
& \mathit{Minimize} \ \ \sum_{i=1}^{m} v_i x_{ik} + \sigma \\
& s.t. \quad \sum_{i=1}^{m} v_i x_{ij} - \sum_{r=1}^{s} u_r g_{rj} + \sigma \geq 0 \quad (j = 1,.., n), \\
& \qquad \sum_{r=1}^{s} u_r g_{rk} = 1, \\
& \qquad v_i \geq 0 (i = 1, \ldots, m), u_r \geq 0 \quad (r = 1, \ldots, s) \ \& \\
& \qquad \sigma : URS.
\end{aligned}
\tag{3.14}
$$

Here, all the descriptions on input-oriented RM(v) in Model (3.5) are applicable to Model (3.14).

Output-oriented RM(*c*) *under constant RTS*: Model (3.9) under constant RTS measures the level of OE_{kc}^* (θ_k^*):

$$
\begin{aligned}
& Maximize \quad \tau_k + \varepsilon_n\left(\sum_{i=1}^{m} d_i^x + \sum_{r=1}^{s} d_r^g\right) \\
& s.t. \quad \sum_{j=1}^{n} x_{ij}\lambda_j + d_i^x = x_{ik} \quad (i = 1, \ldots, m), \\
& \quad -\sum_{j=1}^{n} g_{rj}\lambda_j + d_r^g + \tau_k g_{rk} = 0 \quad (r = 1, \ldots, s), \\
& \quad \lambda_j \geq 0\,(j = 1, \ldots, n), d_i^x \geq 0 \quad (i = 1, \ldots, m), \\
& \quad d_r^g \geq 0\,(r = 1, \ldots, s)\&\tau_k : URS.
\end{aligned}
\tag{3.15}
$$

Model (3.15) drops $\sum_{j=1}^{n} \lambda_j = 1$ from Model (3.9). The OE_{kc}^{*} (θ_k^{*}) is measured by an unrestricted measure (τ_k^{*}) via $\theta^{*} = 1/\left[\tau_k^{*} + \varepsilon_n\left(\sum_{i=1}^{m} d_i^{x*} + \sum_{r=1}^{s} d_r^{g*}\right)\right]$. The elimination of the side constraint makes it possible to measure the output-oriented RM(c) under constant RTS.

The dual formulation of Model (3.15) becomes:

$$
\begin{aligned}
& Minimize \quad \sum_{i=1}^{m} v_i x_{ik} \\
& s.t. \quad \sum_{i=1}^{m} v_i x_{ij} - \sum_{r=1}^{s} u_r g_{rj} \geq 0 \quad (j = 1, \ldots, n), \\
& \quad \sum_{r=1}^{s} u_r g_{rk} = 1, \\
& \quad v_i \geq \varepsilon_n (i = 1, \ldots, m)\ \&\ u_r \geq \varepsilon_n \quad (r = 1, \ldots, s).
\end{aligned}
\tag{3.16}
$$

Here, $V = (v_1, \ldots, v_m)$ and $U = (u_1, \ldots, u_s)$ are two row vectors of dual variables related to the first and second sets of constraints in Model (3.15).

3.4 Comparison Among Radial Models

3.4.1 Comparison Among Input-Oriented and Output-Oriented Radial Models

There are several differences between four RMs, two of which are visually summarized in Fig. 3.1. One of the two differences is that an efficiency score of the input-oriented RM(v) is different from that of the output-oriented RM(v) under variable RTS. In contrast, the efficiency measure of input-oriented RM(c) equals that of output-oriented RM(c) under constant RTS. Proposition 3.1 proves the mathematical claim. The other difference is that Fig. 3.1 depicts a visual difference between efficiency frontiers under constant RTS and variable RTS in the x-g domain. A straight line from the origin indicates an efficiency frontier under constant RTS, while a piecewise linear contour line, or {a}-{b}-{c}-{d}, indicates the efficiency frontier under variable RTS.

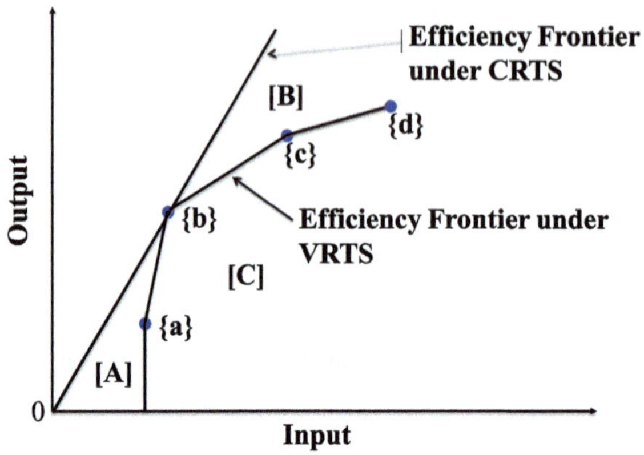

Fig. 3.1 Efficiency frontiers under two RTS types. *Note* **a** We modified the figure prepared by Sueyoshi and Goto (2018). The parenthesis { } indicates an observed DMU. For example, {a} indicates a DMU. The another parenthesis [] indicates a production possibility set. For example, [C] indicates the set for an efficiency frontier under Variable Returns to Scale (VRTS). **b** The union set such as [A] ∪ [B] ∪ [C] consists of the set for an efficiency frontier under Constant Returns to Scale (CRTS). The VRTS incorporates $\sum_{j=1}^{n} \lambda_j = 1$ in RM while the CRTS does not incorporate the restriction in RM. **c** The input minimization for EI projects an inefficient DMU to horizontally left and the output maximization for EE projects an inefficient DMU to vertically up.

As depicted in Fig. 3.1, the two production possibility sets imply two areas for covering a possible combination between inputs and outputs. The figure depicts a single input (x) and a single output (g) for our visual convenience. They are axiomatically specified as follows:

$$P_v(X) = \left\{ (G, X) : G \le \sum_{j=1}^{n} G_j \lambda_j, \mathrm{X} \ge \sum_{j=1}^{n} \mathrm{X_j} \lambda_j, \sum_{j=1}^{n} \lambda_j = 1, \lambda_\mathrm{j} \ge 0 \right\} \text{ and}$$

$$P_c(X) = \left\{ (G, X) : G \le \sum_{j=1}^{n} G_j \lambda_j, \ \mathrm{X} \ge \sum_{j=1}^{n} \mathrm{X_j} \lambda_j, \lambda_\mathrm{j} \ge 0 \right\} \qquad (3.17)$$

The first production possibility set is under variable RTS (VRTS), while the second one is under constant RTS (CRTS) in Eqs. (3.17). The difference between them may be found in only the incorporation of $\sum_{j=1}^{n} \lambda_j = 1$. In Fig. 3.1, the first production possibility set under VRTS consists of the area [C] and the second one under CRTS consists of the three areas expressed by [A] ∪ [B] ∪ [C] where the symbol ∪ indicates a union set.

In examining RM(c), it is necessary for us to prove the following proposition:

Proposition 3-1: The objective value of the input-oriented RM(c) equals that of the output-oriented RM(c) on optimality.

[Proof] Model (3.7), which is the input-oriented RM(c), is equivalent to the following model without slacks:

$$
\begin{aligned}
&\text{Minimize } \theta_k \\
&\text{s.t. } -\sum_{j=1}^{n} x_{ij}\lambda_j + \theta_k x_{ik} \geq 0 \quad (i = 1, \ldots, m), \\
&\sum_{j=1}^{n} g_{rj}\lambda_j \geq g_{rk} \quad (r = 1, \ldots, s), \\
&\theta_k: URS \& \lambda_j \geq 0 \quad (j = 1, \ldots, n),
\end{aligned}
\tag{3.18}
$$

where Model (3.18) drops $\varepsilon_n\left(\sum_{i=1}^{m} d_i^x + \sum_{r=1}^{s} d_r^g\right)$ from Model (3.7) for our descriptive convenience. Let $\theta_k = 1/\tau_k$ and $\lambda_j = \varphi_j/\tau_k$ in Model (3.18), then the model becomes

$$
\begin{aligned}
&\text{Minimize } 1/\tau_k \\
&\text{s.t. } -\sum_{j=1}^{n} x_{ij}(\varphi_j/\tau_k) + (1/\tau_k)x_{ik} \geq 0 \quad (i = 1, \ldots, m), \\
&\sum_{j=1}^{n} g_{rj}(\varphi_j/\tau_k) \geq g_{rk} \quad (r = 1, .., s), \\
&\tau_k: URS \& \varphi_j \geq 0 \quad (j = 1, \ldots, n).
\end{aligned}
\tag{3.19}
$$

Since the minimization of $1/\tau_k$ equals the maximization of τ_k, Model (3.19) becomes as follows:

$$
\begin{aligned}
&\text{Maximize } \tau_k \\
&\text{s.t. } -\sum_{j=1}^{n} x_{ij}\varphi_j + x_{ik} \geq 0 \quad (i = 1, .., m), \\
&\sum_{j=1}^{n} g_{rj}\varphi_j \geq \tau_k g_{rk} \quad (r = 1, .., s), \\
&\tau_k: URS \& \varphi_j \geq 0 \quad (j = 1, \ldots, n).
\end{aligned}
\tag{3.20}
$$

The comparison between (3.18) and (3.20) identifies that the output-oriented model (3.20) equals the input-oriented model (3.18) in terms of their optimal efficiency measures. Thus, the efficiency score of the input-oriented RM(c) equals that of the output-oriented RM(c) under constant RTS. Q.E.D.

It is important to note that the proposed proposition is valid only for the two RM models under constant RTS, but it does not work in other variable RTS cases (so, no assumption on RTS). This book will explain the concern in the next subsection.

3.4.2 From Energy Economics

Table 3.1 summarizes the four RM measures from "energy economics". The purpose of the table is to describe how they may link to concepts widely used in energy economics.

Energy Intensity: The first concept widely used in energy economics is "EI (Energy Intensity) that we define the amount of each "energy source" divided by the amount of "GDP". Energy sources may include coal, oil, natural gas, nuclear power, renewable energy (e.g., solar photovoltaic and wind power) and other energy source. The EI represents the ratio (= each energy source / GDP), indicating the importance of each energy to GDP. The single denominator is the level of GDP, where we compute GDP = consumptions + government expenditures + investments + exports—imports. The main contributor to GDP for many countries is usually consumption, which is usually more than half of many countries. Given a level of GDP, we minimize each energy by the input-oriented DEA models because we look for the lower bound of energy source. Then, we measure EI = an estimated amount of each input (energy source) / an estimated amount of GDP, both are measured on the optimality of an input-oriented RM model.

Energy Efficiency: The second concept is "Energy Efficiency (EE)". We define it as an amount of "GDP" divided by the "a total amount of energy sources". The ratio (= GDP / the total sum of energy sources) is an opposite concept of EI. Given the total amount of energy sources, we maximize the level of GDP by the output-oriented models with multiple inputs (energy sources).

Finally, the last concept is "Operational Efficiency *(OE)*" which we minimize the total energy sources or maximize the amount of GDP, depending upon the formulation

Table 3.1 Four radial measures and three concepts in energy economics

	Method			
Economic Concept	RM(v)-Input	RM(v)-Output	RM(c)-Input	RM(c)-Output
Energy Intensity (EI)	GDP is a single output and an energy source is a single input	No	GDP is a single output and an energy source is a single input	No
Energy Efficiency (EE)	No	GDP is a single output and energy sources are multiple inputs	No	GDP is a single output and energy sources are multiple inputs
Operational Efficiency (OE)	Multiple outputs and Multiple inputs (No restriction on RTS)		Multiple outputs and Multiple inputs (Restriction on constant RTS)	

Note (a) RM stands for a radial model. The "v" and "c" imply variable and constant RTS, respectively. (b) GDP implies Gross Domestic Product. (c) All concepts (EI, EE and OE) need to be determined on an efficiency frontier so that we use DEA, not assuming that all DMUs are on the frontier

orientation (input or output oriented). We may use multiple inputs and multiple outputs for the efficiency measurement, not a single output (GDP) and not multiple inputs (energy sources).

To discuss EI and EE from DEA, we need to note the two concerns. One of the two concerns is that previous economic studies on EI and EE assume the efficiency of all entities. We cannot accept the assumption so that we use DEA, not econometrics or statistics, in measuring IE and EE because DEA can measure the level of efficiency/inefficiency. The other concern is that EI and EE are based upon GDP as a single output in DEA measurement. It is possible for us to compute the two measures under both constant and variable RTS as summarized at the bottom of Table 3.1.

DEA Computation for Two Measures: Both EI and EE are calculated as special cases of *OE* measurement where GDP is a single output and energy sources are multiple inputs. The computation of EI and EE has as the following process:

EI: We measure EI $= \overline{x}_i/\overline{GDP}$ where $\overline{x}_i$ is the i th estimated energy factor ($i = 1,.., m$) and $\overline{GDP}$ is the estimated (minimized, not observed) level of GDP. Using input-oriented DEA models: Models (3.1) or (3.7), we measure the level of EI_{ik} on the i th input of k th DMU as follows:

$$EI_{ik} = (\theta_k^* x_{ik} - d_i^{x*})/(g_k + d^{g*}) \text{ for } i = 1, \ldots, m. \tag{3.21}$$

where we determine θ_k^*, d_i^{x*} and d^{g*} on the optimality of Model (3.1) or Model (3.7). The g_k is the observed GDP of the k th DMU and the x_{ik} is the observed i th input of k th DMU. Equation (3.21) indicates that DEA models adjust such observed values into the ones on an efficiency frontier.

EE: We measure EE $= \overline{\text{GDP}} / \sum_{i=1}^{m} \overline{x}_i$ implying “an estimated level of GDP” divided by “the total sum of estimated energy factors” where both are on the output-based DEA models: Models (3.9) and (3.15). We determine the level of EE_k on the k th DMU as follows:

$$EE_k = \tau_k^* g_k / \sum_{i=1}^{m} (x_{ik} - d_i^{x*}), \tag{3.22}$$

where τ_k^* and d_i^{x*} are determined on the optimality of Model (3.9) and (3.15). Equation (3.22) indicates that DEA models adjust such observed values into the ones on an efficiency frontier.

Illustrative Example: Readers may find an illustrative example on EI and EE in the following article:

Sueyoshi, T. Goto, M. (2023) Energy intensity, energy efficiency and economic growth among OECD nations from 2000–2009. Energies Vol. 16, Issue 4, pp. 1–29.

3.5 Efficiency Reexamination

3.5.1 Multiplier Restriction

An empirical difficulty in DEA applications is that they often suffer from an occurrence of many efficient DMUs. For example, 98 DMUs are efficient and 2 DMUs are inefficient among 100 DMUs in a computation result. Such an occurrence is mathematically acceptable, but practically unacceptable, from our economics and business perspectives, because we cannot determine the rank of efficient DMUs. The degree of *OE* is not so important among corporate leaders. In many cases, the rank of DMUs is more important than the degree of *OE* in a competitive market.

Assurance Region (AR) Analysis: To reduce the number of efficient DMUs by restricting the range of multipliers (i.e., dual variables), Thompson et al. (1986), Dyson and Thanassoulis (1988) and others have proposed the use of AR analysis. The analysis incorporates the following multiplier restrictions into the proposed dual formulations:

$$\begin{aligned} \underline{lv}_i \le v_i \big/ v_1 \le \overline{uv}_i (i = 2, 3, \ldots, m) \text{ and } \underline{lu}_r \\ \le u_r \big/ u_1 \le \overline{uu}_r (r = 2, 3, \ldots, s), \end{aligned} \tag{3.23}$$

where the left-hand side of (3.23) indicates the ratio of the i th input multiplier to the first one between lower (l) and upper (u) bounds. The ratio combinations are applicable to the r th output to the first one as specified in the right-hand side of Eq. (3.23). We expect the multipliers to be positive in many cases, whose magnitudes are larger than ε_n.

Equations (3.23) are further extendable by the following input and output weighted measure on the specific k th DMU:

$$\begin{aligned} &\underline{lv}_i \le x_{ik} v_i \Big/ \sum_{i=1}^{m} x_{ik} v_i \le \overline{uv}_i (i = 1, 2, \ldots, m) \text{ and} \\ &\underline{lu}_r \le y_{rk} u_r \Big/ \sum_{r=1}^{s} y_{rk} u_r \le \overline{uu}_r \ (r = 1, 2, \ldots, s), \end{aligned} \tag{3.24}$$

where the ratio is determined by the i th weighted input divided by the sum of the total weighted inputs. In a similar manner, we may apply the ratio to the r th output as formulated in Eqs. (3.24). Each equation indicates the importance of the i th input and the r th output among these production factors. The bars upper and under indicate upper and lower limits of these ratios.

This study considers that SDGs belong to a future potential direction in multiplier region which we can specify by the two bounds for AR. The remaining task is that we need to incorporate a time horizon to express an annual change for expressing

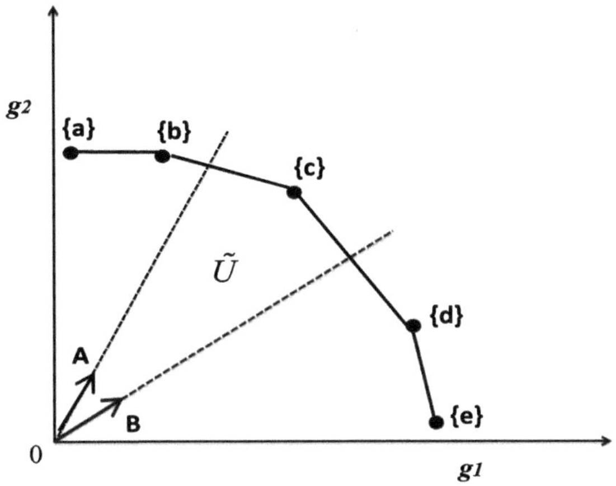

Fig. 3.2 Multiplier restriction for SDGs. *Note* The number of efficient DMUs decreases from the five DMUs: {a}-{b}-{c}-[d]-{e} on the efficiency frontier to a single DMU {c}. We understand that strong multiplier restriction often produces an infeasible solution on optimality. The two-directional vectors (A and B) are used to restrict the direction of output multipliers. The production possibility set is expressed by $\tilde{U}$ via restricting multipliers. This figure assumes that all DMUs use the same amount of an input. The input-based restriction may be found in Sueyoshi and Goto (2018). The multiplier restriction may be used for SDGs because the direction toward sustainability is expressed by the upper and lower vectors

the level of expected sustainability. This aspect of SDGs will be discussed in the proceeding chapters (after Chap. 4).

Figure 3.2 visually describes an implication of multiplier restriction in the data domain of two outputs. All DMUs from {a} to {e}, consisting of an efficiency frontier, have the same magnitude of an input so that the figure drops it. Let us consider A and B as the two vectors to restrict output multipliers. They are used as the upper and lower bounds for multiplier restriction, expressed by $\tilde{U}$ in Fig. 3.2. As a result of such multiplier restriction, the number of efficient DMUs decreases from five to one, i.e., {c} because only the DMU can exist within the multiplier range ($\tilde{U}$) for outputs.

The proposed multiplier restriction has two concerns from the practical uses. One of the two concerns is that the approach depends upon prior information (e.g., experience and previous empirical evidence) for multiplier restriction. It is often difficult for us to access such prior information. The other is that the approach may produce an infeasible solution on optimality as a result of strict multiplier restriction. We must carefully consider how to restrict multipliers on the use of the AR approach[5].

[5] We have discussed multiplier restriction by AR. We know that there is another approach, referred to as "Cone Ratio (CR)", to restrict multipliers to a given range. See Charnes et al (1989) for a detailed discussion on CR. See Sueyoshi and Goto (2018) as well.

3.5.2 Cross Reference Analysis

Besides the multiplier restriction, many different applications have used a cross reference method to classify efficient DMUs into two groups. One of the two groups is efficient DMUs, located on a vertex of an efficiency frontier. The other group includes the other efficient DMUs, locating on the efficiency frontier, but not on the vertex. See Charnes et al., (1986, 1991) for the original DMU classification.

This chapter classifies the three groups of DMUs by an optimal solution of RM regarding the k th DMU. The assumption on constant RTS is necessary for the classification. The proposed cross reference method, using RM(c), can produce a feasible solution on optimality under the assumption. In contrast, RM(v) may produce an infeasible solution in the case of variable RTS.

The three groups of DMU classifications[6] have the following specification:

$$\begin{aligned} &E = \{k \in J \,|\, \theta_{\mathrm{k}}^{*} = 1,\ \lambda_{\mathrm{k}}^{*} = 1,\ \lambda_{j}^{*} = 0\ (\text{all j} \neq \text{k} \in \text{J}), \\ &\text{all zero slacks, and unique solution}\}, \\ &E' = \{k \in J \,|\, \theta_{\mathrm{k}}^{*} = 1,\ \lambda_{\mathrm{k}}^{*} \leq 1,\ \lambda_{j}^{*} > 0\ (\text{some j} \in \text{J}), \\ &\text{all zero slacks, and multiple solutions}\}\ \& \\ &IF = \{k \in J \,|\, \theta_{\mathrm{k}}^{*} = 1\ \text{, and at least one positive slack}\} \end{aligned} \tag{3.25}$$

Here, a whole set (J) consists of all DMUs. See our description on the structure of Model (3.1).

The first two groups of efficient DMUs are located on an efficiency (OE) frontier. The efficient group of DMUs (E) locates on the vertexes of an efficiency frontier. The efficient DMUs in the other group (E') are located between such efficient DMUs in E. They (in E') may suffer from an occurrence of multiple solutions on a combination(s) of a reference set. As long as DEA uses linear programming, it cannot escape from the occurrence of multiple solutions. The last group (IF) consists of inefficient DMUs, but they exist on the efficiency frontier. They are not efficient because there is at least one positive slack. Therefore, DEA users need to examine both efficiency scores and slacks.

---

[6] See Charnes et al., (1986, 1981) for DMU classification. Note that in addition to E and E', inefficient DMUs have the following DMU group:

$$\begin{aligned} IF' &= \{k \in J_n \,|\, \theta_k^* = 1\ \text{, at least one positive slack \& multiple solutions}\}, \\ IE' &= \{k \in J_n \,|\, \theta_k^* < 1,\ \lambda_k^* = 0\ \&\ \lambda_j^* > 0\ (\exists j \in E)\}, \\ IF &= \{k \in J_d \,|\, \theta_k^* = 1\ \&\ \text{at least one positive slack}\}, \\ IE &= \{k \in J_d \,|\, \theta_k^* < 1,\ \lambda_k^* = 0\ \&\ \lambda_j^* > 0\ (\exists j \in E)\} \end{aligned}$$

We pay attention on an occurrence of multiple efficient DMUs so that we do not make any comment on the inefficient DMUs.

As mentioned previously, DEA may produce many efficient DMUs in *E* U *E'*. Therefore, it is necessary for us to classify them further if we want to prepare their ranking assessment. That is the purpose of the cross reference method.

To describe the proposed approach, let us select a DMU$\{a\}$, belonging to *E* U *E'* and return to input-based RM(c) to obtain computational feasibility. The cross-reference efficiency ($\theta^*_{a,b}$) of the *b* th DMU in *J* (a whole DMU set) is measured by the following RM (e.g., Doyle & Green, 1994; Green et al., 1996):

$$
\begin{aligned}
&Minimize \quad \theta_b \\
&s.t. \quad -\sum_{j \in J-a} x_{ij}\lambda_j - d_i^x + \theta_b x_{ib} = 0 \quad (i = 1, \ldots, m), \\
&\qquad \sum_{j \in J-a} g_{rj}\lambda_j - d_r^g = g_{rb} \quad (r = 1, \ldots, s), \\
&\qquad \theta_b : URS \& \lambda_j \geq 0 \quad (j \in J - a), \\
&\qquad d_i^x \geq 0 \, (i = 1, \ldots, m) \;\&\; d_r^g \geq 0 \quad (r = 1, \ldots, s).
\end{aligned}
\tag{3.26}
$$

An important feature of Model (3.26) is that if the efficient DMU$\{a\}$ belongs to *E*, then the elimination changes the shape of an efficiency frontier. As a result, the degree of $\theta^*_{a,b}$ may change from the original efficiency measure. In contrast, if it belongs to *E'*, then the elimination does not make any change on the frontier shape because it does not locate on the vertex of an efficiency frontier. In the case, the degree of $\theta^*_{a,b}$ does not produce any efficiency change. Thus, the cross reference method can provide us with an additional measure on efficient DMUs, based upon which we can classify them. The most important benefit of the proposed approach is that it is possible for us to measure a degree of cross reference of the *a* th DMU in *E* U *E'* by examining the degree of $D^*_{a,a} = \theta^*_{a,a} - \theta^*_a$. In the case, $\theta^*_{a,a}$ may be more than unity so that $D^*_{a,a}$ becomes positive. Thus, we reevaluate all efficient DMUs in the group (*E*) on the vertex of an efficiency frontier by using the degree of $D^*_{a,a}$. The cross reference can provide us with information to classify efficient DMUs for ranking analysis.

Finally, it is important to note the three concerns on the use of the cross reference. First, the proposed RM approach is feasible under constant RTS, but it may produce an infeasible solution under variable RTS. Second, there is no theoretical rationale on the validity of the cross reference although it intuitively appeals to us. Finally, the assessment on efficient DMUs is based upon local evaluation by considering a limited number of efficient DMUs in a reference set. It does not cover the group-wide performance assessment of all DMUs by using a single set of common multipliers (weights) on efficient DMUs. Thus, the cross-reference has a high level of computational tractability on DMU ranking analysis but lacks any theoretical rationale within the framework of RM(c).

3.6 Cost Analysis

3.6.1 Cost Efficiency

A methodological benefit of RM is that it can conceptually connect it to cost efficiency analysis that minimizes the amount of total production cost (Sueyoshi, 1999). The development of ESG and SDGs needs a financial support for their practice. The cost-based efficiency will be important for such environmental assessment.

Assuming that we can access an input price vector, $P_j = (p_{1j}, p_{2j}, \ldots, p_{mj})$, of all DMUs ($j = 1,.., n$), the cost efficiency of the k th DMU is measured by the following model:

$$\begin{aligned} &\textit{Minimize} \sum_{i=1}^{m} p_{ik}x_i \\ &s.t. \quad -\sum_{j=1}^{n} x_{ij}\lambda_j + x_i \geq 0 \quad (i = 1,.., m), \\ &\qquad \sum_{j=1}^{n} g_{rj}\lambda_j \geq g_{rk} \quad (r = 1,.., s), \\ &\qquad \sum_{j=1}^{n} \lambda_j = 1, \\ &\qquad \lambda_j \geq 0\,(j = 1, \cdots, n) \,\&\, x_i \geq 0 \quad (i = 1,.., m). \end{aligned} \tag{3.27}$$

where $X = (x_1, x_2, .., x_m)^{Tr}$ is an unknown input quantity vector, not an observed vector as previously discussed for the RM measurement. Here, Model (3.27) does not incorporate slacks into the formulation because it looks for an input vector that attains cost minimum, not an efficiency score. Moreover, dual variables become positive, as discussed below, because an input-related dual vector corresponds to an input price vector. Therefore, this chapter drops a slack vector in the objective function of Model (3.27).

The cost efficiency of the k th DMU is determined by the following manner (Farrell, 1957):

$$\mu^* = c_k^* / c_k = \sum_{i=1}^{m} p_{ik}x_i^* \Big/ \sum_{i=1}^{m} p_{ik}x_{ik} \tag{3.28}$$

The cost efficiency implies the minimized cost divided by an observed cost regarding the k th DMU.

The dual formulation of (3.27) becomes

$$\begin{aligned} & Maximize \ \sum_{r=1}^{s} u_r g_{rk} + \sigma \\ & s.t. \quad -\sum_{i=1}^{m} v_i x_{ij} + \sum_{r=1}^{s} u_r g_{rj} + \sigma \le 0 \quad (j = 1, \ldots, n), \\ & \qquad v_i \le p_{ik} \quad (i = 1, \ldots, m), \\ & \qquad v_i \ge 0 (i = 1, \ldots, m), u_r \ge 0 \quad (r = 1, \ldots, s) \& \\ & \qquad \sigma : URS. \end{aligned} \tag{3.29}$$

On optimality, both primal and dual models have the cost minimum expressed by $\sum_{i=1}^{m} p_{ik} x_i^* = \sum_{r=1}^{s} u_r^* g_{rk} + \sigma^*$. Moreover, $x_i^*(p_{ik} - v_i^*) = 0$ (i = 1, ..., m) always exist between the two models as a part of Complementary Slackness Conditions (CSCs) of linear programming. If $x_i^* > 0$ for all *i*, then Model (3.29) becomes the following condensed model:

$$\begin{aligned} & Maximize \quad \sum_{r=1}^{s} u_r g_{rk} + \sigma \\ & s.t. \qquad \sum_{r=1}^{s} u_r g_{rj} + \sigma \le \sum_{i=1}^{m} p_{ik} x_{ij} \quad (j = 1, \ldots, n), \\ & \qquad\quad u_r \ge 0 \quad (r = 1, \ldots, s) \end{aligned} \tag{3.30}$$

because $p_{ik} = v_i^*$ exists on the optimality of Model (3.30). Equation (3.28) indicates that the cost minimum of the *k* th DMU is less than or equal all the cost estimates measured by its observed input price vector.

3.6.2 Efficiency Measures in Production and Cost Analyses

The previous discussions have used the term "efficicncy". Hereafter, we separate the concept of efficiency into more specific classifications related to the proposed input-oriented RM. Farrell (1957) has conceptually specified some of these efficiency mcasures in the case of a single output with multiple inputs under constant and diminishing RTS. Then, Sueyoshi (1999) has elaborated them by extending these production factors under Constant RTS (CRTS) and Variable RTS (VRTS).

The efficiency measures used here are as follows:

(a) Operational Efficiency (OE_v) under Variable RTS (VRTS): Implying the degree of operational efficiency that exists on the optimal objective value of RM(v), e.g., Model (3.1),
(b) Operational and Scale Efficiency (OE_c) under constant RTS (CRTS): Implying the degree of operational efficiency that exists on the optimal objective valuc of RM(c), e.g., Model (3.7),
(c) Production-based Scale Efficiency (*PSE*): $PSE = OE_c / OE_v$.
(d) Cost Efficiency (CE_v) under VRTS: $OE_v = \mu^*$ from Eq. (3.28) via Model (3.27).

(e) Cost and Scale Efficiency (CE_c) under CRTS: $OE_c = \mu^*$ from Eq. (3.28) via Model (3.27) without $\sum_{j=1}^{n} \lambda_j = 1$.
(f) Cost-based Scale Efficiency (CSE): $CSE = CE_c/CE_v$
(g) Allocative Efficiency (AE_v) under VRTS: $AE_v = CE_v/OE_v$ and
(h) Allocative and Scale Efficiency (AE_c) under CRTS: $AE_c = CE_c/OE_c$.

The output-oriented measures have another type of efficiency classifications. We describe only the input-oriented measures because they can directly link to cost-based efficiency concepts.

Figure 3.3 visually describes eight efficiency measures, (a) to (h), discussed above. The figure has two efficiency frontiers, depending upon the assumption on RTS (i.e., constant or variable RTS). The efficiency frontier, consisting of a piece-wise linear contour line, DMUs: {f}-{g}-{b}-{h}-{i}-{j}, is under variable RTS, while the other curve is under constant RTS. For our descriptive convenience, we start with a visual explanation on OE_V. The degree of OE_V is visually specified by the distance {ob}/{oa} under variable RTS, where {ob} stands for a distance between the origin {o} and DMU{b}. In a similar manner, {oa} indicates the distance between the origin {o} and DMU{a}. This section may drop the term (DMU) if a specified point in the figure is used to indicate a projected point, so not indicating a DMU. Shifting from variable to constant RTS, OE_c is measured by {oc}/{oa}. The difference between the two measures is expressed by $PSE = OE_c/OE_v$ = {oc/oa}/{ob/oa} = {oc/ob}. For example, DMU{a} needs to reduce the amount of an input vector from {a} to {b} under variable RTS. The level of such input reduction, indicating an amount of inefficiency, is expressed by the distance of ({oa}-{ob})/{oa}. By controlling the operation size, the DMU{a} can attain the input decrease until it attains a projected point{c}. The inefficiency due to an inappropriate operation size becomes ({ob}-{oc})/{oa}. Thus, we separate OE_C into two components, so being $OE_c = (OE_v)(PSE)$.

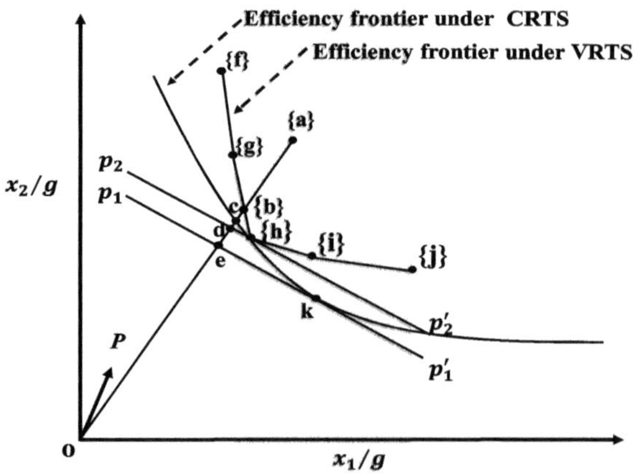

Fig. 3.3 Efficiency measures. *Note* This study modifies the figure prepared by Sueyoshi (1999). See also Sueyoshi and Goto (2018). This book reorganizes these works. A DMU with the parenthesis { } is an observed one and without it is a projected DMU

Next, we change the production-based description to the cost-based one such as CE_v, CE_c and CSE. Given an input price vector (P), the DMU {h} indicates the cost minimum for DMU{a} in the case of variable RTS. Here, lines p_1-p_1' and p_2-p_2' indicate a level of cost under a fixed ratio of input prices with p_1/p_2. The DMUs {d} and {h} are located on the line (p_2 and p_2'), so both having the same value of cost minimum. Therefore, CE_v = {od}/{oa}. If the line is closer to the origin, the level of cost is lower. Meanwhile, under constant RTS, the point {k} indicates such cost minimum. The total production cost becomes the same on {k} and {e} because both points are located on the line (p_1 and p_1'). Therefore, CE_c = {oe}/{oa}. The degree of CSE is determined by the ratio between CE_v and CE_c. Thus, we have $CSE = CE_c/CE_v$ = ({oe}/{oa})/({od}/{oa}) = {oe}/{od}. The decomposition related to the cost minimization process indicates that DMU{a} needs to attain {h} by an effort for cost minimization and further attain {k} by controlling its operational size.

In addition to these efficiency concepts, AE_v and AE_c have unique features that we cannot find in the other efficiency measures. For example, we determine the degree of AE_v by $AE_v = CE_v/OE_v$ and AE_V = ({od}/{oa}) / ({ob}/{oa} = {od}/{ob} in Fig. 3.3. Given an input price vector (P), the efficiency measure indicates how each DMU controls the ratio of input allocation by itself for cost minimization under variable RTS. The degree of AE_C has the same implication under constant RTS.

3.7 Illustrative Examples

Table 3.2 lists a data set to discuss three efficiency measures related to two RMs. The table contains eight DMUs from {a} to {h}, each of which uses a single input to produce a single output. This is for our illustrative purpose. Table 3.3 summarizes computational results on OE_v, OE_c and PSE where OE_v is measured under variable RTS and OE_c is measured under constant RTS, both are associated with the two efficiency frontiers.

The formulation to measure OE_V of DMU{a}, for example, is formulated as follows:

Table 3.2 A simple illustrative example

DMU	{a}	{b}	{c}	{d}	{e}	{f}	{g}	{h}
Input	5	8	6	7	5	4	9	10
Desirable output	3	5	6	4	9	7	4	5

Note DMUs are listed by {a}-{h}

Table 3.3 Production-based efficiency measures

DMU	{a}	{b}	{c}	{d}	{e}	{f}	{g}	{h}
OE_v	0.800	0.500	0.667	0.571	1.000	1.000	0.444	0.400
OE_c	0.333	0.347	0.556	0.317	1.000	0.972	0.247	0.278
PSE	0.417	0.694	0.833	0.556	1.000	0.972	0.556	0.694

Note OE_v and OE_c are operational efficiency under variable RTS and constant RTS, respectively

$$\begin{aligned}
&\textit{Minimize}\ \theta \\
&s.t.\quad -5\lambda_a - 8\lambda_b - 6\lambda_c - 7\lambda_d - 5\lambda_e - 4\lambda_f - \lambda_g - 10\lambda_h + 5\theta \geq 0 \\
&\qquad 3\lambda_a + 5\lambda_b + 6\lambda_c + 4\lambda_d + 9\lambda_e + 7\lambda_f + 4\lambda_g + 5\lambda_h \geq 1 \\
&\qquad \lambda_a + \lambda_b + \lambda_c + \lambda_d + \lambda_e + \lambda_f + \lambda_g + \lambda_h = 1 \\
&\qquad \lambda_j \geq 0\,(j = a, b, \cdots, h)\ \&\ \theta : URS.
\end{aligned}$$

We need to repeat the computation process on DMU{a} to measure the other DMUs from {b} to {h}. This computation of DEA is tedious due to the nature of relative comparison among DMUs.

As listed in Table 3.3, only DMU{e} attains the status of efficiency in the three measures. The DMU {f} attains the status of efficiency on OE_v under variable RTS. The other DMUs {a, b, c, d, g and h} have exhibited some level of inefficiency on OE_v. To describe the implication of PSE, measured by OE_C/OE_V, let us pay attention to the inefficient DMU{d}. Since the computational results of the table originate from the input-oriented measurement, we find that the ideal performance of the DMU{d} is a projected point{r} on the efficiency frontier under variable RTS and is another projected point {q} under constant RTS. The degree of OE_V on DMU{d} is {pr}/{pd} = 0.571. The degree of OE_c is {pq}/{pd} = 0.317. Based upon the two efficiency measures, we determine the degree of PSE on the DMU by OE_c/OE_v = ({pq}/{pd})/({pr}/{pd}) = {pq}/{pr} = 0.643/0.810 = 0.794. The description on DMU{d} in terms of the three efficiency measures is applicable regarding the other DMUs.

$$\begin{aligned}
&\textit{Minimize}\ 1x_1 + 6x_2 \\
&s.t.\quad -6\lambda_a - 5\lambda_b - 8\lambda_c - 3\lambda_d \\
&\qquad -7\lambda_e - 4\lambda_f - 8\lambda_g - 2\lambda_h + x_1 \geq 0, \\
&\qquad -5\lambda_a - 8\lambda_b - 4\lambda_c - 9\lambda_d - 5\lambda_e - 6\lambda_f \\
&\qquad -5\lambda_g - 6\lambda_h + x_2 \geq 0, \\
&\qquad 6\lambda_a + 10\lambda_b + 6\lambda_c + 8\lambda_d \\
&\qquad +2\lambda_e + 10\lambda_f + 7\lambda_g + 4\lambda_h \geq 2, \\
&\qquad \lambda_a + \lambda_b + \lambda_c + \lambda_d + \lambda_e + \lambda_f + \lambda_g + \lambda_h = 1, \\
&\qquad \lambda_j \geq 0\ (j = a, b, \ldots, h)\&\ x_i \geq 0 \quad (i = 1, 2).
\end{aligned}$$

Table 3.4 lists another data set to discuss eight efficiency measures related to production and cost-based efficiency measures. First, let us describe the following formulation to measure the level of CE_v on DMU{d}, for example:

Table 3.4 Illustrative example

DMU	{a}	{b}	{c}	{d}	{e}	{f}	{g}	{h}
Input 1	6	5	8	3	7	4	8	2
Input 2	5	8	4	9	5	6	5	6
Desirable output	6	10	6	8	2	10	7	4
Price of input 1	5	6	8	1	6	3	7	3
Price of input 2	3	3	8	6	4	4	3	7

Note {a}-{h} are DMUs

Table 3.5 summarizes eight efficiency measures related to production and cost analyses. As summarized in the table, DMU{f} is efficient in terms of the eight measures. The other DMUs {b, c, d, and h} have mixed efficiency measures in the eight measures and the remaining DMUs {a, e, and g} are inefficient in these measures.

Returning to energy economics, Fig. 3.4 visually describes OE_v measures under variable RTS and OE_c masures under constant RTS, both are associated with the two efficiency frontiers. We minimize an energy factor as an input to decrease the energy intensity (EI). An output is GDP in measuring EI and EE. In the figure, the degree of EI is measured on the two projected points (f and g) and the degree of EE is measured on those h and i. Note that both are on the efficiency frontiers, so that we need DEA-based frontier analysis to measure EI and EE.

Table 3.5 Production and cost-based efficiency measures

DMU	{a}	{b}	{c}	{d}	{e}	{f}	{g}	{h}
OE_v	0.966	0.800	1.000	1.000	0.909	1.000	0.900	1.000
OE_c	0.720	0.796	0.900	1.000	0.240	1.000	0.840	0.750
PSE	0.746	0.996	0.900	1.000	0.264	1.000	0.933	0.750
CE_v	0.696	0.778	0.722	0.632	0.581	1.000	0.549	1.000
CE_c	0.507	0.778	0.500	0.561	0.155	1.000	0.454	0.450
CSE	0.728	1.000	0.692	0.889	0.267	1.000	0.826	0.450
AE_v	0.721	0.972	0.722	0.632	0.639	1.000	0.610	1.000
AE_c	0.704	0.977	0.556	0.561	0.645	1.000	0.540	0.600

Note Operational efficiency under variable RTS, OE_c: Operational and scale efficiency (OE_c) under constant RTS, PSE: Production-based scale efficiency $PSE = OE_c/OE_v$, CE_v Cost efficiency under variable RTS, CE_c: Cost and scale efficiency under constant RTS, CSE: Cost-based scale efficiency $CSE = CE_c/CE_v$, AE_v: Allocative efficiency under variable RTS $AE_v = CE_v/OE_v$, and AE_c: Allocative and scale efficiency under constant RTS $AE_c = CE_c/OE_c$

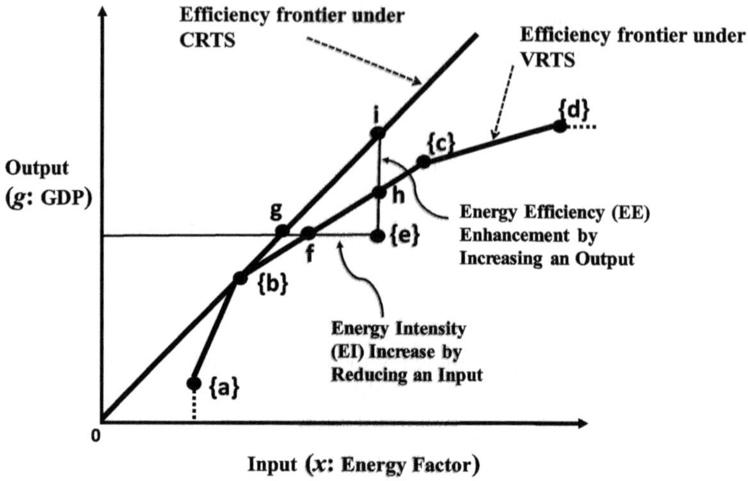

Fig. 3.4 Projections for EI and EE under two efficiency frontiers. *Note* An efficiency frontier under VRTS consists of {a}-{b}-{c}-{d}. Efficient DMUs are {a, b, c and d}. An inefficient DMU is {e}. Projected DMUs (f and g) are determined by input-based minimization (e.g., EI). The other projected DMUs DMU (h and i) may be projected on the two frontiers by output-based maximization (e.g., EE)

3.8 Discussion

This chapter has reviewed the standard use of DEA that serves as a methodological basis for preparing DEA-EA in the remaining chapters. We have the three concerns to be noted, here. First, the use of DEA (RM in this chapter) is conventionally classified into input-based or output-based model, both have different unique features in their applications. Second, we have reexamined the two types of DEA from the perspective of energy economics, in particular EI and EE. The two measures serve as major concepts for discussing energy economics and energy policy. Finally, the chapter adds multiplier restriction and cost analysis, which are later methodologically linked to ESG and SDGs after incorporating the existence of undesirable outputs.

References

Banker, R. D., Charnes, A., & Cooper, W. W. (1984). Some models for estimating technical and scale inefficiencies in data envelopment analysis. *Management Science, 30*, 1078–1092.

Charnes, A., Cooper, W. W., & Rhodes, E. (1978). Measuring the efficiency of decision making units. *European Journal of Operational Research, 6*, 429–444.

Charnes, A., Cooper, W. W., Golany, B., Seiford, L., & Stutz, J. (1985). Foundations of data envelopment analysis for Pareto-Koopmans efficient empirical production functions. *Journal of Econometrics, 30*, 91–107.

Charnes, A., Cooper, W. W., & Thrall, R. M. (1986). Classifying and characterizing efficiencies and inefficiencies in data envelopment analysis. *Operations Research Letters, 5*, 105–110.

Charnes, A., Cooper, W. W., & Thrall, R. M. (1991). A structure for classifying and charactering efficiency and inefficiency in data envelopment analysis. *Journal of Productivity Analysis, 2*, 197–237.

Charnes, A., Cooper, W. W., Wei, Q. L., & Huang, Z. M. (1989). Cone ratio data environmental analysis and multi-objective programming. *International Journal of System Science, 20*, 1099–1118.

Debreu, G. (1951). The Coefficient of Resource Utilization. *Econometrica, 19*, 273–292.

Debreu, G. (1959). *Theory of Value*. Colonial Press Inc.

Doyle, J., & Green, R. (1994). Efficiency and cross-efficiency in DEA: Derivations, meanings and uses. *The Journal of the Operational Research Society, 45*, 567–578.

Dyson, R. G., & Thanassoulis, E. (1988). Reducing weight flexibility in data environmental analysis. *Journal of the Operational Research Society, 39*, 563–576.

Farrell, M. J. (1954). An application of activity analysis to the theory of the firm. *Econometrica, 22*, 291–302.

Farrell, M. J. (1957). The measurement of productive efficiency. *Journal of the Royal Statistical Society*, Series A, 120. *Part, 3*, 253–329.

Farrell, M.J. & Fieldhouse, M. (1962) Production functions under increasing returns to scale. *Journal of the Royal Statistical Society*, Series A (General)125, 252–267.

Green, R., Doyle, J. R., & Cook, W. D. (1996). Preference voting and project ranking using DEA and cross-evaluation. *European Journal of Operational Research, 90*, 461–472.

Glover, F., & Sueyoshi, T. (2009). Contributions of Professor William W. Cooper in operations research and management science. *European Journal of Operational Research, 197*, 1–16.

Ijiri, Y., & Sueyoshi, T. (2010). Accounting essays by Professor William W. Cooper: Revisiting in commemoration of his 95th birthday. ABACUS: A Journal of Accounting. *Finance and Business Studies, 46*, 464–505.

Koopmans, T.C. (1951) Analysis of production as an efficient combination of activities. Activity Analysis of Production and Allocation, Edited by T.C. Koopmans. Wiley, New York.

Russell, R. R. (1985). Measures of technical efficiency. *Journal of Economic Theory, 35*, 109–126.

Russell, R. R. (1990). Continuity of measures of technical efficiency. *Journal of Economic Theory, 51*, 255–267.

Sueyoshi, T. (1999). DEA duality on returns to scale (RTS) in production and cost analyses: An occurrence of multiple solutions and differences between production based and cost-based RTS estimates. *Management Science, 45*, 1593–1608.

Sueyoshi, T., & Goto, M. (2018). *Environment Assessment an Energy and Sustainability by Data Envelopment Analysis*. Wiley.

Sueyoshi, T., & Goto, M. (2023). Energy intensity, energy efficiency and economic growth among OECD nations from 2000–2009. *Energies, 16*, 1–29.

Sueyoshi, T., & Yuan, Y. (2016). Marginal rate of transformation and rate of substitution measured by DEA environmental assessment: Comparison among European and North American nations. *Energy Economics, 56*, 270–287.

Sueyoshi, T., & Yuan, Y. (2017). Social sustainability measured by intermediate approach for DEA environmental assessment: Chinese regional planning for economic development and pollution prevention. *Energy Economics, 66*, 154–166.

Thompson, R. G., Singleton, F. D., Thrall, R. M., & Smith, B. A. (1986). Comparative site evaluation for locating a high-energy physics lab in Texas. *Interface, 16*, 35–49.

Chapter 4
Radial, Non-radial and Intermediate Models for Environmental Assessment (ESG)

Abstract This chapter compares three DEA approaches for EA (Environmental Assessment) which examines the level of simultaneous achievement on economic prosperity and environmental protection. Chap. 2 has discussed that ESG and SDGs are important concepts for the sustainability enhancement in our societies, but they are imprecise in terms of practicality. To handle the impreciseness, Chap. 3 has first discussed DEA from energy economics and production economics. In this chapter, we incorporate "undesirable outputs" into the DEA framework to develop a new type of approach which is referred to as "DEA-EA". The DEA approach measures the performance of many entities which use multiple inputs to produce not only multiple desirable outputs (e.g., electricity) but also multiple undesirable outputs (e.g., CO_2). The incorporation of undesirable outputs makes it possible that we measure the level of ESG by DEA-EA. We conventionally classified DEA-EA into radial or non-radial categories in the previous studies. Recently, a new "intermediate" model, analytically locating between the radial and non-radial measures, has been proposed as the third alternative. The new approach measures a degree of unified inefficiency on each production factor so that it can determine the level of unified efficiency from the total of these inefficiency scores. This chapter discusses the analytical features of the three (radial, non-radial and intermediate) approaches by comparing their analytical structures. The methodological comparison conveys a message that DEA-EA is applicable to various ESG issues from economic prosperity and environmental protection. However, it may be true that many DEA-EA applications often suffer from a methodological bias, implying that different models produce different empirical results. In guiding large policy issues on ESG, we need to compare several different models to obtain reliable empirical evidences. This chapter discusses such a methodological issue from the practicality of these models in assessing various concerns on energy and environment. We analytically describe how DEA-EA can determine ESG from "investment", using non-radial model. The other two (radial and intermediate) models may follow the similar process on ESG investments as discussed for the non-radial model.

Keywords Radial measure · Non-radial measure · Intermediate measure · Unified efficiency

T. Sueyoshi and M. Goto, *Environment and Sustainability for ESG and SDGs*,
https://doi.org/10.1007/978-981-96-2464-5_4

4.1 Introduction

Our difficulty to attain a low-carbon society, as a part of ESG, is that we do not have a practical methodology to properly assess both economic development and pollution prevention in a unified framework. The economic development usually increases a level of pollutions if we do not develop any technology for environmental protection. Here, we need to mention two concerns on environment protection. One of the two concerns is that methodologically, it is almost impossible to use the standard RMs (Radial Models in Chap. 3) for discussing the environmental protection. Because these models do not incorporate undesirable outputs (e.g., CO_2 and NO_x) in their computational process. The other concern is that we must consider a technology progress and its shift among nations. See Chaps. 7 and 8 for technology dissemination.

To partly deal with the methodological difficulty (because of no undesirable outputs), we propose a new type of DEA that has conventionally served as a practical methodology for performance evaluation from ESG and SDGs enhancements. The standard DEA previously characterizes economic activities by considering only the relationship between desirable outputs (e.g., electricity) and inputs (e.g., the number of employees).[1]

The purpose of this chapter is to extend the DEA method, discussed in Chap. 3, into DEA-EA which has a high level of practicality by incorporating the amount of CO_2 emission and other types of pollutions (e.g., marine pollution and nuclear waste) as "undesirable output(s)" into the proposed framework. The incorporation of undesirable outputs implies that DEA-EA can handle the "quantitative" exploration on ESG. Here, we must admit that the practicality of DEA-EA is not perfect and the scope is limited within the quantitative analysis for approximation. However, we believe that it may be better than nothing and it is a promising approach.

To discuss DEA-EA applied to ESG, we start with a review on previous studies prepared by Sueyoshi and Goto (2018). In their review, this study finds that they have analytically separated various models for DEA-EA into "radial" or "non-radial" categories. Acknowledging the importance of such previous classification and developments, this chapter newly adds an "intermediate" model and its related mathematical formulations. The discussion in Chap. 4 will be a basis for Chap. 5 in the manner that we can discuss how the intermediate model can deal with SDGs in a time horizon of DEA-EA.

The intermediate model, first proposed by Sueyoshi and Yuan (2017), analytically locates between the radial and non-radial models, so being referred to as the intermediate in their study. The model can incorporate the radial properties as found

[1] See Chap. 2, along with Glover and Sueyoshi (2009) and Ijiri and Sueyoshi (2009), for a historical perspective of DEA and Sueyoshi et al., (2017a, 2017b) for environmental assessment. A problem associated with DEA applications was that the standard use was very limited in its applicability, so lacking practicality in terms of environmental assessment because it did not have a computational capability to handle the existence of undesirable outputs (e.g., CO2). See Chap. 3 reviews the framework and standard use of DEA.

in Debreu-Farrell type of efficiency measurement and the non-radial properties as found in the Pareto–Koopmans type of efficiency measurement. The intermediate model can measure the degree of unified inefficiency on each production factor and determines the level of total unified inefficiency from the average of the sum of these factor-based inefficiency measures. This type of efficiency belongs to Russell (1985, 1990) measure. Note that we separate outputs into desirable and undesirable ones in this chapter. Then, we combine them into a unification process in the proposed efficiency/inefficiency measurement.

The remainder of this chapter has the following structure: Sect. 4.2 discusses underlying concepts used for the development of the three DEA models for economic prosperity and environment protection. Section 4.3 describes the radial model. Section 4.4 discusses the non-radial model. Section 4.5 describes the intermediate model. Section 4.6 describes methodological differences among the three models in their unification processes. Section 4.7 discusses how DEA-EA can handle ESG investment. The investment for eco-technology is the gist of ESG. Section 4.8 discusses how DEA-EA can deal with SDGs in a time horizon. We discuss both sections under managerial disposability. Section 4.9 summarizes this chapter along with future extensions. Appendix describes how to handle an occurrence of zero or negative values in a data set.

4.2 Underlying Concepts

4.2.1 Disposability Concepts

The DEA-EA, different from the standard DEA, is characterized by two disposability concepts. Figure 4.1 prepares a visual description on the two concepts.

Figure 4.1, obtained and modified from Sueyoshi and Goto (2018), depicts an analytical structure to measure the degree of unified (operational and environmental) efficiency. We use the figure to describe the three approaches for environmental assessment. For our visual convenience, the figure considers the observed achievement, listed as {k}, for example, of a DMU that uses a single component of an input vector (x in the horizontal axis) to produce both a single component of a desirable output vector (g on the left vertical axis) and an undesirable output vector (b on the right vertical axis). There are two DMUs {k} because we need to express the performance of {k} in the two coordinates: x-g and x-b. It should be in the three dimensions. Such a treatment is due to our visual convenience. Our description is easily extendable to a more general case where DMUs have multiple components of the three vectors in the proposed formulation.

Let us consider that (x_{ik}, g_{rk}, b_{fk}) indicates the achievement of the k th DMU. Here, DMU stands for a specific organization to be evaluated by DEA-EA. To measure the level of its unified efficiency, we need to incorporate the two efficiency frontiers into the proposed analytical scheme, as depicted in Fig. 4.1. One of the two frontiers is

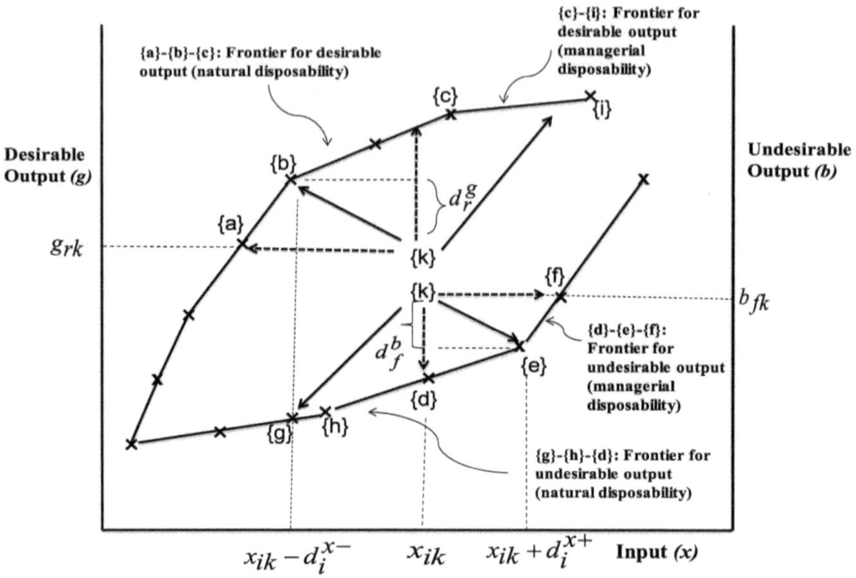

Fig. 4.1 Two efficiency frontiers for measuring unified efficiency. *Note* (a) Fig. 4.1 has three production factors: x: an input, g: a desirable output, and b: an undesirable output. (b) The direction of NW (North-West) indicates a projection of {k} toward an efficiency frontier ({a}-{b}-{c}) that is incorporated into the standard DEA framework and modern economics. This study extends the conventional use into the four projection regions, as depicted in Fig. 4.1. (c) DEA-EA incorporates the projection of SW (South-West) from {k} toward an efficiency frontier ({g}-{h}-{d}) under natural disposability and the projection of SE (South-East) from {k} toward an efficiency frontier ({d}-{e}-{f}) under managerial disposability. The projection of NW serves as a basis for the performance assessment of standard DEA. The projection of NE (North-East) toward an efficient frontier ({c}-{i}) has been excluded from the conventional use. The proposed environmental assessment incorporates the projection toward NE along with an increase in components of an input vector (x). (d) NW + SW: natural disposability and NE + SE: managerial disposability. The proposed DEA-EA incorporates both natural and managerial disposability concepts.

an efficiency (top) frontier for a desirable output (g) and an input (x). The other is an efficiency (bottom) frontier for an undesirable output (b) and an input (x).

An important feature of DEA-EA is that it incorporates two disposability concepts to measure a degree of unified (operational and environmental) efficiency. Sueyoshi and Goto (2018) have referred to them as "natural disposability" and "managerial disposability", both of which the standard DEA does not have in the analytical framework. The natural disposability and the managerial disposability visually correspond to the left hand side and the right hand side from DMU $\{k\}$ in Fig. 4.1.

The natural disposability has the two efficiency frontiers. One of the two is for undesirable output is the left hand side (bottom) of the efficiency frontier: {g}-{h}-{d}. The other frontier for desirable output is the left hand side (upper) of the efficiency frontier: {a}-{b}-{c}. Meanwhile, the managerial disposability has two efficiency frontiers. One of the two is for undesirable output is the right hand side (bottom) of the efficiency frontier: {d}-{e}-{f}. The other frontier for desirable output is the right hand side (upper) of the efficiency frontier: {c}-{i}.

Using Fig. 4.1, we may classify possible ESG enhancements by the following four types of projections (Sueyoshi & Goto, 2018):

(a) NW (North West) projections to enhance operational performance: If the *k* th DMU is inefficient in operational performance, then it needs to improve the degree of *OE* (Operational Efficiency) by increasing the amount of a desirable output and/or decreasing the amount of an input. A possible projection may be found on {b} as an example. A piece-wise linear contour line ({a}-{b}-{c}) indicates an efficiency frontier where DMU{*k*} needs to be projected. We may express the direction of such possible projections toward {a}-{b}-{c} by both the sign of an input-related slack and that of a desirable output-related slack, along with the direction of a unified inefficiency measure, as depicted in Fig. 4.1. This type of projections belongs to "NW" which indicates the enhancement of operational performance. Such projections serve as a conceptual basis for enhancing the level of *OE* within standard DEA based upon modern production economics. The projection looks for the best strategy for the increase in desirable outputs and the reduction in inputs. The reduction naturally implies a decrease of an undesirable output (i.e., industrial pollution), so indicating the concept of "natural disposability". The standard use of DEA incorporates this type of disposability concept.

(b) NE (North East) projections to enhance operational performance: The projection of NE does not exist in the standard use of DEA. The proposed DEA assessment incorporates the type of projections toward NE on the piece-wise linear contour line ({c}-{i}), along with an increase in both an input and a desirable output, as depicted in the right hand side of Fig. 4.1. The type of projection for enhancing the level of operational performance implies "economic growth" of the *k* th DMU. The economic growth is usually associated with various industrial pollutions. Therefore, we must consider how to make a balance between them. We clearly understand that it is not easily attainable such a balance because it needs to make a considerable effort, so being referred to as "managerial disposability". This type of performance enhancement has been never discussed in the standard DEA. The contribution of DEA-EA is that it incorporates the type of projections toward NE.

(c) SW (South West) projections to enhance environmental performance as part of ESG: Shifting our interest from operational to environmental protection enhancement, Fig. 4.1 visually describes a projection to enhance the performance in the input (on a horizontal coordinate) and the undesirable output (on a right vertical coordinate) whose type of projections direct toward SW along with an input decrease. One of such directions is the projection from {k} to {g} in Fig. 4.1. Here, {g} stands for the performance on an efficiency frontier on an undesirable output and an input. The piece-wise linear contour line ({g}-{h}-{d}) indicates such a frontier for unified efficiency. This type of projection, occurring with an input decrease, naturally decreases an amount of the undesirable output. Thus, we consider the projection as "natural disposability" to enhance environmental effort so that it increases the level of ESG.

(d) SE (South East) projections to enhance environmental performance: The type of projection from {k} to {e} indicates an opposite case of the SW projection, but indicating an enhancement of environmental protection as part of ESG. In the case, an efficiency frontier for the k th DMU can be found on the piece-wise linear contour line ({d}-{e}-{f}) where the DMU needs to reduce the amount of the undesirable output by green technology and/or managerial effort, along with an input increase. This type of projections, under managerial disposability, has been never explored in the previous DEA studies.

Lower and upper bounds on an input vector: We need to specify the lower and upper bounds on the change of an input vector. As depicted in Fig. 4.1, each DMU can reduce the amount of an input until it reaches an efficiency frontier on a desirable output and an input. Thus, the efficiency frontier indicates the lower bound for the input reduction. In contrast, the DMU can increase an input until it can reach an efficiency frontier on an undesirable output and an input. Here, the efficiency frontier on the bottom line at the right hand indicates the upper bound for an input increase. This upper bound indicates the limit of "economic growth" under current green technology. The advancement of green technology shifts the upper bound for the right hand side in the manner that we can attain a maximum level of input increase, so indicating the maximum enhancement of economic growth. The importance of green technology innovation is that it can shift the upper bound in the manner that an input increase can enhance the amount of a desirable output with a reduced undesirable output (i.e., less pollution). Thus, the green technology makes it possible that we can attain the status of sustainability. See Sueyoshi and Goto (2018) for a detailed discussion on the two limits on input decrease and increase. In contrast, the conventional use of DEA based upon modern economics has never considered such an analytical scheme that is necessary for sustainability development by economic growth and pollution reduction. As depicted in Fig. 4.1, the standard use of DEA, expressed only by the projections toward NW, does not have any practicality on sustainability development.

Relationship with ESG: An important feature of DEA-EA is that it incorporates undesirable outputs (e.g., CO_2) in the computational framework. As a result, DEA-EA can measure the level of ESG on the two efficiency frontiers and the four economic conditions (EW, ES, SE and SW) as depicted in Fig. 4.1. Thus, we discuss DEA-EA for ESG enhancement on DMUs in this chapter.

4.2.2 *Axiomatic Expression*

The DEA-EA utilizes economic concepts such as "natural disposability", expressed by projections toward NW and SW, as well as "managerial disposability", expressed by projections toward NE and SE, as depicted in Fig. 4.1. To describe them more analytically, let us consider $X \in R^m_+$ as an input vector with m components, $G \in R^s_+$ as a desirable output vector with s components and $B \in R^h_+$ as an undesirable output vector with h components. In these column vectors, the subscript (j) is used to indicate the j th DMU, whose vector components are all strictly positive.

In the previous chapters, we did not consider the existence of desirable and undesirable outputs. This chapter describes the existence of undesirable outputs for environmental protection. The reduction is required for ESG enhancement.

First, using an axiomatic expression, we need to clearly specify unified production and pollution possibility sets to express natural (N) disposability and that for managerial (M) disposability by the two types of output vectors and an input vector, respectively, as follows:

$$P_c^N(X) = \left\{ (G, B) : G \leq \sum_{j=1}^{n} G_j\lambda_j,\ B \geq \sum_{j=1}^{n} B_j\lambda_j,\ X \geq \sum_{j=1}^{n} X_j\lambda_j \ \&\ \lambda_j \geq 0\ (j = 1, \ldots, n) \right\} \text{and}$$

$$P_c^M(X) = \left\{ (G, B) : G \leq \sum_{j=1}^{n} G_j\lambda_j,\ B \geq \sum_{j=1}^{n} B_j\lambda_j,\ X \leq \sum_{j=1}^{n} X_j\lambda_j \ \&\ \lambda_j \geq 0\ (j = 1, \ldots, n) \right\} \quad (4.1)$$

$P_c^N(X)$ stands for a production and pollution possibility set under natural disposability (N). Meanwhile, $P_c^M(X)$ is that of managerial disposability (M). The subscript (c) stands for constant Returns to Scale (RTS) or constant Damages to Scale (DTS) because the two axiomatic expressions do not incorporate the constraint ($\sum_{j=1}^{n} \lambda_j = 1$) in Eq. (4.1). See Sueyoshi and Goto (2018) on a detailed description on RTS and DTS.[2]

The difference between the two disposability concepts is that the production technology under natural disposability, or $P_c^N(X)$, has $\mathrm{X} \geq \sum_{j=1}^{n} \mathrm{X_j}\lambda_j$, implying that a DMU can attain an efficiency frontier by reducing a directional vector of inputs. We determine the "lower bound for input decrease" by an efficiency frontier for desirable outputs and inputs. Meanwhile, that of the managerial disposability, or $P_c^M(X)$, has $\mathrm{X} \leq \sum_{j=1}^{n} \mathrm{X_j}\lambda_j$, implying that a DMU can attain a status of an efficiency frontier by increasing a directional vector of inputs. We determine the "upper bound for input increase" by an efficiency frontier for undesirable outputs and inputs.

Porter and van der Linde (1995) have implicitly indicated the concept of manage rial disposability from the perspective of corporate social responsibility and corporate strategy. They think that economic achievement and environmental protection are not mutually exclusive. So, it is possible for corporate leaders and managers can attain their economic success by investing in environmental protection. Their opinion is similar to the ESG principle. See Sueyoshi and Goto (2018), as well. In short, the natural disposability uses the operational performance as the first priority and the

[2] To simplify our discussion, here, this study considers three production factors with a single component, so being listed as x: an input, g: a desirable output and b: an undesirable output. The degree of RTS is defined as (dg/dx)/(g/x) where a mathematical symbol (d) stands for the derivative of a functional form. In a similar manner, the degree of DTS (Damages to Scale) is defined as (db/dx)/(b/x). The degree of DTR (Damages to Return) is defined as (db/dg)/(b/g) and the degree of RTD (Returns to Damage) is defined as (dg/db)/(g/b). This study discusses only RTS, so being not necessary to consider DTS, DTR and RTD because of no existence of an undesirable output.

environmental performance as the second priority. In contrast, the managerial disposability has an opposite priority. The DEA-EA analytically incorporates the priority into the conceptual framework for measuring ESG. It also measures the simultaneous achievement by examining distances from the two efficiency frontiers.

Besides the above difference, the two disposability concepts have a common feature that both have $G \le \sum_{j=1}^{n} G_j\lambda_j$ and $B \ge \sum_{j=1}^{n} B_j\lambda_j$ in these axiomatic expressions. These conditions intuitively appeal to us because an efficiency frontier for desirable outputs should locate above or on all observations (DMUs), while that of undesirable outputs should locate below or on these observations.

By incorporating the constraint ($\sum_{j=1}^{n} \lambda_j = 1$) into the two axiomatic expressions, these production and pollution possibility sets become as follows:

$$P_v^N(X) = \left\{ (G, B) : G \le \sum_{j=1}^{n} G_j\lambda_j,\ B \ge \sum_{j=1}^{n} B_j\lambda_j,\ X \ge \sum_{j=1}^{n} X_j\lambda_j, \sum_{j=1}^{n} \lambda_j = 1\ \&\ \lambda_j \ge 0\ (j = 1, \ldots, n) \right\} \text{and}$$

$$P_v^M(X) = \left\{ (G, B) : G \le \sum_{j=1}^{n} G_j\lambda_j,\ B \ge \sum_{j=1}^{n} B_j\lambda_j,\ X \le \sum_{j=1}^{n} X_j\lambda_j, \sum_{j=1}^{n} \lambda_j = 1\ \&\ \lambda_j \ge 0\ (j = 1, \ldots, n) \right\} \quad (4.2)$$

The subscript (v) stands for variable RTS or variable DTS. The description on Eq. (4.1) is applicable to Eq. (4.2).

The nomenclatures used in this chapter are as follows: j is a subscript of the j th DMU ($j = 1,\ldots,n$), k is a subscript of the specific k th DMU ($k = 1,\ldots,n$) whose performance is measured by DEA, ξ_k an inefficiency score in unified efficiency of the k th DMU, ε_s is a very small number (e.g., 0.00001) to be prescribed by a DEA user, R_i^x is a data range related to the i th input, R_r^g is a data range related to the r th desirable output, R_f^b is a data range related to the f th undesirable output, x_{ij} is an observed value of the i th input on the j th DMU, g_{rj} is an observed value of the r th desirable output on the j th DMU, b_{fj} is an observed value of the f th undesirable output on the j th DMU, λ_j is an intensity or structural variable related to the j th DMU, d_i^x is a slack related to the i th input, d_i^{x-} is a part of d_i^x under natural disposability, d_i^{x+} is a part of d_i^x under managerial disposability, d_r^g is a slack related to the r th desirable output and d_f^b is a slack related to the f th undesirable output.

4.3 Radial Model (R)

4.3.1 Unified Efficiency Under Natural Disposability

The previous research (e.g., Sueyoshi & Goto, 2012a, 2012b, 2012c, 2015a, 2018, Sueyoshi & Wang, 2014) proposed the following radial model to measure the degree of UEN_{kv}^{R} (Unified Efficiency) on the k th DMU under natural disposability and variable (v) RTS:

$$\begin{aligned}
&Maximize\ \ \xi_k + \varepsilon_s\Big(\sum_{i=1}^{m} R_i^x d_i^{x-} + \sum_{r=1}^{s} R_r^g d_r^g + \sum_{f=1}^{h} R_f^b d_f^b\Big) \\
&s.t.\quad \sum_{j=1}^{n} x_{ij}\lambda_j + d_i^{x-} = x_{ik} \quad (i = 1, \dots, m), \\
&\qquad \sum_{j=1}^{n} g_{rj}\lambda_j - d_r^g - \xi_k g_{rk} = g_{rk} \quad (r = 1, \dots, s), \\
&\qquad \sum_{j=1}^{n} b_{fj}\lambda_j + d_f^b + \xi_k b_{fk} = b_{fk} \quad (f = 1, \dots, h), \\
&\qquad \sum_{j=1}^{n} \lambda_j = 1, \\
&\qquad \lambda_j \geq 0\ (j = 1, \dots, n),\ \xi_k : URS,\ d_i^{x-} \geq 0 \quad (i = 1, \dots, m), \\
&\qquad d_r^g \geq 0\ (r = 1, \dots, s)\ \&\ d_f^b \geq 0\ (f = 1, \dots, h).
\end{aligned} \tag{4.3}$$

Under natural disposability, we determine the level of UEN_{kv}^{R} on the k th DMU by

$$UEN_{kv}^{R} = 1 - \Big[\xi_k^* + \varepsilon_s\Big(\sum_{i=1}^{m} R_i^x d_i^{x-*} + \sum_{r=1}^{s} R_r^g d_r^{g*} + \sum_{f=1}^{h} R_f^b d_f^{b*}\Big)\Big], \tag{4.4}$$

where the inefficiency measure (ξ_k^*) and all slack variables are on the optimality of Model (4.3). Thus, we find the equation value within Eq. (4.4) on the optimality of Model (4.3). After subtracting the level of unified inefficiency from unity, we measure the degree of unified efficiency.

Model (4.3) has the following dual formulation:

$$
\begin{aligned}
&Minimize \ \sum_{i=1}^{m} v_i x_{ik} - \sum_{r=1}^{s} u_r g_{rk} + \sum_{f=1}^{h} w_f b_{fk} + \sigma \\
&s.t. \quad \sum_{i=1}^{m} v_i x_{ij} - \sum_{r=1}^{s} u_r g_{rj} + \sum_{f=1}^{h} w_f b_{fj} + \sigma \geq 0 \quad (j = 1, \ldots, n), \\
&\sum_{r=1}^{s} u_r g_{rk} + \sum_{f=1}^{h} w_f b_{fk} = 1, \\
&v_i \geq \varepsilon_s R_i^x \quad (i = 1, \ldots, m), \\
&u_r \geq \varepsilon_s R_r^g \quad (r = 1, \ldots, s), \\
&w_f \geq \varepsilon_s R_f^b \quad (f = 1, \ldots, h)\& \\
&\sigma : URS.
\end{aligned}
\tag{4.5}
$$

where v_i ($i = 1, \ldots, m$), u_r ($r = 1, \ldots, s$), w_f ($f = 1, \ldots, h$) are all positive dual variables (i.e., multipliers) related to the first, second and third groups of constraints in Model (4.3). We obtain the unrestricted dual variable (σ) from the fourth constraint of Model (4.3).

The comparison between Models (4.3) and (4.5) provides us with the following three concerns: First, the objective value of Model (4.3) equals that of Model (4.5) on optimality. Thus, we have the following relationship:

$$
\xi_k^* + \varepsilon_s \left[\sum_{i=1}^{m} R_i^x d_i^{x-*} + \sum_{r=1}^{s} R_r^g d_r^{g*} + \sum_{f=1}^{h} R_f^b d_f^{b*} \right] = \sum_{i=1}^{m} v_i^* x_{ik} - \sum_{r=1}^{s} u_r^* g_{rk} + \sum_{f=1}^{h} w_f^* b_{fk} + \sigma^* \tag{4.6}
$$

on optimality. Second, an important feature of Model (4.3) is that all dual variables are positive as formulated in Model (4.5). Thus, information on the three groups of production factors is fully utilized in Model (4.3). Finally, each dual variable indicates an amount of change in unified inefficiency under natural disposability due to a unit change in the corresponding production factor.

Under constant RTS: The concept of natural disposability under constant RTS is expressed by the following formulation that slightly reorganizes Model (4.3):

$$
\begin{aligned}
&Maximize \ \xi_k + \varepsilon_s \left(\sum_{i=1}^{m} R_i^x d_i^{x-} + \sum_{r=1}^{s} R_r^g d_r^g + \sum_{f=1}^{h} R_f^b d_f^b \right) \\
&s.t. \quad same\ constraints\ in\ (4-3)\ without \sum_{j=1}^{n} \lambda_j = 1.
\end{aligned}
\tag{4.7}
$$

The elimination of $\sum_{j=1}^{n} \lambda_j = 1$ from Model (4.3) changes the dual formulation (4.5) as follows:

$$
\begin{aligned}
\text{Minimize} \quad & \sum_{i=1}^{m} v_i x_{ik} - \sum_{r=1}^{s} u_r g_{rk} + \sum_{f=1}^{h} w_f b_{fk} \\
s.t. \quad & \sum_{i=1}^{m} v_i x_{ij} - \sum_{r=1}^{s} u_r g_{rj} + \sum_{f=1}^{h} w_f b_{fj} \geq 0\,(j = 1, \ldots, n)\& \\
& \textit{same constraints in } (4-5).
\end{aligned} \tag{4.8}
$$

Here, Model (4.8) drops the dual variable (σ), originated from $\sum_{j=1}^{n} \lambda_j = 1$ in Model (4.3). There is almost no other difference between Models (4.5) and (4.8). The unified efficiency (UEN_c^R), like Eq. (4.4), becomes as follows:

$$
UEN_{kc}^{R} = 1 - [\xi_k^* + \varepsilon_s(\sum_{i=1}^{m} R_i^x d_i^{x-*} + \sum_{r=1}^{s} R_r^g d_r^{g*} + \sum_{f=1}^{h} R_f^b d_f^{b*})], \tag{4.9}
$$

where all variables are on the optimality of Model (4.7). The subscript (c) implies the constant RTS that is replaced by the subscript (v).

4.3.2 Unified Efficiency Under Managerial Disposability

Shifting our research description from natural to managerial disposability, where the first priority is environmental performance and the second priority is operational performance, we utilize the following radial model that measures the efficiency status on the k th DMU under managerial disposability:

$$
\begin{aligned}
\text{Maximize} \quad & \xi_k + \varepsilon_s(\sum_{i-1}^{m} R_i^x d_i^{x+} + \sum_{r=1}^{s} R_r^g d_r^g + \sum_{f=1}^{h} R_f^b d_f^b) \\
s.t. \quad & \sum_{j=1}^{n} x_{ij}\lambda_j - d_i^{x+} = x_{ik} \quad (i = 1, \ldots, m), \\
& \sum_{j=1}^{n} g_{rj}\lambda_j - d_r^g - \xi_k g_{rk} = g_{rk} \quad (r = 1, \ldots, s) \\
& \sum_{j=1}^{n} b_{fj}\lambda_j + d_f^b + \xi_k b_{fk} = b_{fk} \quad (f = 1, \ldots, h), \\
& \sum_{j=1}^{n} \lambda_j = 1, \\
& \lambda_j \geq 0 (j = 1, \ldots, n), \xi_k : URS, d_i^{x+} \geq 0 \quad (i = 1, \ldots, m), \\
& d_r^g \geq 0 (r = 1, .., s)\ \&\ d_f^b \geq 0 \quad (f = 1, \ldots, h).
\end{aligned} \tag{4.10}
$$

An important feature of Model (4.10) is that it changes $+d_i^{x-}$ of Model (4.3) to $-d_i^{x+}$ in Model (4.10) to attain the managerial disposability. We formulate Model (4.10) under variable DTS. A unified efficiency measure (UEM_{kv}^{R}) on the k th DMU becomes as follows:

$$UEM_{kv}^{R} = 1 - \left[\xi_k^* + \varepsilon \left(\sum_{i=1}^{m} R_i^x d_i^{x+*} + \sum_{r=1}^{s} R_r^g d_r^{g*} + \sum_{f=1}^{h} R_f^b d_f^{b*} \right) \right], \tag{4.11}$$

where the inefficiency score and all slacks are on the optimality of Model (4.10). Thus, the equation value within the parenthesis, obtained from the optimality of Model (4.10), indicates the degree of unified inefficiency under managerial disposability. We obtain the UEM_{kv}^{R} by subtracting the level of inefficiency from unity.

Model (4.10) has the following dual formulation:

$$\begin{aligned}
&\text{Minimize} && -\sum_{i=1}^{m} v_i x_{ik} - \sum_{r=1}^{s} u_r g_{rk} + \sum_{f=1}^{h} w_f b_{fk} + \sigma \\
&s.t. && -\sum_{i=1}^{m} v_i x_{ij} - \sum_{r=1}^{s} u_r g_{rj} + \sum_{f=1}^{h} w_f b_{fj} + \sigma \geq 0 \quad (j = 1, \ldots, n), \\
& && \sum_{r=1}^{s} u_r g_{rk} + \sum_{f=1}^{h} w_f b_{fk} = 1, \\
& && v_i \geq \varepsilon_s R_i^x \quad (i = 1, \ldots, m), \\
& && u_r \geq \varepsilon_s R_r^g \quad (r = 1, \ldots, s), \\
& && w_f \geq \varepsilon_s R_f^b \quad (f = 1, \ldots, h) \& \\
& && \sigma : URS,
\end{aligned} \tag{4.12}$$

where v_i ($i = 1, \ldots, m$), u_r ($r = 1, \ldots, s$), w_f ($f = 1, \ldots, h$) are all dual variables related to the first, second and third groups of constraints in Model (4.10). We obtain the dual variable (σ) from the fourth constraint of Model (4.10). The objective value of Model (4.10) equals that of Model (4.12) on optimality. Consequently, we have the following relationship:

$$\begin{aligned}
&\xi_k^* + \varepsilon_s \left[\sum_{i=1}^{m} R_i^x d_i^{x+*} + \sum_{r=1}^{s} R_r^g d_r^{g*} + \sum_{f=1}^{h} R_f^b d_f^{b*} \right] \\
&\qquad = -\sum_{i=1}^{m} v_i^* x_{ik} - \sum_{r=1}^{s} u_r^* g_{rk} + \sum_{f=1}^{h} w_f^* b_{fk} + \sigma^*
\end{aligned} \tag{4.13}$$

on optimality.

Under constant DTS: The concept of managerial disposability under constant DTS is expressed by the following formulation that slightly reorganizes Model (4.10):

$$\begin{aligned} & Maximize \quad \xi_k + \varepsilon_s\left(\sum_{i=1}^{m} R_i^x d_i^{x+} + \sum_{r=1}^{s} R_r^g d_r^g + \sum_{f=1}^{h} R_f^b d_f^b\right) \\ & s.t. \qquad same\ constraints\ in\ (4-10)\ without\ \sum_{j=1}^{n} \lambda_j = 1. \end{aligned} \tag{4.14}$$

The elimination of $\sum_{j=1}^{n} \lambda_j = 1$ from Model (4.10) changes the dual formulation (4.12) as follows:

$$\begin{aligned} Minimize \quad & -\sum_{i=1}^{m} v_i x_{ik} - \sum_{r=1}^{s} u_r g_{rk} + \sum_{f=1}^{h} w_f b_{fk} \\ s.t. \quad & -\sum_{i=1}^{m} v_i x_{ij} - \sum_{r=1}^{s} u_r g_{rj} + \sum_{f=1}^{h} w_f b_{fj} \geq 0 \quad (j = 1, \ldots, n)\ \& \\ & same\ constraints\ in\ (4-10). \end{aligned} \tag{4.15}$$

Here, Model (4.15) drops the dual variable (σ) originated from $\sum_{j=1}^{n} \lambda_j = 1$ in Model (4.10). There is no other difference between Models (4.10) and (4.14). The unified efficiency (UEM_{kc}^{R}), like Model (4.11), becomes as follows:

$$UEM_{kc}^{R} = 1 - \left[\xi^* + \varepsilon_s\left(\sum_{i=1}^{m} R_i^x d_i^{x+*} + \sum_{r=1}^{s} R_r^g d_r^{g*} + \sum_{f=1}^{h} R_f^b d_f^{b*}\right)\right], \tag{4.16}$$

where all variables are on the optimality of Model (4.14). The previous discussions on formulation under natural disposability are applicable to those under managerial disposability.

At the end of this subsection, we note that readers may find a detailed description on both RTS and DTS in the book prepared by Sueyoahi and Goto (2018).

4.4 Non-radial Model (NR)

4.4.1 Unified Efficiency Under Natural Disposability

The non-radial model under natural disposability, which measures the unified efficiency (UEN_{kv}^{NR}) of the k th DMU, utilizes the following model (e.g., Sueyoshi & Goto, 2012a, 2015b, 2015c, 2018):

$$
\begin{aligned}
& Maximize\ \varepsilon\Big(\sum_{i=1}^{m} R_i^x d_i^{x-} + \sum_{r=1}^{s} R_r^g d_r^g + \sum_{f=1}^{h} R_f^b d_f^b\Big) \\
& s.t. \quad \sum_{j=1}^{n} x_{ij}\lambda_j + d_i^{x-} = x_{ik} (i = 1, \ldots, m), \\
& \qquad \sum_{j=1}^{n} g_{rj}\lambda_j - d_r^g = g_{rk} \quad (r = 1, \ldots, s), \\
& \qquad \sum_{j=1}^{n} b_{fj}\lambda_j + d_f^b = b_{fk} \quad (f = 1, \ldots, h), \\
& \qquad \sum_{j=1}^{n} \lambda_j = 1, \\
& \qquad \lambda_j \geq 0 \, (j = 1, \ldots, n), d_i^{x-} \geq 0 \, (i = 1, \ldots, m), \\
& \qquad d_r^g \geq 0 \, (r = 1, \ldots, s) \;\&\; d_f^b \geq 0 \, (f = 1, \ldots, h).
\end{aligned}
\tag{4.17}
$$

Model (4.17) considers only deviations $+d_i^{x-}$ ($i = 1,\ldots, m$) related to inputs to attain the status of natural disposability. Aida et al. (1998) that first discussed a methodical difficulty on this type of non-radial approach within the standard non-radial model. Model (4.17) uses ε (a subjective number) to control the magnitude of unified inefficiency, so being different from the use of ε_s (a very small number) found in Model (4.3).

The unified efficiency (UEN_{kv}^{NR}) of the k th DMU under natural disposability and variable RTS is measured by

$$
UEN_{kv}^{NR} = 1 - \varepsilon\Big(\sum_{i=1}^{m} R_i^x d_i^{x-*} + \sum_{r=1}^{s} R_r^g d_r^{g*} + \sum_{f=1}^{h} R_f^b d_f^{b*}\Big), \tag{4.18}
$$

where all slack variables are on the optimality of Model (4.17). The superscript (NR) stands for Non-Radial and the subscript (v) stands for variable RTS. The equation within the parenthesis, obtained from the optimality of Model (4.17), indicates the level of unified inefficiency. The unified efficiency is obtained by subtracting the level of inefficiency from unity, as formulated in Eq. (4.18).

Model (4.17) has the following dual formulation:

$$
\begin{aligned}
&\textit{Minimize} \sum_{i=1}^{m} v_i x_{ik} - \sum_{r=1}^{s} u_r g_{rk} + \sum_{f=1}^{h} w_f b_{fk} + \sigma \\
&s.t. \quad \sum_{i=1}^{m} v_i x_{ij} - \sum_{r=1}^{s} u_r g_{rj} + \sum_{f=1}^{h} w_f b_{fj} + \sigma \geq 0 \quad (j = 1, \ldots, n), \\
&\quad v_i \geq \varepsilon R_i^x \quad (i = 1, \ldots, m), \\
&\quad u_r \geq \varepsilon R_r^g \quad (r = 1, \ldots, s), \\
&\quad w_f \geq \varepsilon R_f^b \quad (f = 1, \ldots, h), \\
&\quad \sigma : URS,
\end{aligned}
\tag{4.19}
$$

where v_i ($i = 1, \ldots, m$), u_r ($r = 1, \ldots, s$) and w_f ($f = 1, \ldots, h$) are all dual variables related to the first, second and third groups of constraints in Model (4.17). We obtain the dual variable (σ) from the fourth equation of Model (4.17). An important feature of Model (4.19), as discussed previously, is that all dual variables are positive so that all the production factors are fully utilized in the proposed DEA-EA assessment.

On optimality, the primal and dual models have

$$
\begin{aligned}
&\varepsilon\left(\sum_{i=1}^{m} R_i^x d_i^{x-*} + \sum_{r=1}^{s} R_r^g d_r^{g*} + \sum_{f=1}^{h} R_f^b d_f^{b*}\right) \\
&\quad = \sum_{i=1}^{m} v_i^* x_{ik} - \sum_{r=1}^{s} u_r^* g_{rk} + \sum_{f=1}^{h} w_f^* b_{fk} + \sigma^*
\end{aligned}
\tag{4.20}
$$

Equation (4.20) indicates the level of unified inefficiency measured by either Model (4.17) or (4.19).

Under constant RTS: The concept of natural disposability under constant RTS has the following formulation that slightly reorganizes Model (4.17):

$$
\begin{aligned}
&\textit{Maximize } \varepsilon\left(\sum_{i=1}^{m} R_i^x d_i^{x-} + \sum_{r=1}^{s} R_r^g d_r^g + \sum_{f=1}^{h} R_f^b d_f^b\right) \\
&s.t. \quad \textit{same constraints in } (4-17) \textit{ without } \sum_{j=1}^{n} \lambda_j = 1.
\end{aligned}
\tag{4.21}
$$

The elimination of $\sum_{j=1}^{n} \lambda_j = 1$ from Model (4.17) changes the dual formulation (4.19) as follows:

$$
\begin{aligned}
&\textit{Minimize} \sum_{i=1}^{m} v_i x_{ik} - \sum_{r=1}^{s} u_r g_{rk} + \sum_{f=1}^{h} w_f b_{fk} \\
&s.t. \quad \sum_{i=1}^{m} v_i x_{ij} - \sum_{r=1}^{s} u_r g_{rj} + \sum_{f=1}^{h} w_f b_{fj} \geq 0 \quad (j = 1, \ldots, n)\ \& \\
&\quad \textit{same constraints in } (4-19).
\end{aligned}
\tag{4.22}
$$

Here, Model (4.22) drops the dual variable (σ), originated from $\sum_{j=1}^{n} \lambda_j = 1$ in Model (4.17). There is no other difference between Models (4.17) and (4.21). The unified efficiency (UEN_{kc}^{NR}) becomes as follows:

$$UEN_{kc}^{NR} = 1 - [\varepsilon(\sum_{i=1}^{m} R_i^x d_i^{x-*} + \sum_{r=1}^{s} R_r^g d_r^{g*} + \sum_{f=1}^{h} R_f^b d_f^{b*})], \tag{4.23}$$

where we obtain all variables from the optimality of Model (4.21).

4.4.2 Unified Efficiency Under Managerial Disposability

To measure the unified efficiency (UEM_{kv}^{NR}) of the k th DMU under managerial disposability, Sueyoshi and Goto (2012a, 2015b, 2015c) have proposed the following non-radial model:

$$\begin{aligned}
&Maximize\ \varepsilon(\sum_{i=1}^{m} R_i^x d_i^{x+} + \sum_{r=1}^{s} R_r^g d_r^g + \sum_{f=1}^{h} R_f^b d_f^b) \\
&s.t. \quad \sum_{j=1}^{n} x_{ij}\lambda_j - d_i^{x+} = x_{ik} \quad (i = 1, \ldots, m), \\
&\qquad \sum_{j=1}^{n} g_{rj}\lambda_j - d_r^g = g_{rk} \quad (r = 1, \ldots, s), \\
&\qquad \sum_{j=1}^{n} b_{fj}\lambda_j + d_f^b = b_{fk} \quad (f = 1, \ldots, h), \\
&\qquad \sum_{j=1}^{n} \lambda_j = 1, \\
&\qquad \lambda_j \geq 0\ (j = 1, \ldots, n), d_i^{x+} \geq 0 (i = 1, \ldots, m), \\
&\qquad d_r^g \geq 0\ (r = 1, \ldots, s)\ \&\ d_f^b \geq 0 \quad (f = 1, \ldots, h).
\end{aligned} \tag{4.24}$$

Model (4.24) incorporates only deviations $-d_i^{x+}$ ($i = 1,\ldots, m$) related to inputs to attain the status of managerial disposability. The ε indicates a small number which controls the degree of unified inefficiency in the range between 0 and 1. The model has the formulation structured under variable (v) DTS.

We measure the unified efficiency (UEM_{kv}^{NR}) of the k th DMU by

$$UEM_{kv}^{NR} = 1 - \varepsilon(\sum_{i=1}^{m} R_i^x d_i^{x+*} + \sum_{r=1}^{s} R_r^g d_r^{g*} + \sum_{f=1}^{h} R_f^b d_f^{b*}), \tag{4.25}$$

where all slack variables are on the optimality of Model (4.24). The equation value within the parenthesis, obtained from the optimality of Model (4.24), indicates the degree of unified inefficiency under managerial disposability. We obtain the unified efficiency by subtracting the level of inefficiency from unity, as formulated in Eq. (4.25).

Model (4.24) has the following dual formulation:

$$
\begin{aligned}
& \textit{Minimize} \ -\sum_{i=1}^{m} v_i x_{ik} - \sum_{r=1}^{s} u_r g_{rk} + \sum_{f=1}^{h} w_f b_{fk} + \sigma \\
& s.t. \quad -\sum_{i=1}^{m} v_i x_{ij} - \sum_{r=1}^{s} u_r g_{rj} + \sum_{f=1}^{h} w_f b_{fj} + \sigma \ge 0 \quad (j = 1, \ldots, n), \\
& \qquad v_i \ge \varepsilon R_i^x \quad (i = 1, \ldots, m), \\
& \qquad u_r \ge \varepsilon R_r^g \quad (r = 1, \ldots, s), \\
& \qquad w_f \ge \varepsilon R_f^b \quad (f = 1, \ldots, h), \\
& \qquad \sigma : URS,
\end{aligned}
\tag{4.26}
$$

where v_i $(i = 1, \ldots, m)$, u_r $(r = 1, \ldots, s)$ and w_f $(f = 1, \ldots, h)$ are all dual variables related to the first, second and third groups of constraints in Model (4.24). The dual variable (σ) is due to the fourth equation of Model (4.24).

Models (4.24) and (4.26) measure the level of unified inefficiency under managerial disposability. The following condition exists on the optimality between the two models:

$$
\begin{aligned}
& \varepsilon\Big(\sum_{i=1}^{m} R_i^x d_i^{x+*} + \sum_{r=1}^{s} R_r^g d_r^{g*} + \sum_{f=1}^{h} R_f^b d_f^{b*}\Big) \\
& \quad = -\sum_{i=1}^{m} v_i^* x_{ik} - \sum_{r=1}^{s} u_r^* g_{rk} + \sum_{f=1}^{h} w_f^* b_{fk} + \sigma^*.
\end{aligned}
\tag{4.27}
$$

Equation (4.27) indicates that each dual variable specifies a change in the degree of unified inefficiency, due to one-unit increase in each production factor, under managerial disposability.

Under constant DTS: The concept of managerial disposability under constant DTS is expressed by the following formulation that slightly reorganizes Model (4.24):

$$
\begin{aligned}
& \textit{Maximize} \ \varepsilon\Big(\sum_{i=1}^{m} R_i^x d_i^{x+} + \sum_{r=1}^{s} R_r^g d_r^g + \sum_{f=1}^{h} R_f^b d_f^b\Big) \\
& s.t. \quad \textit{same constraints in } (4-24) \textit{ without } \sum_{j=1}^{n} \lambda_j = 1.
\end{aligned}
\tag{4.28}
$$

The elimination of $\sum_{j=1}^{n} \lambda_j = 1$ from Model (4.24) changes the dual formulation (4.26) as follows:

$$\begin{aligned} &Minimize \quad -\sum_{i=1}^{m} v_i x_{ik} - \sum_{r=1}^{s} u_r g_{rk} + \sum_{f=1}^{h} w_f b_{fk} \\ &s.t. \quad -\sum_{i=1}^{m} v_i x_{ij} - \sum_{r=1}^{s} u_r g_{rj} + \sum_{f=1}^{h} w_f b_{fj} \geq 0 \quad (j = 1, \ldots, n)\ \& \\ &\qquad same\ constraints\ in\ (4-26). \end{aligned} \tag{4.29}$$

Here, the dual variable (σ), originated from $\sum_{j=1}^{n} \lambda_j = 1$ in Model (24), does not exist in Model (4.29). There is no other difference between Models (4.26) and (4.29). We measure the unified efficiency (UEM_{kc}^{NR}), like Model (4.25), as follows:

$$UEM_{kc}^{NR} = 1 - [\varepsilon(\sum_{i=1}^{m} R_i^x d_i^{x+*} + \sum_{r=1}^{s} R_r^g d_r^{g*} + \sum_{f=1}^{h} R_f^b d_f^{b*})], \tag{4.30}$$

where all variables are obtained from the optimality of Model (4.28).

4.5 Intermediate Model (I)

4.5.1 Unified Efficiency Under Natural Disposability

As the third alternative of DEA-EA, we may apply the concept of natural disposability under variable RTS to the intermediate model. The following formulation (Sueyoshi & Goto, 2019; Sueyoshi & Yuan, 2017) measures the level of unified efficiency (UEN_v^I) of the k th DMU:

$$\begin{aligned} &Maximize \ \tfrac{1}{s+h}(\sum_{r=1}^{s} \xi_{rk}^g + \sum_{f=1}^{h} \xi_{fk}^b) + \varepsilon_s(\sum_{i=1}^{m} R_i^x d_i^{x-} + \sum_{r=1}^{s} R_r^g d_r^g + \sum_{f=1}^{h} R_f^b d_f^b) \\ &s.t. \quad \sum_{j=1}^{n} x_{ij}\lambda_j + d_i^{x-} = x_{ik} \quad (i = 1, \ldots, m), \\ &\qquad \sum_{j=1}^{n} g_{rj}\lambda_j - d_r^g - \xi_{rk}^g g_{rk} = g_{rk} \quad (r = 1, \ldots, s), \\ &\qquad \xi_{rk}^g \leq 1 \quad (r = 1, \ldots, s), \\ &\qquad \sum_{j=1}^{n} b_{fj}\lambda_j + d_f^b + \xi_{fk}^b b_{fk} = b_{fk} \quad (f = 1, \ldots, h), \\ &\qquad \xi_{fk}^b \leq 1 \quad (f = 1, \ldots, h), \\ &\qquad \sum_{j=1}^{n} \lambda_j = 1, \\ &\qquad \xi_{rk}^g \geq 0\ (r = 1, \ldots, s),\ \xi_{fk}^b \geq 0\ (f = 1, \ldots, h),\ \lambda_j \geq 0\ (j = 1, \ldots, n), \\ &\qquad d_i^{x-} \geq 0\ (i = 1, \ldots, m),\ d_r^g \geq 0\ (r = 1, \ldots, s)\ \&\ d_f^b \geq 0\ (f = 1, \ldots, h). \end{aligned} \tag{4.31}$$

where ξ_{rk}^{g} ($r = 1, \ldots, s$) and ξ_{fk}^{b} ($f = 1, \ldots, h$), respectively, stand for subcomponents of an inefficiency score (ξ_k) related to desirable and undesirable outputs. The input slack $+d_i^{x-}$ in Model (4.31) indicates that the k th DMU can attain an efficiency frontier by decreasing the amount of inputs under natural disposability.

As mentioned previously, we separate the level of unified inefficiency into its subcomponents. The average of the sum of these inefficiency subcomponents, $\frac{1}{s+h}\left(\sum_{r=1}^{s}\xi_{rk}^{g}+\sum_{f=1}^{h}\xi_{fk}^{b}\right)$, is used as the final unified inefficiency measure by Model (4.31). We measure a unified efficiency score (UEN_{kv}^{I}) of the k th DMU by

$$UEN_{kv}^{I} = 1 - \left[\frac{1}{s+h}\left(\sum_{r=1}^{s}\xi_{rk}^{g*} + \sum_{f=1}^{h}\xi_{fk}^{b*}\right) + \varepsilon_s\left(\sum_{i=1}^{m}R_i^x d_i^{x-*} + \sum_{r=1}^{s}R_r^g d_r^{g*} + \sum_{f=1}^{h}R_f^b d_f^{b*}\right)\right], \quad (4.32)$$

where inefficiency components and slacks are on the optimality of Model (4.31). The superscript (I) and subscript (v) stand for Intermediate (I) and variable (v) RTS.

The intermediate model has originated from Russell (1985, 1990) as a nonlinear programing formulation. We cannot solve the formulation by linear programing. Thus, the original formulation had a computational difficulty. We had to solve it by a special non-linear programming approach. For example, Sueyoshi and Sekitani (2007) have discussed how to solve it by a nonlinear programming approach, referred to as "SOCP (Second-Order Cone Programming)". Meanwhile, a contribution of Sueyoshi and Yuan (2017) was that they have changed the Russell type of intermediate model in the manner that we can solve it by liner programing. Sueyoshi and Goto (2019) have provided a detailed description on analytical differences between the Russell measure and the intermediate model.

The dual formulation of Model (4.31) becomes as follows:

$$\begin{aligned}
& Minimize \ \sum_{i=1}^{m} v_i x_{ik} - \sum_{r=1}^{s}(u_r g_{rk} - \eta_r) + \sum_{f=1}^{h}(w_f b_{fk} + \mu_f) + \sigma \\
& s.t. \quad \sum_{i=1}^{m} v_i x_{ij} - \sum_{r=1}^{s} u_r g_{rj} + \sum_{f=1}^{h} w_f b_{fj} + \sigma \geq 0 \quad (j = 1, \ldots, n), \\
& \qquad u_r g_{rk} + \eta_r \geq 1/(s+h) \quad (r = 1, \ldots, s), \\
& \qquad w_f b_{fk} + \mu_f \geq 1/(s+h) \quad (f = 1, \ldots, h), \\
& \qquad v_i \geq \varepsilon_s R_i^x \quad (i = 1, \ldots, m), \\
& \qquad u_r \geq \varepsilon_s R_r^g \quad (r = 1, \ldots, s), \\
& \qquad w_f \geq \varepsilon_s R_f^b \quad (f = 1, \ldots, h) \& \\
& \qquad \sigma : URS.
\end{aligned} \quad (4.33)$$

Here, v_i ($i = 1, \ldots, m$), u_r ($r = 1, \ldots, s$), η_r ($r = 1, \ldots, s$), w_f ($f = 1, \ldots, h$), μ_f ($f = 1, \ldots, h$) and σ are dual variables (i.e., multipliers) related to the first, second, third, fourth, fifth and sixth groups of constraints in Model (4.31). As formulated in the last three groups of constraints, they are all strictly positive in Model (4.33). Thus, the intermediate model (4.31) can fully utilize all production factors as found in the last four constraints from the bottom of Model (4.33).

The objective value of Model (4.31) equals that of Model (4.33) on optimality so that we can identify the unified inefficiency measure from their optimal objective values:

$$\frac{1}{s+h}\left(\sum_{r=1}^{s}\xi_{\mathrm{rk}}^{g*}+\sum_{f=1}^{h}\xi_{\mathrm{fk}}^{b*}\right)+\varepsilon_s\left(\sum_{i=1}^{m}R_i^x d_i^{x-*}+\sum_{r=1}^{s}R_r^g d_r^{g*}+\sum_{f=1}^{h}R_f^b d_f^{b*}\right)$$
$$=\sum_{i=1}^{m}v_i^* x_{\mathrm{ik}}-\sum_{r=1}^{s}(u_r^* g_{\mathrm{rk}}-\eta_r^*)+\sum_{f=1}^{h}(w_f^* b_{\mathrm{fk}}+\mu_f^*)+\sigma^*. \quad (4.34)$$

Thus, each dual variable indicates an amount of change in unified inefficiency under natural disposability due to a unit change in the corresponding production factor.

Constant RTS: The natural disposability under constant RTS reorganizes Model (4.31) by the following formulation:

$$\begin{aligned} &\textit{Maximize}\ \tfrac{1}{s+h}\left(\sum_{r=1}^{s}\xi_{rk}^{g}+\sum_{f=1}^{h}\xi_{fk}^{b}\right)+\varepsilon_s\left(\sum_{i=1}^{m}R_i^x d_i^{x-}+\sum_{r=1}^{s}R_r^g d_r^{g}+\sum_{f=1}^{h}R_f^b d_f^{b}\right) \\ &s.t. \quad \textit{same constraints in}\ (4-31)\ \textit{without}\ \sum_{j=1}^{n}\lambda_j=1. \end{aligned} \quad (4.35)$$

The elimination of $\sum_{j=1}^{n}\lambda_j = 1$ in Model (4.31) changes the dual formulation (4.33) as follows:

$$\begin{aligned} &\textit{Minimize}\ \sum_{i=1}^{m}v_i x_{ik}-\sum_{r=1}^{s}(u_r g_{rk}-\eta_r)+\sum_{f=1}^{h}(w_f b_{fk}+\mu_f) \\ &s.t.\quad \sum_{i=1}^{m}v_i x_{ij}-\sum_{r=1}^{s}u_r g_{rj}+\sum_{f=1}^{h}w_f b_{fj}\ge 0\quad (j=1,\ldots,n)\ \& \\ &\qquad \textit{same constraints in}\ (4-33). \end{aligned} \quad (4.36)$$

Here, Model (4.36) drops the dual variable (σ), originated from $\sum_{j=1}^{n}\lambda_j = 1$ of Model (4.33). There is no other difference between Models (4.31) and (4.35). The unified efficiency measure under natural disposability and constant RTS, like Eq. (4.32), becomes as follows

$$UEN_{kc}^{I}=1-\left[\frac{1}{s+h}\left(\sum_{r=1}^{s}\xi_{\mathrm{rk}}^{g*}+\sum_{f=1}^{h}\xi_{\mathrm{fk}}^{b*}\right)+\varepsilon_s\left(\sum_{i=1}^{m}R_i^x d_i^{x-*}+\sum_{r=1}^{s}R_r^g d_r^{g*}+\sum_{f=1}^{h}R_f^b d_f^{b*}\right)\right], \quad (4.37)$$

where all variables are on the optimality of Model (4.35). The subscript (c) stands for constant RTS.

4.5.2 Under Managerial Disposability

Shifting our description from natural to managerial disposability, we change Model (4.31) to the following intermediate model under managerial disposability (Sueyoshi & Yuan, 2017):

$$
\begin{aligned}
&Maximize\ \tfrac{1}{s+h}\Big(\sum_{r=1}^{s}\xi_{rk}^{g}+\sum_{f=1}^{h}\xi_{fk}^{b}\Big)+\varepsilon_s\Big(\sum_{i=1}^{m}R_i^x d_i^{x-}+\sum_{r=1}^{s}R_r^g d_r^g+\sum_{f=1}^{h}R_f^b d_f^b\Big)\\
&s.t.\quad \sum_{j=1}^{n}x_{ij}\lambda_j-d_i^{x+}=x_{ik}\quad (i=1,\ldots,m),\\
&\qquad \sum_{j=1}^{n}g_{rj}\lambda_j-d_r^g-\xi_{rk}^{g}g_{rk}=g_{rk}\quad (r=1,\ldots,s),\\
&\qquad \xi_{rk}^{g}\le 1\quad (r=1,\ldots,s),\\
&\qquad \sum_{j=1}^{n}b_{fj}\lambda_j+d_f^b+\xi_{fk}^{b}b_{fk}=b_{fk}\quad (f=1,\ldots,h),\\
&\qquad \xi_{fk}^{b}\le 1\quad (f=1,\ldots,h),\\
&\qquad \sum_{j=1}^{n}\lambda_j=1\\
&\qquad \xi_{rk}^{g}\ge 0(r=1,\ldots,s),\xi_{fk}^{b}\ge 0\,(f=1,\ldots,h),\lambda_j\ge 0\quad (j=1,\ldots,n),\\
&\qquad d_i^{x+}\ge 0(i=1,\ldots,m),d_r^g\ge 0\,(r=1,\ldots,s)\,\&\,d_f^b\ge 0\quad (f=1,\ldots,h).
\end{aligned}
\tag{4.38}
$$

Model (4.38) changes $+d_i^{x-}$ in Model (4.31) to $-d_i^{x+}$ in the formulation. Such a change indicates that the k th DMU can attain an efficiency frontier by increasing the amount of inputs under managerial disposability.

The dual formulation of Model (4.38) has the following structure:

$$
\begin{aligned}
&Minimize\quad -\sum_{i=1}^{m}v_i x_{ik}-\sum_{r=1}^{s}(u_r g_{rk}-\eta_r)+\sum_{f=1}^{h}(w_f b_{fk}+\mu_f)+\sigma\\
&s.t.\qquad -\sum_{i=1}^{m}v_i x_{ij}-\sum_{r=1}^{s}u_r g_{rj}+\sum_{f=1}^{h}w_f b_{fj}+\sigma\ge 0\quad (j=1,\ldots,n),\\
&\qquad\quad u_r g_{rk}+\eta_r\ge 1/(s+h)\,(r=1,\ldots,s),\\
&\qquad\quad w_f b_{fk}+\mu_f\ge 1/(s+h)(f=1,\ldots,h),\\
&\qquad\quad v_i\ge \varepsilon_s R_i^x\quad (i=1,\ldots,m),\\
&\qquad\quad u_r\ge \varepsilon_s R_r^g\quad (r=1,\ldots,s),\\
&\qquad\quad w_f\ge \varepsilon_s R_f^b\quad (f=1,\ldots,h)\&\\
&\qquad\quad \sigma : URS.
\end{aligned}
\tag{4.39}
$$

A unified efficiency score (UEM_{kv}^{I}) of the k th DMU under variable DTS becomes

$$UEM_{kv}^{I} = 1 - [\frac{1}{s+h}(\sum_{r=1}^{s} \xi_{rk}^{g*} + \sum_{f=1}^{h} \xi_{fk}^{b*}) + \varepsilon_s(\sum_{i=1}^{m} R_i^x d_i^{x+*} + \sum_{r=1}^{s} R_r^g d_r^{g*} + \sum_{f=1}^{h} R_f^b d_f^{b*})]. \quad (4.40)$$

Here, we obtain all variables from the optimality of Model (4.38). The superscript (I) and the subscript (v) stands for Intermediate and the subscript (v) stand for variable DTS.

Constant DTS: The following formulation expresses the concept of managerial disposability under constant DTS which slightly reorganizes Model (4.38):

$$\begin{aligned} &Maximize \ \tfrac{1}{s+h}(\sum_{r=1}^{s} \xi_r^g + \sum_{f=1}^{h} \xi_f^b) + \varepsilon_s(\sum_{i=1}^{m} R_i^x d_i^{x+} + \sum_{r=1}^{s} R_r^g d_r^g + \sum_{f=1}^{h} R_f^b d_f^b) \\ &s.t. \quad same\ constraints\ in\ (4-38)\ without\ \sum_{j=1}^{n} \lambda_j = 1. \end{aligned} \quad (4.41)$$

The elimination of $\sum_{j=1}^{n} \lambda_j = 1$ from Model (4.38) changes the dual formulation as follows:

$$\begin{aligned} &Minimize \quad -\sum_{i=1}^{m} v_i x_{ik} - \sum_{r=1}^{s} (u_r g_{rk} - \eta_r) + \sum_{f=1}^{h} (w_f b_{fk} + \mu_f) \\ &s.t. \quad -\sum_{i=1}^{m} v_i x_{ij} - \sum_{r=1}^{s} u_r g_{rj} + \sum_{f=1}^{h} w_f b_{fj} \geq 0 \quad (j = 1, \ldots, n)\ \& \\ &\qquad same\ constraints\ in\ (4-39). \end{aligned} \quad (4.42)$$

Model (4.42) drops the dual variable (σ), originated from $\sum_{j=1}^{n} \lambda_j = 1$ in Model (4.38). There is no other difference between Models (4.39) and (4.42). The unified efficiency measure under managerial (M) disposability and constant (c) DTS, like Eq. (4.40), becomes the following structure:

$$UEM_{kc}^{I} = 1 - \left[\frac{1}{s+h}\left(\sum_{r=1}^{s} \xi_{rk}^{g*} + \sum_{f=1}^{h} \xi_{fk}^{b*}\right) + \varepsilon_s\left(\sum_{i=1}^{m} R_i^x d_i^{x+*} + \sum_{r=1}^{s} R_r^g d_r^{g*} + \sum_{f=1}^{h} R_f^b d_f^{b*}\right)\right], \quad (4.43)$$

where all variables are on the optimality of Model (4.41).

4.5.3 Visual Description on Intermediate Model

A research inquiry to be addressed here is how the proposed three model can unify desirable and undesirable outputs, both of which have opposite directional vectors for performance betterment. Since both radial and non-radial models are well known among DEA researchers, this section focuses upon a visual description on the intermediate model.

To visually reply to the question on unification between the two types of outputs, we obtain two figures from Sueyoshi and Yuan (2017) and modify them for our descriptions. One of the two figures corresponds to Fig. 4.2 that consists of a single input (x) and two desirable outputs (g_1 and g_2). The horizontal axis of Fig. 4.2 is for g_1/x and the vertical axis is for g_2/x. In the case, we assume that all DMUs produce the same amount of an undesirable output (b). The other one is Fig. 4.3 that extends Fig. 4.2 to the case of two undesirable outputs (b_1 and b_2).

The horizontal axis of Fig. 4.3 is for b_1/x and the vertical axis is for b_2/x under the assumption that all DMUs produce the same amount of a desirable output (g). In the two figures, {b}, {c}, {d} and {e} indicate the observed performance of four efficient DMUs. A piece-wise linear contour line ({b}-{c}-{d}-{e}) indicates an efficiency frontier in each figure. The projected performance {a'} is a projected point of an inefficient DMU {a}.

In the two figures, an inefficient DMU {a} directs its location toward a projected point a' to enhance the joint performance between operational and environmental achievements. The directional vector of desirable outputs is $(g_1^{\{a\}}, g_2^{\{a\}})$ in Fig. 4.2 and that of undesirable outputs becomes $(-b_1^{\{a\}}, -b_2^{\{a\}})$ in Fig. 4.3. The two vector directions $(g_1^{\{a\}}, g_2^{\{a\}}, -b_1^{\{a\}}, -b_2^{\{a\}})$ indicate for its performance enhancement. However, none knows the magnitude of the two directional vectors between {a} and a'. It is

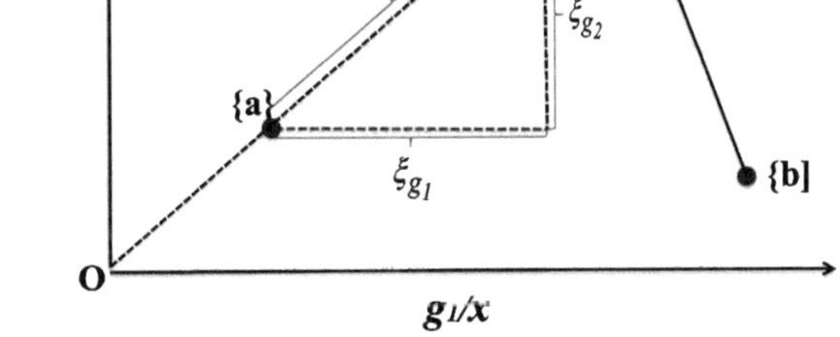

Fig. 4.2 Projection onto efficiency frontier for desirable outputs. *Note* a' is a projected point of the observed DMU {a}. An efficiency frontier is {b}-{c}-{d}-{e}

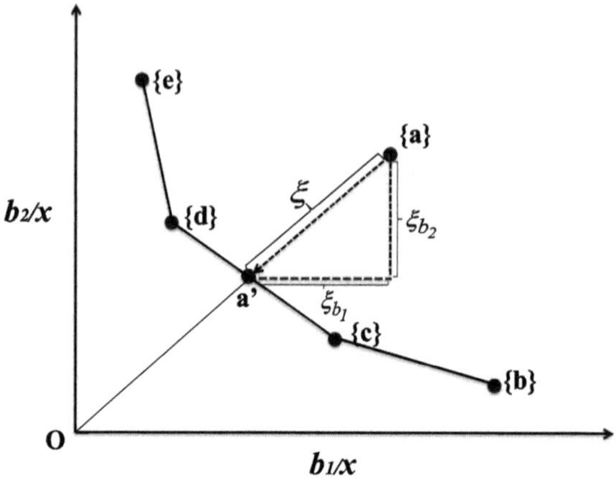

Fig. 4.3 Projection onto efficiency frontier for undesirable outputs. *Note* a' is a projected point of the observed DMU {a}. An efficiency frontier is {b}-{c}-{d}-{e}

true that the two figures visually indicate such a magnitude. However, if the number of coordinates is more than two, then none knows how to determine the magnitude of such a directional vector for performance betterment. A purpose, not all, of DEA environmental assessment is to mathematically identify the distance between the observed and projected performances ({a} and a') by DEA-based relative comparison.

To visually explain the distance measurement, let us consider the ratio (oa)/(oa') in Fig. 4.2 that indicates the magnitude on unified efficiency of DMU{a}. The ratio becomes

$$\frac{oa}{oa'} = \frac{oa}{oa + aa'} = \frac{1}{1 + \frac{aa'}{oa}} \cong \frac{1}{1 + \frac{aa'}{oa'}} = \frac{1}{1 + \xi} = 1 - \xi + \xi^2 - \xi^3 + \cdots \cong 1 - \xi.$$

The above equation considers that DMU {a} locates near a' so that oa can be replaced by oa' in the equation. In other words, if a DMU locates on or near an efficiency frontier, then the ratio measure is reliable. In contrast, if the DMU locates far from the efficiency frontier, then the ratio measure is just an approximation. The ratio (aa'/oa'), or ξ (i.e., a degree of unified inefficiency), indicates the magnitude on a directional vector of DMU {a} for improving the operational performance of DMU {a}, as visually specified in Fig. 4.2. An approximation error is specified by $\sum_{z=2}^{\infty} (-\xi)^z = \xi^2/(1+\xi) \cong 0$ because $\xi \leq 1$. Thus, it is acceptable that the measurement of $1 - \xi$ may approximate the degree of unified efficiency.

The proposed intermediate model separates the magnitude of unified inefficiency (ξ) into ξ_{g_1} and ξ_{g_2} as the two subcomponents of the inefficiency measure. Such a visual separation is on the two coordinates of Fig. 4.2. Thus, we consider that the proposed approach is "intermediate" because it incorporates analytical features of the radial and non-radial approaches. In the non-radial measurement, each subcomponent corresponds to a slack because it does not have an inefficiency score and the level of unified inefficiency is measured by the sum of total slacks. The feature is different from the radial measurement that directly measures the level of a unified inefficiency.

Figure 4.3 depicts another type of projection of DMU{a} in the case of two undesirable outputs (b_1 and b_2). In this case, our description is a straightforward manner. That is, the ratio (oa'/oa) indicates the degree of unified efficiency of DMU {a} by

$$\frac{oa'}{oa} = \frac{oa - aa'}{oa} = 1 - \xi.$$

The ratio (aa'/oa), or ξ, indicates a magnitude of the directional vector of DMU{a} to improve the environmental performance in the two undesirable outputs. Thus, it is possible for us to unify desirable and undesirable outputs and to measure the magnitude of unified efficiency by $1 - \xi$, as visually discussed in Fig. 4.3. As mentioned previously in Fig. 4.2, Fig. 4.3 also depicts the disaggregation of ξ into its two components, ξ_{b_1} and ξ_{b_2}, as visually specified in the two coordinates. Such a disaggregation is due to the computational framework of the intermediate approach. Each subcomponent corresponds to a slack in the case of non-radial measurement.

At the end of this section, we need to add that the level of unified inefficiency is separated into its subcomponents (ξ_{g_1}, ξ_{g_2}, ξ_{b_1} and ξ_{b_2}), as depicted in Figs. 4.2 and 4.3, respectively. Therefore, this study uses an average of these inefficiency components. In the case of multiple components, the average is specified by $\frac{1}{s+h}\left(\sum_{r=1}^{s} \xi_r^g + \sum_{f=1}^{h} \xi_f^b\right)$ in the proposed intermediate approach.

4.6 Structural Differences Among Three Models

Table 4.1 summarizes analytical differences among the three different models for DEA-EA. Sueyoshi et al., (2017a, 2017b) has first prepared the table. This study updates their table based upon the current knowledge on environmental assessment. The eight differences among three approaches are as follows:

First, as discussed in Table 4.1, the three approaches have originated from these optimality concepts, which we first classify into radial (i.e., "Debreu-Farrell" type of efficiency measurement) or non-radial (i.e., "Pareto–Koopmans" type of efficiency measurement) category. Sueyoshi and Goto (2018) provided a detailed description on the differences between the two types of efficiency measurement. The radial measurement determines the level of efficiency by an efficiency score assigned to a directional (so, radial) vector of production factors. Meanwhile, the non-radial

Table 4.1 Comparison among three models in DEA-EA

Criterion	Radial	Non-radial	Intermediate
(a) Type of Efficiency Measurement	Debreu-Farrell (Efficiency = 1—inefficiency)	Pareto–Koopmans (Efficiency = 1—inefficiency)	Russel (Efficiency = 1—inefficiency)
(b) Objective Function	Maximization of an inefficiency score assigned to a vector of desirable and undesirable outputs	Maximization of the total amount of slacks related to all inputs, desirable and undesirable outputs	Maximization of an average of inefficiency scores assigned to desirable and undesirable outputs
(c) Model Orientation	All outputs oriented formulation	All outputs and inputs oriented formulation	All outputs oriented formulation
(d) Production Factor Utilization	All production factors are fully utilized	All production factors are fully utilized	All production factors are fully utilized
(e) Assumption	Uniqueness on an optimal solution (An occurrence of multiple solutions)	Uniqueness on an optimal solution (An occurrence of multiple solutions)	Uniqueness on an optimal solution (An occurrence of multiple solutions)
(f) Influence of a size difference among DMUs	A size difference among DMUs may produce a limited influence on their inefficiency scores	A size difference among DMUs may produce an influence on a slack(s), but a limited influence on their inefficiency scores because these scores are determined by multiple slacks	A size difference among DMUs may produce an influence on a component of the inefficiency score. Consequently, the difference may influence their efficiency scores
(g) Zero and Negative Values	No analytical capability	Property of "translation invariance" can handle an occurrence of zero in a data set	No analytical capability
(h) Small number	ε_s (a very small number) to reduce an influence of slacks on unified efficiency	ε (a small number) to control the degree of unified efficiency. It serves as a magnitude control factor	ε_s (a very small number) to reduce an influence of slacks on unified efficiency

measurement calculates the inefficiency level by a sum of slacks associated with productions factors. We determine the level of efficiency by subtracting the inefficiency level from unity. Such a difference may exist in the objective function of these approaches. In a similar manner, we classify the proposed models, incorporating undesirable outputs, into radial or non-radial category for environmental assessment. This study adds an intermediate model between them as the third alternative. The model measures the degree of unified inefficiency on each production factor and determines the level of total unified inefficiency from the average of the sum of these inefficiency scores. We measure the level of unified efficiency by subtracting the inefficiency level from unity. Thus, it structurally belongs to "Russell" type of efficiency measure.

Here, it is important to note the following three differences between standard models and these extensions for environmental assessment. First, the standard DEA measures the performance of DMUs which use inputs to yield only desirable outputs, so excluding the existence of undesirable outputs. In contrast, DEA-EA incorporates undesirable outputs in the DEA scheme. As a result, the output unification produces a difficulty in developing the analytical structure because the vector direction of undesirable outputs is opposite to that of desirable outputs. Second, the standard DEA (radial models) measures the level of *OE*. In contrast, these models for DEA-EA determine the level of unified (operational and environmental) inefficiency. The radial-based unified efficiency measurement is due to a unification process between desirable and undesirable outputs in the DEA-EA. Finally, the intermediate model, we discuss here, does not exist in the standard DEA. It is possible for us to consider that the approach is originated from the Russell measure because it determines the level of efficiency by measuring the average of efficiency scores related to all production factors (i.e., inputs and desirable outputs). Note that the proposed intermediate model is based upon inefficiency, not efficiency as found in the Russell measure. The standard Russell measure for DEA has an analytical structure of non-linear programming (Sueyoshi & Sekitani, 2007). Meanwhile, the intermediate model for DEA-EA is formulated by linear programming. See Sueyoshi and Goto (2018) for a detailed description on the Russell measure and the importance in DEA-EA assessment.

Second, the three approaches for environmental assessment have different objective functions. The radial model is designed to maximize a level of unified inefficiency. We need to incorporate the sum of slacks related to all production factors into the objective function to avoid an occurrence of zero in their corresponding dual variables (i.e., multipliers). The occurrence of zero means that the DEA assessment does not utilize the corresponding production factor. Thus, such an occurrence is problematic. Furthermore, the non-radial approach maximizes the total amount of slacks, indicating the level of unified inefficiency in the objective function(s). Finally, the intermediate approach separates all the components of an inefficiency score and maximizes them along with the sum of all slacks. These inefficiency components function like slacks, as depicted in Figs. 4.2 and 4.3. The purpose of slacks is to avoid the occurrence of zero in these corresponding dual variables.

Third, the radial model incorporates the unification process between desirable and undesirable output vectors, which have opposite directions on optimization. Thus, the approach is output-oriented measurement. In contrast, the non-radial model measures a level of inefficiency by the sum of slacks so that the unification is output-oriented and input-oriented combined measurement. The intermediate model separates the components of an inefficiency measure related to desirable and undesirable outputs and then it measures the average of these components. Thus, the model is output-oriented measurement.

Fourth, an important feature of the three models is that they incorporate the data range adjustment on all slacks in their objective functions. As a result, all dual variables (i.e., multipliers) are strictly positive. Thus, all production factors are fully utilized in these models. However, as discussed by Sueyoshi and Goto (2018), it is possible for these approaches to incorporate additional multiplier restriction based upon prior information (e.g., previous results and mathematical requirements) in order to enhance the reality of performance assessment. Such multiplier restriction technique may reduce the number of efficient DMUs because DEA often produces many efficient DMUs. Moreover, such technique is useful in measuring the level of SDGs,

Fifth, a drawback of the three models is that they need to assume the uniqueness on an optimal solution (e.g., a unique reference set, a unique projection and a unique intercept of a supporting hyperplane). The three models may suffer from an occurrence of multiple solutions as a computational problem. In the case of such an occurrence, we need to incorporate SCSCs (Strong Complementary Slackness Conditions) of linear programming in these formulations. See, for example, the book of Sueyoshi and Goto (2018) that explains how to incorporate the SCSCs into the radial and non-radial formulations for DEA-EA. Their book (2018) did not discuss the intermediate approach.

Sixth, the magnitude difference in DMUs may influence the degree of unified efficiency scores of the three models. A first discussed by Aida et al. (1998), the non-radial model usually produces efficient DMUs and inefficient ones whose magnitudes are close to unity. To handle the problem, they suggested a use of "slack-adjusted radial measure", which serves as a conceptual basis of the radial measurement. The proposed intermediate approach can separate the degree of unified inefficiency by decomposing its inefficiency components so that the degree of unified efficiency may have a wide range of distribution than the radial and non-radial measures.

Seventh, it is possible for the non-radial model to handle "zero and negative values" in a data set by the property of "translation invariance". The property indicates that an efficiency measure does not influenced even if we shift production factors toward a same direction by adding or subtracting a specific real number. Appendix of this chapter explains the "translation invariance". Sueyoshi et al. (2015c) provided the mathematical proof on the desirable property. Both radial and intermediate models do not have the property. The two models depend upon the "data disaggregation" as discussed by Sueyoshi and Goto (2018). See also Sueyoshi and Yuan (2015).

Finally, the radial and intermediate models use a very small number (e.g., $\varepsilon_s = 0.0001$) to reduce an influence of slacks on their unified efficiency measures. Meanwhile, the non-radial model uses a small number (e.g., $\varepsilon = 1$ or 2) to control the degree of a unified efficiency measure as a magnitude control factor.

Illustrative example: Readers may find an illustrative example of the three models for DEA-EA in the following article:

Sueyoshi, T., Yuan, Y., Li A., Wang D. (2017) Methodological comparison among radial, non-radial and intermediate approaches for DEA environmental assessment. Energy Economics 67: 439-453.

They have discussed the analytical features of the intermediate model by comparing it with the radial and non-radial ones. The previous book (Sueyoshi & Goto, 2018) have not described the intermediate model of DEA-EA.

4.7 How DEA-EA Handles ESG Under Managerial Disposability

The ESG has the two quantitative features, obtained from the application of DEA-EA. One of the two features is that we need to incorporate "undesirable outputs" (e.g., CO_2) into the DEA-EA computation process. The other aspect is "investment" that is an important part of ESG. This section describes an analytical rationale on how the proposed DEA-EA can determine investment opportunities for the ESG enhancement.

This section first intuitively describes the analytical rationale by using the non-radial approach under managerial disposability. We may use the similar process to describe how the other two (radial and intermediate) models can handle ESG under the managerial disposability. The natural disposability does not have the similar function on ESG because the disposability is interested in economic prosperity as the first priority and environmental protection is the second priority.

To intuitively describe the importance of Model (4.26) for measuring ESG enhancement, we prepare Fig. 4.4 which depicts an influence of investment on eco-technology innovation to prevent industrial pollution. The figure has the horizontal axis to represent a desirable output (g) and the vertical axis to represent an undesirable output (b). Figure 4.4 visually specifies the three types of a supporting hyperplane in the g-b dimensions. The objective function of Model (4.26) indicates that we express the supporting hyperplane by $wb = vx + ug - \sigma$ when all production factors have a single component. See the research of Sueyoshi and Goto (2014) that has provided a detailed description on how to express a supporting hyperplane in production factors with multiple components.

The supporting hyperplane has three types, each of which indicates positive, zero and negative DTR (Damages to Return), respectively, where we measure the degree of DTR by $(db/dg)/(b/g)$ in the case of a single component. The three hyperplane have positive, zero and negative slopes, respectively, so indicating positive, zero and negative DTR. As indicated in Fig. 4.4, the eco-technology innovation occurs on negative DTR because an increase in a desirable output (g) decreases an amount of an undesirable output (b). The increase in the desirable output (g) is due to an increase in an input (x).

According to Sueyoshi and Goto (2014), Model (4.26) can identify an occurrence of eco-technology innovation by the following rule:

(a) if $u_r = 0$ for some (at least one) r, then "week eco-innovation" occurs on the k th DMU,
(b) if $u_r < 0$ for some (at least one) r, then "strong eco-innovation" occurs on the k th DMU &
(c) if $u_r > 0$ for all r, then "no eco-innovation" occurs on the k th DMU.

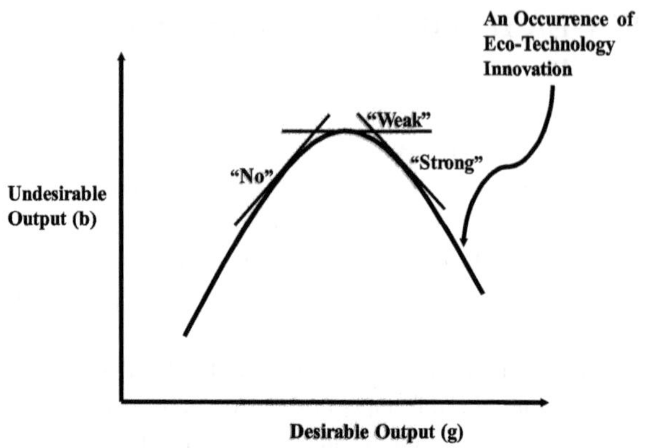

Fig. 4.4 An occurrence of eco-technology innovation. *Note* (a) Fig. 4.4 visually describes the economic implication of DTR (Damages to Return) which we determine by $(db/dg)/(b/g)$ in the case of a single production factor. The DTR implies the relationship between desirable and undesirable outputs. Thus, the scale measure is different from RTS (Returns to Scale) measured by $(dg/dx)/(g/x)$ which we use in the context of economics. The occurrence of eco-technology corresponds to DC (Desirable Congestion) in DEA-EA. See Sueyoshi and Goto (2018) that describes the theoretical background on DTR and DC

We invest on DMU in the second case because it has a high likeliness on eco-innovation, so increasing the status of ESG.

Note that if $u_r < 0$ for some r and $u_{r'} = 0$ for other r', then we consider that the strong eco- innovation occurs on the k th DMU, indicating a status of eco-technology innovation on undesirable outputs. Thus, DEA-EA can determine the investment opportunity to which DMU we can invest.

Here, it is important to describe that we need to modify Model (4.26) slightly to attain the above classification as follows:

$$
\begin{aligned}
\text{Minimize} \quad & -\sum_{i=1}^{m} v_i x_{ik} - \sum_{r=1}^{s} u_r g_{rk} + \sum_{f=1}^{h} w_f b_{fk} + \sigma \\
s.t. \quad & -\sum_{i=1}^{m} v_i x_{ij} - \sum_{r=1}^{s} u_r g_{rj} + \sum_{f=1}^{h} w_f b_{fj} + \sigma \geq 0 \quad (j = 1, \ldots, n), \\
& v_i \geq \varepsilon R_i^x \quad (i = 1, \ldots, m), \\
& u_r : URS \quad (r = 1, \ldots, s), \\
& w_f \geq \varepsilon R_f^b \quad (f = 1, \ldots, h), \\
& \sigma : URS,
\end{aligned}
\tag{4.44}
$$

where Model (4.44) changes $u_r \geq \varepsilon R_r^g$ to u_r : URS in the formulation so that u_r may take positive, zero and negative in the sign.

To discuss a mathematical rationale on why Model (4.44) can identify a possible occurrence of eco-technology innovation, we need to discuss the following proposition:

Proposition: A supporting hyperplane of the k th DMU, measured by Model (4.44), under managerial disposability becomes $-\sum_{i=1}^{m} v_i x_{ij} - \sum_{r=1}^{s} u_r g_{rj} + \sum_{f=1}^{h} w_f b_{fj} + \sigma = 0$ where $v_i \geq \varepsilon_s R_i^x$ $(i = 1,\ldots, m)$, u_r : URS $(r = 1,\ldots, s)$ and $w_f \geq \varepsilon_s R_f^b$ $(f = 1, \ldots, h)$ are parameters (slopes) for indicating the direction of a supporting hyperplane and σ indicates an intercept of the supporting hyperplane. The parameters of the supporting hyperplane are all unknown and need to be measured by the following equations:

$$-\sum_{i=1}^{m} v_i x_{ij} - \sum_{r=1}^{s} u_r g_{rj} + \sum_{f=1}^{h} w_f b_{fj} + \sigma = 0, \ j \in \mathrm{RS}_k, \tag{4.45}$$

where RS_k stands for a reference set of the k th DMU which is measured by the primal model of Model (4.45).

[Proof] The CSCs (Complementary Slackness Conditions) between primal and dual models contain the following equations on optimality:

$$(-\sum_{i=1}^{m} v_i^* x_{ij} - \sum_{r=1}^{s} u_r^* g_{rj} + \sum_{f=1}^{h} w_f^* b_{fj} + \sigma^*)\lambda_j^* = 0 \text{ for } j \in \mathrm{RS}_k \tag{4.46}$$

A reference set for the k th DMU (RS_k) consists of DMUs that have $\lambda_j > 0$ for $j \in \mathrm{RS}_k$.

The supporting hyperplane is expressed by $-v*x - u*g + w*b + \sigma* = 0$ on an efficiency frontier in the case when three production factors have a single component. The supporting hyperplane is expressed by $b = (v*x + u*g - \sigma*)/w*$. Since both $w*$ and $v*$ are positive, the slope of a supporting hyperplane is determined by $u*$ and $\sigma*$, both are unrestricted in their signs.

After solving Model (4.44), this chapter can identify a possible occurrence of DC (Desirable Congestion), or an occurrence of eco-technology innovation, by the following rule along with the assumption on a unique optimal solution:

Illustrative examples: Readers may find illustrative examples of DEA-EA for ESG in the following articles:

(a) Sueyoshi, T., Goto, M. (2014) Investment strategy for sustainable society by development of regional economies and prevention of industrial pollutions in Japanese manufacturing sectors. Energy Economics 42: 299–312.
(b) Wang, D. Li, S., Sueyoshi, T. (2014) DEA environmental assessment on U.S. industrial sectors: investment for improvement in operational and environmental performance for corporate sustainability. Energy Economics 45: 254–267.
(c) Sueyoshi, T., Goto, M. (2016) Undesirable congestion under natural disposability and desirable congestion under managerial disposability in U.S. electric power industry measured by DEA environmental assessment. Energy Economics 55: 173–188.

4.8 How DEA-EA Handles SDGs Under Managerial Disposability

In addition to ESG, let us consider how to handle SDGs within the framework of DEA-EA under managerial disposability. To analytically examine the level of SDGs, we need to consider the two concerns. One of the two concerns is that if SDGs may contain specific goals with these priorities, then we can depend upon AR (Assurance Region) analysis that is discussed in Sect. 3. The other concern is that we must examine the SDGs from a time horizon as an extension of ESG. This chapter does not discuss the important feature of SDGs. Rather, Chap. 5 will discuss such exploration on SDGs over time.

After solving SDGs by the AR analysis, we need to discuss how to handle the SDGs solutions. Here, let us consider a case that we use a non-radial model as an illustrative model. Note that all discussion here may be applicable to the other two DEA-EA approaches (i.e., radial and intermediate). First, the SDGs may be classified into desirable goals (g_r for $r = 1,.., s$) and undesirable goals (b_f for $f = 1, ..., h$). For example, the level of GDP is a desirable measure (as SDG 8) that we need to increase and the amount of CO_2 emission (as SDG 13) is an undesirable goal that we need to reduce the magnitude. The two types of goals provide us with specific goal levels that we need to attain at the final stage.

Model (4.24) have the following equations on optimality:

$$\begin{aligned} &\sum\nolimits_{j=1}^{n} g_{rj}\lambda_j^* = g_{rk}+d_r^{g*} \ (r = 1, \ldots, s) \text{ and} \\ &\sum\nolimits_{j=1}^{n} b_{fj}\lambda_j^* = b_{fk} - d_f^{b*} \ (f = 1, \ldots, h). \end{aligned} \tag{4.47}$$

The above two equations indicate the "attainable" performance of desirable outputs and that of undesirable outputs. Both are on a frontier for desirable outputs and that of undesirable outputs. The differences between the goals (g_r and b_f) specified by SDGs and the attainable performances may be expressed by the following absolute value:

$$\begin{aligned} &\delta_k^g = \left|g_{r-(}g_{rk}+d_r^{g*})\right| \ (r = 1, \ldots, s) \text{ and} \\ &\delta_k^b = \left|b_f - (b_{fk} - d_f^{b*})\right| \ (f = 1, \ldots, h) \end{aligned} \tag{4.48}$$

Here, the symbol || indicates the absolute value. The left hand sides of Eqs. (4.48) indicate the distances to SDGs requirements on the k th DMU.

The Eqs. (4.48) produce the following new SDGs index (ρ_k) on the k th DMU:

$$\rho_k = \left((\sum_{r=1}^{s} \delta_k^g / g_r) + (\sum_{f=1}^{h} \delta_k^b / b_f) \right) / (s + h). \tag{4.49}$$

The SDGs index indicates a total percentage on how much the k th DMU needs to improve the performance to attain the sustainable goals required by SDGs.

4.9 Discussion

This chapter compared the three models for DEA-EA, all of which examined a level of simultaneous achievement on economic prosperity and environmental protection so that it can measure the level of ESG. The SDGs is considered as an extension of ESG in this chapter. The standard DEA examines the performance assessment of DMUs which use "inputs" to produce "desirable outputs". Meanwhile, DEA-EA evaluates the assessment of DMUs which produces not only desirable outputs but also "undesirable outputs" by their economic activities. As a consequence, DEA-EA measures the level of ESG on DMUs by identifying investment opportunities to reduce the amount of undesirable outputs.

We have previously classified the DEA-EA into radial or non-radial category (Sueyoshi & Goto, 2018). The new "intermediate" model, analytically locating between the radial and non-radial categories, becomes as the third alternative (Sueyoshi & Yuan, 2017). A use of the intermediate model has several important features for measuring ESG, all of which are not found in the radial and non-radial models (Sueyoshi & Goto, 2018; Sueyoshi et al., 2017a, 2017b).

For assessing the sustainability of DMUs, the methodological comparison conveys a message to the audience that "DEA may be not a perfect methodology for environmental assessment. Rather, it is an approximation method to understand the performance of many organizations in public and private sectors. DEA-EA often faces difficulties in its applications, resulting from a methodological bias, implying that different approaches produce different empirical results. Therefore, in guiding large policy and business issues such as the global warming and climate change, we need to compare several different approaches to obtain a reliable empirical result(s) for preparing policy guidance on ESG and SDGs.

Appendix

Translation Invariance of Non-radial Model

In real DEA applications, we often face to an occurrence of zero or negative in the data set of *G*. For example, GDP (Gross Domestic Product) is always positive in measuring the EI (Energy Intensity) and EE (Energy Efficiency) comparisons among all nations. However, when we consider the amount of sales and/or that of profit in business assessment, the output may become zero or negative values in *G*. Another example is that we find the occurrence of zero in the amount of nuclear power generation because many countries do not have such power plants.

Considering such real cases, we need to consider how to handle an occurrence of zero and negative values in a data set. Such an effort may be mathematically useful. In this chapter, we fully utilize the property of "translation invariance" of the non-radial models. The non-radial models have the desirable property. The other DEA models (e.g., radial and intermediate models) do not have the property.

For applying the property of "translation invariance" for DEA-EA, we start with a description on the following data shift on all DMUs ($j = 1, \ldots, n$):

$$\begin{aligned} &\overline{x}_{\mathrm{ij}} = x_{\mathrm{ij}} + \alpha_i (i = 1, \ldots, m), \overline{g}_{\mathrm{rj}} = g_{\mathrm{rj}} + \beta_r (r = 1, \ldots, s) \text{ and} \\ &\overline{b}_{\mathrm{fj}} = b_{\mathrm{fj}} + \delta_f (f = 1, \ldots, h). \end{aligned} \tag{4.A}$$

The three Greek symbols are specific positive numbers (e.g., 1 and 2) that are subjectively selected by a DEA user(s). As a result of these data shifts, all production factors of the *j* th DMU become $\overline{x}_{\mathrm{ij}} > 0$ ($i = 1, \ldots, m$), $\overline{g}_{\mathrm{rj}} > 0$ ($r = 1, \ldots, s$) and $\overline{b}_{\mathrm{fj}} > 0$ ($f = 1, \ldots, h$), where the symbol (>) implies strict positivity in all components of the three vectors of production factors.

The symbols should be selected within the boundary of our common sense. For example, let us consider a case in which $\alpha_i = 100{,}000$, $\beta_r = 1$ and $\delta_f = 1$ are selected for Eqs. (4.44). In the case, the adjusted large data on inputs ($\overline{x}_{ij}$) dominates the other desirable and undesirable outputs ($\overline{g}_{rj}$ and $\overline{b}_{fj}$) in the computation of DEA-EA. Consequently, the non-radial model does not produce any reliable result on EA. This is not a mathematical problem, indeed, rather being a computational problem. In addition, the selection of $\alpha_i = \beta_r = \delta_f$ is acceptable as long as such a selection fits with the mathematical requirement that all production factors become strictly positive on their components.

Under Natural Disposability: To examine the property of translation invariance, let us modify the three groups of constraints as follows:

$$\sum_{j=1}^{n} (x_{\mathrm{ij}} + \alpha_i)\lambda_j + d_i^{x-} = x_{\mathrm{ik}} + \alpha_i (i = 1, \ldots, m),$$

$$\sum_{j=1}^{n}(g_{rj}+\beta_r)\lambda_j - d_r^g = g_{rk}+\beta_r (r=1,\ldots,s) \text{ and}$$

$$\sum_{j=1}^{n}(b_{fj}+\delta_f)\lambda_j + d_f^b = b_{fk}+\delta_f (f=1,\ldots,h). \quad (4.B)$$

Equations (4.A) add a specific positive number to each production factor so that all observations become positive, shifting from zero or negative to positive, in their signs.

Equations (4.B) maintain the following three conditions: $\sum_{j=1}^{n}\alpha_i\lambda_j = \alpha_i$, $\sum_{j=1}^{n}\beta_r\lambda_j = \beta_r$ and $\sum_{j=1}^{n}\delta_f\lambda_j = \delta_f$ because of $\sum_{j=1}^{n}\lambda_j = 1$. Consequently, the three constraints of Eqs. (4.B) become

$$\sum_{j=1}^{n} x_{ij}\lambda_j + d_i^{x-} = x_{ik}(i=1,\ldots,m),$$

$$\sum_{j=1}^{n} g_{rj}\lambda_j - d_r^g = g_{rk}(r=1,\ldots,s) \text{ and}$$

$$\sum_{j=1}^{n} b_{fj}\lambda_j + d_f^b = b_{fk}(f=1,\ldots,h). \quad (4.C)$$

Next, paying attention to the objective function, the data shifts change the three types of slacks as follows:

$$\sum_{i=1}^{m} R_i^x[(x_{ik}+\alpha_i) - \sum_{j=1}^{n}(x_{ij}+\alpha_i)\lambda_j] = \sum_{i=1}^{m} R_i^x(x_{ik} - \sum_{j=1}^{n} x_{ij}\lambda_j) = \sum_{i=1}^{m} R_i^x d_i^{x-}$$

$$\sum_{r=1}^{s} R_r^g[\sum_{j=1}^{n}(g_{rj}+\beta_r)\lambda_j - g_{rk}+\beta_r)] = \sum_{r=1}^{s} R_r^g(\sum_{j=1}^{n} g_{rj}\lambda_j - g_{rk}) = \sum_{r=1}^{s} R_r^g d_r^g \text{ and}$$

$$\sum_{f=1}^{h} R_f^b[(b_{fk}+\delta_f) - \sum_{j=1}^{n}(b_{fj}+\delta_f)\lambda_j] = \sum_{f-1}^{h} R_f^b(b_{fk} - \sum_{j=1}^{n} b_{fj}\lambda_j) = \sum_{f=1}^{h} R_f^b d_f^b \quad (4.D)$$

Equations (4.D) clearly indicate the translation invariance in the objective valuc of non-radial model. Thus, the proposed data shifts from zero or negative to positivc do not influence the objective value of non-radial model under natural disposability.

Under Managerial Disposability: In a similar manner discussed above, the non-radial model under managerial disposability has the property of translation invariance.

References

Aida, K., Cooper, W. W., Pastor, J. T., & Sueyoshi, T. (1998). Evaluating water supply services in Japan with RAM: A range-adjusted measure of inefficiency. *Omega, 26*, 207–232.

Glover, F., & Sueyoshi, T. (2009). Contributions of Professor William W. Cooper in operations research and management science. *European Journal of Operational Research, 197*, 1–16.

Ijiri, Y., & Sueyoshi, T. (2010). Accounting essays by Professor William W. Cooper: Revisiting in commemoration of his 95th birthday. *ABACUS: A Journal of Accounting Finance and Business Studies, 46*, 464–505.

Porter, M. E., & van der Linde, C. (1995). Toward a new conception of the environment competitiveness relationship. *Journal of Economic Perspectives, 9*, 97–118.

Russell, R. R. (1985). Measures of technical efficiency. *Journal of Economic Theory, 35*, 109–126.

Russell, R. R. (1990). Continuity of measures of technical Efficiency. *Journal of Economic Theory, 51*, 255–267.

Sueyoshi, T., & Goto, M. (2012a). Data envelopment analysis for environmental assessment: Comparison between public and private ownership in petroleum industry. *Eurupen Journal of Operational Research, 216*, 668–678.

Sueyoshi, T., & Goto, M. (2012b). DEA radial and non-radial models for unified efficiency under natural and managerial disposability: Theoretical extension by strong complementary slackness conditions. *Energy Economics, 34*, 700–713.

Sueyoshi, T., & Goto, M. (2012c). DEA radial measurement for environmental assessment and planning: Desirable procedures to evaluate fossil fuel power plants. *Energy Policy, 41*, 422–432.

Sueyoshi, T., & Goto, M. (2014). Investment strategy for sustainable society by development of regional economies and prevention of industrial pollutions in Japanese manufacturing sectors. *Energy Economics, 42*, 299–312.

Sueyoshi, T., & Goto, M. (2015a). DEA environmental assessment in time horizon: Radial approach for Malmquist index measurement on petroleum companies. *Energy Economics, 51*, 329–345.

Sueyoshi, T., & Goto, M. (2015b). Environmental assessment on coal-fired power plants in U.S. north-east region by DEA non-radial measurement. *Energy Economics, 50*, 125–139.

Sueyoshi, T., & Goto, M. (2015c). Japanese fuel mix strategy after disaster of Fukushima Daiichi nuclear power plant: Lessons from international comparison among industrial nations measured by DEA environmental assessment in time horizon. *Energy Economics, 52*, 87–103.

Sueyoshi, T., & Goto, M. (2016). Undesirable congestion under natural disposability and desirable congestion under managerial disposability in U.S. electric power industry measured by DEA environmental assessment. *Energy Economics, 55*, 173–188.

Sueyoshi T., Goto, M. (2018) Environment Assessment an Energy and Sustainability by Data Envelopment Analysis. Wiley, NJ in USA and West Sussex, UK.

Sueyoshi, T., & Goto, M. (2019). Intermediate approach for sustainability enhancement and scale related measures in environmental assessment. *European Journal of Operational Research, 276*, 744–756.

Sueyoshi, T., & Sekitani, K. (2007). Computational strategy for Russell measure in DEA: Second-order cone programming. *European Journal of Operational Research, 180*, 459–471.

Sueyoshi, T., & Wang, D. (2014). Radial and non-radial approaches for environmental assessment by data envelopment analysis: Corporate sustainability and effective investment for technology innovation. *Energy Economics, 45*, 537–551.

Sueyoshi, T., & Yuan, Y. (2015). Comparison among U.S. industrial sectors by DEA environmental assessment: Equipped with analytical capability to handle zero or negative in production factors. *Energy Economics, 52*, 69–86.

Sueyoshi, T., & Yuan, Y. (2017). Social sustainability measured by intermediate approach for DEA environmental assessment: Chinese regional planning for economic development and pollution prevention. *Energy Economics, 66*, 154–166.

Sueyoshi, T., Yuan, Y., & Goto, M. (2017a). A literature study for DEA applied to energy and environment. *Energy Economics, 62*, 104–124.

Sueyoshi, T., Yuan, Y., Li, A., & Wang, D. (2017b). Methodological comparison among radial, non-radial and intermediate approaches for DEA environmental assessment. *Energy Economics, 67*, 439–453.

Wang, D. Li, S., Sueyoshi, T. (2014) DEA environmental assessment on U.S. industrial sectors: investment for improvement in operational and environmental performance for corporate sustainability Energy Economics 45: 254–267.

Chapter 5
Intermediate Model for SDGs: Three Time Structures

Abstract As an extension of Chap. 4, this chapter discusses a use of DEA-EA (Environmental Assessment) in a time horizon so that we may discuss how to measure the level of SDGs, as important part of ESG, within the framework of DEA-EA. Chapter 4 did not discuss the approach over time. The data sets on EA for ESG and SDGs often have an analytical structure with time series. In applying DEA to EA, we need to examine an efficiency shift among different periods because it indicates "technology transfer" due to its progress on desirable and undesirable outputs. This chapter thinks that the gist of SDGs is the gradual improvement of ESG over time, focusing upon our sustainability goals. This chapter focuses upon the intermediate model among the three approaches (cross sectional, window efficiency and window index) of DEA-EA, all of which we have not discussed in Chap. 4. An important feature of these approaches is that they incorporate the concepts of natural and managerial disposability into these analytical frameworks and then extends them under the two disposability concepts over time. To capture the shift of efficiency measures (not frontier shifts as found in Chap. 6) in a time horizon, we propose the three different structures of DEA-EA over time. Focusing upon the intermediate model, we discuss the improvement of SDGs under managerial disposability in a time horizon. We apply the proposed DEA-EA to a data set on US coal-fired power plants during 1995–2007 for our illustration. The application finds that managers of the coal-fired power plants have gradually paid attention to environmental protections under US CAA (Clean Air Act). Consequently, their performance under managerial disposability has increased during the observed periods. This indicates the importance of CAA and strict implementation for US environmental protection. It is necessary to extend the scope of CAA for controlling the amount of CO_2 emission because current regulation has a policy influence on the source of global warming and climate change in our modern societies which are directing toward the enhancement of ESG and SDGs.

Keywords Environmental assessment · Time series · Electricity

T. Sueyoshi and M. Goto, *Environment and Sustainability for ESG and SDGs*,
https://doi.org/10.1007/978-981-96-2464-5_5

5.1 Introduction

Chapter 4 has introduced the three different (i.e., radial, non-radial and intermediate) models of DEA-EA. See Sueyoshi and Yuan (2017) and Sueyoshi et al. (2017) for a detailed description on the three models. We may apply them to various environmental issues to empirically measure the level of ESG enhancement. As an extension of such research efforts, this chapter will discuss its new applicability toward the enhancement of SDGs by incorporating a time horizon into the computational framework of the intermediate model. The approach is one of the three ones for ESG enhancement, discussed in Chap. 4. Note that all discussions in this chapter are applicable to the other two alternatives.

A contribution of DEA-EA is that it methodologically discusses the importance of separating outputs into desirable and undesirable categories because all production activities have produced not only desirable (good) outputs but also undesirable (bad) outputs such as CO_2 emission. Thus, DEA-EA is closely related to ESG enhancement. A problem is that the previous research works on ESG, as discussed in Chap. 4, did not clearly document any assessment in a dynamic time shift so that it could not discuss its contribution to the SDGs enhancement.

To proceed the research issue further, this chapter focuses upon a use of intermediate model over time. The approach has been not yet well explored at the level that it becomes a practical tool for the measurement of SDGs. Before discussing the intermediate model over time, we first describe the historical and current situations of an electric power industry which is an important example of SDGs in the world. That is, the electricity generation by fossil fuels may contribute to a large portion of CO_2 emission so that we have historically considered as a source of air pollution.

In a recent trend of the electric power industry, many industrial nations attempt to assess the performance of fossil fuel generation from the amount of CO_2 emission reduction. For instance, previous studies (e.g., Xie et al., 2019; Zhang and Chen, 2018) analyzed an emission reduction potential of electricity generation in various countries. They assumed that the fossil fuel electricity generation was able to improve its performance by reducing CO_2 emission along with a fuel mix strategy to change from coal to natural gas, renewable and nuclear generation.[1]

When discussing the fuel mix change in the electric power industry, we need to describe a recent structural change. Before the disaster at Fukushima Daiichi on March 11, 2011, many industrial nations, including Japan, directed themselves toward nuclear power generation to reduce the amount of CO_2 emission (Goto & Sueyoshi, 2016). The nuclear power generation was the most promising technology to combat the climate change and global warming (so, enhancing the level of ESG and SDGs) in the world. However, after the Fukushima's disaster, many policy makers and individuals, who are interested in the electric power industry, have realized that the nuclear power generation has extremely high risk and very expensive opportunity cost, along with high operation cost.

[1] See Chap. 2 of this book which we have discussed current socio-economic issues from the perspectives on ESG and EDGs.

To substitute for the nuclear power generation, many industrial nations have paid serious attention to renewable energy (e.g., wind power and solar photovoltaic generations) and natural gas generations. However, these energy densities of renewable energy are low so that they cannot satisfy most of the demand from end users. The cost of renewable energy is expensive. The energy is influenced by external factors (e.g., a weather condition and a number of sunny days). To promote the generation by renewable energy technologies, many nations have introduced FIT (Feed-in Tariff) program[2] in which electric power companies need to purchase all electricity produced by renewable energy sources by a fixed price.

To compensate the high risk of nuclear power technology and the high cost of renewable energy, many nations have considered a fuel mix among nuclear, renewable and fossil fuel generations. Among fossil fuel generations, several nations (e.g., the United States and Japan) have attempted to utilize coal combustion because they have recently developed clean coal technology at the level that it may effectively reduce the amount of CO_2 emission (so, ESG enhancement).

To assess the performance of coal-fired power plants, previous studies (e.g., Sueyoshi & Goto, 2013) proposed an application of DEA-EA as a managerial methodology for environmental assessment. The previous studies pooled all annual data sets on coal-fired power plants and treated it as a cross-sectional data set, so not incorporating any time horizon in their DEA assessments. Consequently, they could not identify any technology progress for CO_2 reduction. Meanwhile, this chapter incorporates a time horizon to document its importance in DEA-EA assessment. The time shift measurement is an important feature of SDGs.

The remainder of this chapter has the following structure: Sect. 5.2 describes previous studies on DEA-EA in a time horizon, Sect. 5.3 discusses three models based upon the intermediate model, which unify desirable and undesirable outputs under natural and managerial disposability concepts for measuring unified efficiency and unified index. Section 5.4 applies the intermediate-related three approaches to an illustrative example on US coal-fired power plants. Section 5.5 summarizes this chapter.

5.2 Previous Studies

The previous research efforts in the past decade included Zhou et al. (2008) that provided a summary of more than 100 articles in DEA-based environment and energy studies. Sueyoshi and Goto (2018) summarized 699 articles on DEA and DEA-EA

---

[2] Feed in Tariff is, known as standard offer contract or advanced renewable tariff, is policy mechanism that is designed to accelerate investment in renewable energy systems and technologies. They achieve this by offering long-term contracts to renewable energy producers, typically based on the cost of generation of each different technology. Technologies like wind power, for instance, are awarded a lower per-kWh price, whereas technologies like solar, photovoltaic, and tidal or wave power are currently offered a higher price, reflecting their higher costs.

applications that included many tasks for sustainability enhancement. In the literature surveys, the three groups of research were closely related to this chapter.

The first research group included DEA-based performance assessment on power plants. The United States and China became important research areas, because they were large energy consumers and CO_2 emitters in the world. Second, some studies considered undesirable outputs, where CO_2, SO_2 (sulfur dioxide) and NO_x (nitrogen oxides) were important research focuses. Finally, several studies applied DEA-based technique to analyze a data with time series so that they discussed an efficiency shift over time.

As a tool of SDGs, this chapter will utilize the intermediate model proposed by Sueyoshi and Yuan (2017). The approach is relatively new. So, there are a limited number of applications such as Goto and Sueyoshi (2020), Sueyoshi and Goto (2018, 2019) and Sueyoshi et al. (2020). We fully utilize the new model for this empirical study on SDGs because it has unique characteristics (e.g., performance accuracy on efficiency measurement), compared with the other two DEA-EA models (Sueyoshi et al., 2017).[3]

In this chapter, we propose the three schemes for a time horizon, using the intermediate model of DEA-EA. Our application includes the two contributions. One of the two contributions is that no previous study has discussed the intermediate model for efficiency and index measurements over time. The other contribution is that no study has compared the performance of the model with those of the two other extensions (i.e., window efficiency analysis and window index approach) over time. Thus, this chapter may convey a message to audience that DEA-EA can handle partial problems concerning SDGs by considering the three different types of time horizon.

5.3 Formulations

This chapter uses the "intermediate model" for a methodological example for SDGs. We incorporate two disposability concepts (i.e., natural and managerial disposability concepts) into the model and then three time-series schemes for environmental assessment. For these analytical structures, we may refer to Sueyoshi and Yuan (2017), Sueyoshi et al. (2017) and Sueyoshi and Goto (2019). This chapter extends their research efforts by incorporating a time horizon into the proposed model. See Chap. 4 for an analytical description on the intermediate model.

5.3.1 Underlying Concepts

Each DMU (j) transforms m inputs (X) to yield both s desirable outputs (G) and h undesirable outputs (B) in each period. Among multiple inputs and multiple outputs,

---

[3] See Chap. 4 for the three methods for DEA-EA.

DEA does not assume any specific functional form without any assumption on an error distribution, just looking for multipliers (weights) among them. Inputs and two types (desirable and undesirable) of outputs are assumed to be strictly positive at the t th period ($t = 1, ..., T$). Each DMU seeks to maximize its unified efficiency and index measures. We relatively determine them by comparing its performance with efficiency frontiers obtained from several DMUs, including their performances among multiple period(s). Note that this chapter uses the term "unified efficiency" to specify it by unifying desirable and undesirable outputs in the DEA-EA measurement.

The unified production and pollution possibility sets, which combines desirable and undesirable outputs, express natural disposability (N) and managerial disposability (M) at the t th period, respectively, in the following manner:

$$P_t^N(X_t) = \left\{ (G_t, B_t) : G_t \le \sum_{j=1}^{n} G_{jt}\lambda_{jt},\ B_t \ge \sum_{j=1}^{n} B_{jt}\lambda_{jt},\ X_t \ge \sum_{j=1}^{n} X_{jt}\lambda_{jt}\ \&\ \lambda_{jt} \ge 0\ \ (j = 1, \ldots, n) \right\} \tag{5.1}$$

$$P_t^M(X_t) = \left\{ (G_t, B_t) : G_t \le \sum_{j=1}^{n} G_{jt}\lambda_{jt},\ B_t \ge \sum_{j=1}^{n} B_{jt}\lambda_{jt},\ X_t \le \sum_{j=1}^{n} X_{jt}\lambda_{jt}\ \&\ \lambda_{jt} \ge 0\ \ (j = 1, \ldots, n) \right\} \tag{5.2}$$

The above two equations incorporate the time (t) in the previous production and pollution possibility sets expressed by Eqs. (4.1) and (4.2). A difference between natural and managerial disposability relies on the inequality constraint of inputs, because a DMU directs toward the efficiency frontier by decreasing X_t under natural disposability and by increasing X_t under managerial disposability. Both natural and managerial disposability have the same constraints on desirable and undesirable outputs. See Chap. 4 and Sueyoshi and Goto (2018) on a description on disposability concepts.

Intuitively speaking, the concept of natural disposability implies that economic prosperity is the first priority and environmental protection is the second priority. In contrast, the managerial disposability indicates the opposite priority. An underlying position of this chapter is that both are important for our society in terms of ESG which need to incorporate undesirable outputs (e.g., CO_2). In other words, it is difficult for us to develop the pollution reduction without any economic support. The DEA-EA has developed for such sustainable development as specified in ESG (by incorporating undesirable outputs) and SDGs (by incorporating goals in a time horizon).

For data analysis, this chapter specifies the data ranges (R) based on the upper and lower bounds of production factors. We specify these ranges as follows:

$$R_i^x = (m+s+h)^{-1}\left(\max_{j\&t}\{x_{ijt}\} - \min_{j\&t}\{x_{ijt}\} \middle| j=1,\ldots,n \;\&\; t=1,\ldots,T\right)^{-1},$$
$$R_r^g = (m+s+h)^{-1}\left(\max_{j\&t}\{g_{rjt}\} - \min_{j\&t}\{g_{rjt}\} \middle| j=1,\ldots,n \;\&\; t=1,\ldots,T\right)^{-1} \text{ and}$$
$$R_f^b = (m+s+h)^{-1}\left(\max_{j\&t}\{b_{fjt}\} - \min_{j\&t}\{b_{fjt}\} \middle| j=1,\ldots,n \;\&\; t=1,\ldots,T\right)^{-1}. \tag{5.3}$$

The purpose of the data ranges is to avoid an occurrence of zero in multipliers. Such an occurrence implies that the proposed DEA assessment does not fully use these factors so that the computational results are unacceptable to us.

Figure 5.1 depicts the computational process based upon which we discuss the measurement of SDGs. The proposed use of DEA-EA has the three models (i.e., radial, non-radial and intermediate). They have specific formulations that incorporate both natural (N) and managerial (M) disposability concepts which are closely related to ESG. This chapter focuses upon the intermediate model because it is relatively new, compared with the other two, as a method of DEA-EA. Moreover, the previous book (Sueyoshi and Goto, 2018) did not contain the intermediate model. In this chapter, the intermediate one has three different analyses (cross sectional, window efficiency and window index) to deal with a time series data. The time series aspect becomes an analytical basis for examining the development of SDGs. The other models (radial and non-radial) can have the three models for SDGs.

The nomenclatures used in this chapter are as follows: j is a subscript of the j th DMU ($j = 1, \ldots, n$), k is a subscript of the specific k th DMU ($k = 1, \ldots, n$) whose performance is measured by DEA, ξ an inefficiency score in unified efficiency, ξ_{rt}^g and ξ_{ft}^b are inefficiency components on the r th desirable and the f th undesirable outputs at the t th period, ε_s is a very small number (e.g., 0.00001) to be prescribed by a DEA user, R_i^x is a data range related to the i th input, R_r^g is a data range related to the r th desirable output, R_f^b is a data range related to the f th undesirable output, d_{ikt}^{x-} is a deviation of the i th input of the k th DMU at the t th period under natural disposability, d_{ikt}^{x+} is a deviation of the i th input of the k th DMU at the t th period under managerial disposability, d_{rkt}^g is a deviation of the r th desirable output of the k th DMU at the t th period, d_{fkt}^b is a deviation of the f th undesirable output of the k th DMU at the t th period, x_{ijp} is an observed value of the i th input on the j th DMU at the p th period, g_{rjp} is an observed value of the r th desirable output on the j th DMU at the p th period, b_{fjp} is an observed value of the f th undesirable output on the j th DMU at the p th period and λ_{jp} is an intensity or structural variable on the j th DMU at the p th period.

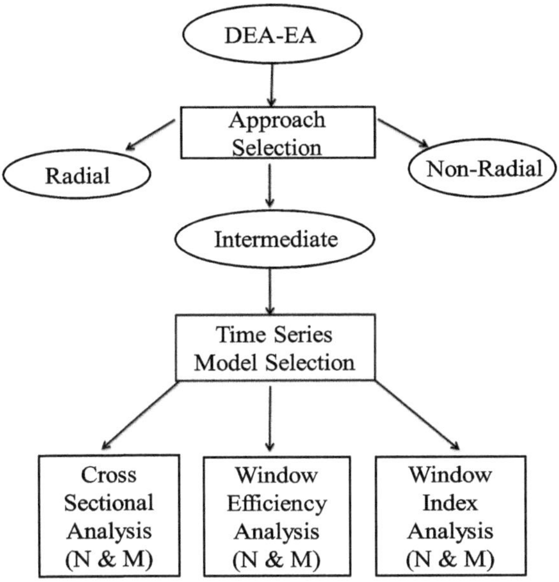

Fig. 5.1 Three analyses selection for intermediate model. *Note* **a** N and M stand for Natural and Managerial disposability, respectively. We need to select one method from 18 alternatives = 3 models (radial, non-radial and intermediate) × 3 analyses (cross sectional, window efficiency and window index) × 2 concepts (natural and managerial). In this chapter, we select the intermediate model for our illustration. **b** See Sueyoshi et al. (2017, 2020) for a description on the three models

5.3.2 Cross-Sectional Analysis

The formulations discussed in Chap. 4 did not include a time horizon. This chapter newly adds the subscript (t) to the previous ones. First, we discuss "cross-sectional" analysis, implying that we pool all DMUs in all observed periods (t) together and treat them as a single data set. An efficiency frontier in this case is for the entire periods ($t = 1, \ldots, T$).

Under Natural Disposability: The intermediate model under natural disposability has the following formulation to measure the unified (operational and environmental) efficiency of the k th DMU at the t th period:

$$
\begin{aligned}
& Maximize \ \tfrac{1}{s+h}\left(\sum_{r=1}^{s}\xi_{rt}^{g}+\sum_{f=1}^{h}\xi_{ft}^{b}\right)+\varepsilon_s\left(\sum_{i=1}^{m}R_i^x d_{ikt}^{x-}+\sum_{r=1}^{s}R_r^g d_{rkt}^{g}+\sum_{f=1}^{h}R_f^b d_{fkt}^{b}\right) \\
& s.t. \quad \sum_{p=1}^{T}\sum_{j=1}^{n} x_{ijp}\lambda_{jp}+d_{ikt}^{x-}=x_{ikt} \quad (i=1,\ldots,m), \\
& \sum_{p=1}^{T}\sum_{j=1}^{n} g_{rjp}\lambda_{jp}-d_{rkt}^{g}-\xi_{rt}^{g}g_{rkt}=g_{rkt} \quad (r=1,\ldots,s), \\
& \xi_{rt}^{g}\le 1, \\
& \sum_{p=1}^{T}\sum_{j=1}^{n} b_{fjp}\lambda_{jp}+d_{fkt}^{b}+\xi_{ft}^{b}b_{fkt}=b_{fkt} \quad (f=1,\ldots,h), \\
& \xi_{ft}^{b}\le 1, \\
& \lambda_{jp}\ge 0 \quad (j=1,\ldots,n \ \&\ p=1,\ldots,T),\ d_{ikt}^{x-}\ge 0 \quad (i=1,\ldots,m), \\
& d_{rkt}^{g}\ge 0 (r=1,\ldots,s) \ \&\ d_{fkt}^{b}\ge 0 \quad (f=1,\ldots,h),
\end{aligned}
\tag{5.4}
$$

where the three equations (i.e., $\sum_{p=1}^{T}\sum_{j=1}^{n} x_{ijp}\lambda_{jp}$, $\sum_{p=1}^{T}\sum_{j=1}^{T} g_{rjp}\lambda_{jp}$ and $\sum_{p=1}^{T}\sum_{j=1}^{n} b_{fjp}\lambda_{jp}$) on the left hand side indicate an efficiency frontier in all the periods ($p = 1, \ldots, T$). The two equations ($\xi_{rt}^{g} \le 1$ and $\xi_{ft}^{b} \le 1$) implies that each inefficiency component is less than or equal to unity. Model (5.4) determines the level of unified inefficiency by comparing between the efficiency frontier and the performance of a specific k th DMU at the t th period. Model (5.4) incorporates ε_s which is a prescribed very small number (e.g., 0.0001). Note that if the small number becomes zero, then corresponding multipliers (i.e., dual variables) may become zero, so indicating that Model (5.4) may not fully utilize some production factors. As a result, the computational results from Model (5.4) become unacceptable.

We determine the degree of the k th DMU at the t th period under natural disposability (UEN_{kt}^{I}) on the optimality of Model (5.4):

$$
UEN_{kt}^{I}=1-\left[\frac{1}{s+h}\left(\sum_{r=1}^{s}\xi_{rt}^{g*}+\sum_{f=1}^{h}\xi_{ft}^{b*}\right)+\varepsilon_s\left(\sum_{i=1}^{m}R_i^x d_{ikt}^{x-*}+\sum_{r=1}^{s}R_r^g d_{rkt}^{g*}+\sum_{f=1}^{h}R_f^b d_{fkt}^{b*}\right)\right]. \tag{5.5}
$$

Model (5.4) has three important features. First, we determine the two groups of inefficiency components (ξ_{rt}^{g} on G and ξ_{ft}^{b} on B) from a given directional vector (g_{rkt} for all r and b_{fkt} for all f). This feature is different from the previous radial model that has a single inefficiency (ξ) measure (Sueyoshi & Yuan, 2017). The measure is an aggregated output-oriented measure. Model (5.4) needs to unify between G (maximization) and B (minimization) for environmental assessment. Second, Model (5.4) incorporates the concept of constant RTS (Returns to Scale) because it excludes $\sum_{j=1}^{n}\lambda_{jt} = 1$. Intuitively, the concept of constant RTS implies that a unit increase in X proportionally increases the amount of G. Finally, as specified in the left hand side of Model (5.4), it covers DMUs in all periods ($t = 1, \ldots, T$) to identify the best efficiency frontier. The efficiency frontier is due to the cross-sectional data structure in all periods ($p = 1, \ldots, T$).

Under Managerial Disposability: The formulation under managerial disposability becomes as follows:

$$
\begin{aligned}
&Maximize\ \frac{1}{s+h}\left(\sum_{r=1}^{s}\xi_{rt}^{g}+\sum_{f=1}^{h}\xi_{ft}^{b}\right)+\varepsilon_s\left(\sum_{i=1}^{m}R_i^x d_{ikt}^{x+}+\sum_{r=1}^{s}R_r^g d_{rkt}^{g}+\sum_{f=1}^{h}R_f^b d_{fkt}^{b}\right)\\
&s.t.\quad \sum_{p=1}^{T}\sum_{j=1}^{n}x_{ijp}\lambda_{jp}-d_{ikt}^{x+}=x_{ikt}\quad (i=1,\ldots,m),\\
&\qquad same\ constraints\ in\ Model\ (5.4),\\
&\qquad \lambda_{jp}\geq 0\ (j=1,\ \ldots,\ n\ \&\ p=1,\ \ldots,\ T),\ d_{ikt}^{x+}\geq 0\ (i=1,\ \ldots,\ m),\\
&\qquad d_{rkt}^{g}\geq 0\ (r=1,\ \ldots,\ s)\ \&\ d_{fkt}^{b}\geq 0\ (f=1,\ \ldots,\ h).
\end{aligned}
\tag{5.6}
$$

There is only a difference between Models (5.4) and (5.6). The input-based constraints change from $+d_{ikt}^{x-}$ to $-d_{ikt}^{x+}$, where such a change attains the status of managerial disposability. The change implies that a DMU attains an efficiency frontier by increasing input(s) under the condition that the DMU has increased desirable output(s) and decreased undesirable output(s). No other difference exists between the two models. See Fig. 4.1 in the previous chapter that visually explains implications of such a change.

We determine the degree of unified efficiency of the k th DMU at the t th period under managerial disposability (UEM_{kt}^{I}) by the following model:

$$
UEM_{kt}^{I}=1-\left[\frac{1}{s+h}\left(\sum_{r=1}^{s}\xi_{rt}^{g*}+\sum_{f=1}^{h}\xi_{ft}^{b*}\right)+\varepsilon_s\left(\sum_{i=1}^{m}R_i^x d_{ikt}^{x+*}+\sum_{r=1}^{s}R_r^g d_{rkt}^{g*}+\sum_{f=1}^{h}R_f^b d_{fkt}^{b*}\right)\right].
\tag{5.7}
$$

Since the description on Eq. (5.5) is applicable to (5.7), we do not describe the feature further here. An exception is that Model (5.6) incorporates the concept of constant DTS (Damages to Scale) in the formulation. Intuitively, the concept of constant DTS implies that a unit increase in X proportionally increases the amount of B. Sueyoshi and Goto (2019) provided a mathematical description on DTS in the intermediate approach.

Strengths and Drawbacks: The strengths and drawbacks of Models (5.4) and (5.6) are as follows: The first strength is that the degree of the unified efficiency measures (i.e., UEN_{kt}^{I} and UEM_{kt}^{I}) may be equal to unity (full efficiency), less than unity (inefficiency), or even 0 (fully inefficiency). Second, these unified efficiency measures originate from the "Russell type of measure" in determining the level of unified efficiency by the sum of efficiency components concerning X, G and B. In Chap. 4, we have discussed the mathematical features (as Russell measure) by comparing it with the other types (i.e., radial and non-radial) measures. Finally, we can easily apply conventional rank sum tests such as Mann–Whitney. See Sueyoshi and Goto (2018) for the rank sum tests.

In contrary, Models (5.4) and (5.6) have three drawbacks. First, they cannot handle a data set that contains zero and/or negative values because they do not have the property of "translation invariance". The property indicates that we can overcome the difficulty by adding a small number into an original data set. The appendix of Chap. 4 discusses the desirable property. Second, the approach can handle an occurrence of a crossover among efficiency frontiers in multiple periods. However, is it appropriate to aggregate DMUs in all periods ($t = 1, \ldots, T$)? For example, DMUs in the first ($t = 1$) cannot access technology of the last ($t = T$). It is trivial that they cannot. This is a drawback of this model. In this study, we apply the proposed model to the electric power industry, as an illustrative example. The industry depends upon a very large generation capacity so that we cannot expect a rapid technology progress. We assume a limited technology progress is practically acceptable. Finally, the proposed approach cannot measure a technological progress of each DMU at the t th period from the previous efficiency frontier of the $t-1$ th period. The next subsection (i.e., window efficiency analysis and window index approach) discusses how to handle the difficulty.

5.3.3 Window Efficiency Analysis

The second approach discusses "window efficiency analysis" for the intermediate model as an alternative of the cross-sectional one. For the approach, we must consider the length of multiple periods for making a window. Importantly, we understand that the length of a window influences an efficiency shift in a time horizon.

Under Natural Disposability: The window efficiency analysis using the intermediate model has the following formulation:

$$
\begin{aligned}
&\text{Maximize } \frac{1}{s+h}\left(\sum_{r=1}^{s}\xi_{rt}^{g}+\sum_{f=1}^{h}\xi_{ft}^{b}\right)+\varepsilon_s\left(\sum_{i=1}^{m}R_i^x d_{ikt}^{x-}+\sum_{r=1}^{s}R_r^g d_{rkt}^{g}+\sum_{f=1}^{h}R_f^b d_{fkt}^{b}\right)\\
&\text{s.t.} \quad \sum_{p=t-L+1}^{t}\sum_{j=1}^{n}x_{ijp}\lambda_{jp}+d_{ikt}^{x-}=x_{ikt}\quad (i=1,\ldots,m),\\
&\qquad \sum_{p=t-L+1}^{t}\sum_{j=1}^{n}g_{rjp}\lambda_{jp}-d_{rkt}^{g}-\xi_{rt}^{g}g_{rkt}=g_{rkt}\quad (r=1,\ldots,s),\\
&\qquad \xi_{rt}^{g}\le 1,\\
&\qquad \sum_{p=t-L+1}^{t}\sum_{j=1}^{n}b_{fjp}\lambda_{jp}+d_{fkt}^{b}+\xi_{ft}^{b}b_{fkt}=b_{fkt}\quad (f=1,\ldots,h),\\
&\qquad \xi_{ft}^{b}\le 1,\\
&\qquad \lambda_{jp}\ge 0\quad (j=1,\ldots,n\ \&\ p=t-L,\ \ldots,\ t),\\
&\qquad d_{ikt}^{x-}\ge 0\quad (i=1,\ldots,m)\ \&\ d_{rkt}^{g}\ge 0\quad (r=1,\ldots,s).
\end{aligned}
\tag{5.8}
$$

Here, p represents a period to make a window in this approach. The L represents the length of window periods. For example, when $L = 2$, the first window contains $t - 1$ and $t - 2$, while the next window has $t - 2$ and $t - 3$ to make an efficiency frontier over the two adjacent periods. When $L = 3$, the first window contains $t - 1$, $t - 2$ and $t - 3$, while the next window has $t - 2$, $t - 3$ and $t - 4$ to make an efficiency frontier over the three adjacent periods. The purpose of Model (5.8) is to examine whether the setting of each window may significantly affect our empirical results. The approach is similar to "moving average" in statistics.

By solving Model (5.8), we compute the unified efficiency $\left(UEN_{kt}^{W}\right)$ of the k th DMU at the t period under natural disposability by the following equation:

$$UEN_{kt}^{W} = 1 - \left[\frac{1}{s+h}\left(\sum_{r=1}^{s}\xi_{rt}^{g*} + \sum_{f=1}^{h}\xi_{ft}^{b*}\right) + \varepsilon_s\left(\sum_{i=1}^{m}R_i^x d_{ikt}^{x-*} + \sum_{r=1}^{s}R_r^g d_{rkt}^{g*} + \sum_{f=1}^{h}R_f^b d_{fkt}^{b*}\right)\right]. \tag{5.9}$$

Here, the superscript (W) indicates the window efficiency analysis. We determine the unknown variables on the optimality of Model (5.8). Our description on Model (5.4) and Eq. (5.5) are applicable to Model (5.8) and Eq. (5.9). This study does not discuss their analytical features, further. An exception is that the degree of the unified efficiency UEN_{kt}^{W} measured by Eq. (5.9) becomes unity (full efficiency) or less than unity (inefficiency).

Under Managerial Disposability: Shifting our description from natural to managerial disposability, we reorganize the formulation as follows:

$$\begin{aligned}
&\text{Maximize } \tfrac{1}{s+h}\left(\sum_{r=1}^{s}\xi_{rt}^{g} + \sum_{f=1}^{h}\xi_{ft}^{b}\right) + \varepsilon_s\left(\sum_{i=1}^{m}R_i^x d_{ikt}^{x+} + \sum_{r=1}^{s}R_r^g d_{rkt}^{g} + \sum_{f=1}^{h}R_f^b d_{fkt}^{b}\right)\\
&s.t. \quad \sum_{p=t-L+1}^{t}\sum_{j=1}^{n} x_{ijp}\lambda_{jp} - d_{ikt}^{x+} = x_{ikt} \quad (i = 1, \dots, m),\\
&\quad \text{same constraints in (5.8)},\\
&\quad \lambda_{jp} \geq 0 \quad (j = 1, \dots, n \;\&\; p = t - L, \dots, t),\; d_{ikt}^{x+} \geq 0 \quad (i = 1, \dots, m)\\
&\quad \&\; d_{rkt}^{g} \geq 0 \quad (r = 1, \dots, s).
\end{aligned} \tag{5.10}$$

A description on Model (5.8) is applicable to Model (5.10). The only difference between Models (5.8) and (5.10) is that the input constraints change from $+d_{ikt}^{x-}$ to $-d_{ikt}^{x+}$. No other difference exists between them.

We measure the unified efficiency (UEM_{kt}^{W}) of the k th DMU at the t th period under managerial disposability by the following equation:

$$UEM_{kt}^{W} = 1 - \left[\frac{1}{s+h}\left(\sum_{r=1}^{s}\xi_{rt}^{g*} + \sum_{f=1}^{h}\xi_{ft}^{b*}\right) + \varepsilon_s\left(\sum_{i=1}^{m}R_i^x d_{ikt}^{x+*} + \sum_{r=1}^{s}R_r^g d_{rkt}^{g*} + \sum_{f=1}^{h}R_f^b d_{fkt}^{b*}\right)\right]. \tag{5.11}$$

The descriptions on Model (5.8) and Eq. (5.10) are applicable to (5.10) and (5.11).

Strengths and Drawbacks: The first strength is that window efficiency analysis can measure an efficiency shift among windows, where a user(s) subjectively determines the length of a window range. Second, an efficiency measure may be less than unity (inefficiency) or equal to unity (full efficiency).

In contrast, the analysis has the following four drawbacks: First, the window efficiency analysis has the same drawbacks (e.g., incapability to handle zero and/or negative data) as discussed in Chap. 4. Second, the approach has a difficulty in determining the best length of window. There is no theoretical justification. To overcome the difficulty, this study recommends several window lengths to examine whether such a change may not influence empirical results. Third, there is no clear linkage between the efficiency shift and technology improvement by a managerial effort to improve the status of unified efficiency (due to a regulatory change). Finally, DEA researches (e.g., Sueyoshi & Goto, 2013) have widely used Malmquist index to measure a frontier shift among different periods. The proposed window efficiency analysis cannot measure such a frontier shift, rather measuring an efficiency change among periods.

5.3.4 Window Index Analysis

Window index analysis is the last (third) alternative, being different from the previous two approaches (i.e., cross-sectional and window efficiency). The analysis can avoid self-evaluation on DMUs in the t period, rather assessing from the previous periods in the formulation. Consequently, it can obtain an index, not an efficiency measure, whose degree indicates a technology shift and/or a managerial change due to a regulatory change.

Under Natural Disposability: The window index analysis has the following formulation for the k th DMU at the t th period:

$$
\begin{aligned}
&Maximize\ \frac{1}{s+h}\left(\sum_{r=1}^{s}\xi_{rt}^{g}+\sum_{f=1}^{h}\xi_{ft}^{b}\right)+\varepsilon_{s}\left(\sum_{i=1}^{m}R_{i}^{x}d_{ikt}^{x-}+\sum_{r=1}^{s}R_{r}^{g}d_{rkt}^{g}+\sum_{f=1}^{h}R_{f}^{b}d_{fkt}^{b}\right)\\
&s.t.\quad \sum_{p=t-L}^{t-1}x_{ijp}\lambda_{jp}+d_{ikt}^{x-}=x_{ikt}(i=1,\ldots,m),\\
&\qquad \sum_{p=t-L}^{t-1}g_{rjp}\lambda_{jp}-d_{rkt}^{g}-\xi_{rt}^{g}g_{rkt}=g_{rkt}(r=1,\ldots,s),\\
&\qquad \xi_{rt}^{g}\leq 1,\\
&\qquad \sum_{p=t-L}^{t-1}b_{fjp}\lambda_{jp}+d_{fkt}^{b}+\xi_{ft}^{b}b_{fkt}=b_{fkt}(f=1,\ldots,h),\\
&\qquad \xi_{ft}^{b}\leq 1,\\
&\qquad \lambda_{jp}\geq 0(j=1,\ldots,n\ \&\ p=t-1-L,\ldots,t-1),\\
&\qquad d_{ikt}^{x-}\geq 0(i=1,\ldots,m)\ \&\ d_{rkt}^{g}\geq 0(r=1,\ldots,s).
\end{aligned}
\tag{5.12}
$$

The difference between Models (5.8) and (5.12) is that the former may contain self-evaluation, but the latter avoids the assessment. This difference comes from our window setting. For example, if we evaluate DMU at the t th period by the use of Model (5.8) and the length of a window is equal to 2 ($L = 2$), then the evaluated window contains all observations in the periods of t and $t - 1$. By comparison, if we use Model (5.12) and the length of a window is equal to 2 ($L = 2$), then the evaluated window contains all observations in the periods of $t - 1$ and $t - 2$. The window index analysis excludes the t th period and thus avoid self-evaluation. As a consequence, Model (5.12) measures the unified index and it may be larger or less than unity. The former case (i.e., larger than unity) indicates an occurrence of a technology progress and/or a managerial change to adjust the DMU for a regulation change.

We measure the degree of unified index (UIN_{kt}) of the k th DMU at the t th period under natural disposability by the following equation.

$$
UIN_{kt}=1-\left[\frac{1}{s+h}\left(\sum_{r=1}^{s}\xi_{rt}^{g*}+\sum_{f=1}^{h}\xi_{ft}^{b*}\right)+\varepsilon_{s}\left(\sum_{i=1}^{m}R_{i}^{x}d_{ikt}^{x-*}+\sum_{r=1}^{s}R_{r}^{g}d_{rkt}^{g*}+\sum_{f=1}^{h}R_{f}^{b}d_{fkt}^{b*}\right)\right],
\tag{5.13}
$$

where all variables are on the optimality of Model (5.12). The previous descriptions on the window efficiency analysis are applicable to Model (5.12) and Eq. (5.13).

Under Managerial Disposability: The formulation under managerial disposability becomes as follows:

$$\begin{aligned}
&Maximize\ \frac{1}{s+h}\left(\sum_{r=1}^{s}\xi_{rt}^{g}+\sum_{f=1}^{h}\xi_{ft}^{b}\right)+\varepsilon_s\left(\sum_{i=1}^{m}R_i^x d_{ikt}^{x+}+\sum_{r=1}^{s}R_r^g d_{rkt}^{g}+\sum_{f=1}^{h}R_f^b d_{fkt}^{b}\right)\\
&s.t.\quad \sum_{p=t-L}^{t-1}x_{ijp}\lambda_{jp}-d_{ikt}^{x+}=x_{ikt}(i=1,\ \ldots,\ m),\\
&\quad\quad same\ constraints\ in\ (5.12),\\
&\quad\quad \lambda_{jp}\geq 0\ (j=1,\ \ldots,\ n\ \&\ pp=t-1-L,\ldots,t-1),\\
&\quad\quad d_{ikt}^{x+}\geq 0\ (i=1,..,m)\ \&\ d_{rkt}^{g}\geq 0\ (r=1,\ldots,s).
\end{aligned} \tag{5.14}$$

The difference between Models (5.12) and (5.14) exists in the constraints on inputs. We cannot find any other difference between them. A description on Model (5.12) is applicable to Model (5.14).

We measure the degree of unified index (UIM_{kt}) by the following equation under managerial disposability:

$$UIM_{kt}=1-\left[\frac{1}{s+h}\left(\sum_{r=1}^{s}\xi_{rt}^{g*}+\sum_{f=1}^{h}\xi_{ft}^{b*}\right)+\varepsilon_s\left(\sum_{i=1}^{m}R_i^x d_{ikt}^{x+*}+\sum_{r=1}^{s}R_r^g d_{rkt}^{g*}+\sum_{f=1}^{h}R_f^b d_{fkt}^{b*}\right)\right]. \tag{5.15}$$

Here, all decision variables (*) are on the optimality of Model (5.14).

Strengths and Drawbacks: The window index analysis measures the performance of a DMU at the t th period based upon how much its observation is different from the frontier of the $t-1$ th period. The window index can measure a technology change and/or a managerial effort for pollution reduction from the $t-1$ th to the t th period, focusing upon a specific DMU. For example, if the index measure is larger than unity, it indicates a technology progress from the $t-1$ th period. This type of analytical capability does not exist in the cross-sectional and the window efficiency analyses.

Meanwhile, the analysis has two drawbacks. For example, it incorporates a possible occurrence of frontier crossover between the two periods ($t-1$ and t) like the window efficiency analysis. No study has discussed the best length for the window index analysis. The other problem is that the analysis produces an index measure larger than or less than unity. It is not easy for us to intuitively understand how to interpret the computational result because the index measure cannot be expressed by a percentage expression. The feature is different from the concept of efficiency in the other two approaches which produce an efficiency measure between 0 (full inefficiency) and 1 (full efficiency). The percentile expression provides us with intuitive rationale on the structure (ranks) of DMUs. The window index analysis does not have such a capability.

5.4 An Illustrative Example

Table 5.1 summarizes descriptive statistics on a data set that we use for an illustrative example. The data set contains the performance of US coal-fired power plants from 1995 to 2007. As summarized in Table 5.1, the operational activity of each power plant is characterized by a single desirable output, four inputs and three undesirable outputs. Avg., Med., Max, Min. and S.D. listed in Table 5.1 stand for average, median, maximum, minimum and standard deviation, respectively.

The data source for the desirable output and the four inputs, obtained by Sueyoshi and Goto (2013). We modify the data set for this illustrative purpose. Their original data sources were Powerdat published by Platts (part of McGraw-Hill Company) and the electric section of FERC (Federal Energy Regulatory Commission: http://www.ferc.gov/docs-filing/eforms.asp). The three undesirable outputs are obtained from US Environmental Protection Agency (Air Markets Program Data: http://ampd.epa.gov/ampd/QueryToolie.html).

The desirable output is annual net generation (MWh: Megawatt hours). The four inputs are (a) the number of employees at each power plant, (b) the sum of all the investment costs at each plant level (this sum represents a running total of all additions, retirements and adjustments at the plant level), (c) the total non-fuel O&M (Operating & Maintenance) that stands for the sum of the total non-fuel operating and maintenance expenses at each plant level, and (d) the fuel consumption that stands for the fuel (coal) consumption of each plant, measured by a weight.

The three undesirable outputs are (a) the total amount of SO_2 released for each year in tons, based on the emission rate per hour and operating hours for each year, (b) the tons of NO_x emitted each year by measuring (or estimating) NO_x emissions as pounds per mmBtu (million British thermal unit) and then calculating the annual total, based on heat input (mmBtu), (c) CO_2 is measured by the annual amount of emission that is computed by the amount of CO_2 emitted each hour times the operation hours of each plant.

For this illustration, the number of DMUs reduces to 10 electric power plants. Hence, we do not make any policy implication here. See Sueyoshi et al. (2017) from both of which we have obtained policy implications on US electric power plants.

In Appendix of this chapter, Tables 5.8 (for 5 DMUs) and 5.9 (for the reaming 5 DMUs) present the data set used for our computation. We divide an observed value divided by the average of each factor to avoid a case that a large data dominates a small data in our computation on DEA-EA. This type of data treatment is due to a computational problem of all DEA assessments, including DEA-EA. It is highly recommended that all users follow the data treatment. This is because we avoid a case which a large data dominates other small data in DEA computation (Sueyoshi & Goto, 2018).

Table 5.2 summarizes *UEN* measures under natural disposability. We have used Model (5.4) along with Eq. (5.5), assuming the cross-sectional structure in the DEA-EA assessment. The table indicates a gradual improvement from 1995 to 2007 in the magnitude of *UEN* on average as found in the bottom of Table 5.2. Since results

Table 5.1 Descriptive statistics (average)

Year	Net generation (MWh)	Average number of employees (number)	Total cost of plant ($)	Total non-fuel O&M ($)	Fuel consumption (1000 ton)	SO_2 (ton)	NO_x (ton)	CO_2 (ton)
1995	4,510,212	184	301,271,730	17,199,343	2149	40,264	20,173	5,518,138
1996	4,616,745	166	304,798,833	17,310,923	2222	40,202	19,859	5,270,345
1997	4,568,390	167	310,854,340	18,281,800	2194	43,175	17,848	5,207,301
1998	4,619,117	162	315,172,787	19,407,419	2216	42,298	17,191	5,210,384
1999	4,527,063	185	327,280,317	19,636,630	2201	37,565	14,257	5,056,999
2000	4,744,551	177	335,593,050	21,015,373	2260	30,850	14,071	5,178,448
2001	4,553,788	185	342,341,021	21,280,507	2211	25,384	12,777	4,989,810
2002	4,285,529	157	351,410,944	24,553,505	2127	24,761	12,123	4,828,038
2003	4,355,317	150	390,181,932	24,011,977	2163	25,182	11,264	4,987,504
2004	4,668,325	160	404,167,373	25,796,224	2315	27,475	11,119	5,199,964
2005	4,525,864	166	419,836,625	29,831,432	2213	30,253	10,311	5,025,529
2006	4,545,589	165	429,534,904	32,397,649	2247	29,186	10,295	5,000,787
2007	4,516,350	164	471,185,046	33,849,195	2209	29,308	9634	4,919,820
Total	4,541,295	168	361,817,608	23,428,614	2210	32,762	13,917	5,107,159

Note We minimize (a) three undesirable outputs, while maximizing a single desirable output in the manner that we can measure the status of EGS by DEA-EA. (b) Total at the bottom of the table means "total average"

in this table are under natural disposability, DMUs (electric power plants) have paid more attention on generation than environment concerns.

Table 5.3 summarizes *UEM* measures under managerial disposability. We have used Model (5.6) along with Eq. (5.7), assuming the cross-sectional structure in the DEA-EA assessment. The table also indicates a gradual improvement from 1995 to 2007 in the magnitude of *UEM* on average as found in the bottom of Table 5.3. Since results in this table are under managerial disposability, DMUs (i.e., electric power plants) have paid more attention to environment concerns than generation. The bottoms of the Tables 5.2 and 5.3 exhibit that the magnitude of Table 5.2 is slightly larger than that of Table 5.3, implying that US regulation might not be effective on electric power plants.

Table 5.4 summarizes *UEN* measures under natural disposability. We used Model (5.8), along with Eq. (5.9), utilizing the window efficiency analysis in the DEA-EA assessment. Meanwhile, Table 5.5 summarizes *UEM* measures under managerial disposability. We used Model (5.10), along with Eq. (5.11), utilizing the window analysis in the DEA-EA assessment.

The length of windows is 5 years so that the starting period for window measurement is 1999 (= 1995 + 5). Then, the window moves it from 2000 until 2007, maintaining the window length with 5 annual periods. A general trend found in Tables 5.4 and 5.5 are almost same as Tables 5.2 and 5.3. However, the window analysis examines their efficiency measures within the limited periods so that the number of efficient DMUs is larger than the cross-sectional approach.

Table 5.6 summarizes Unified Index (*UI*) measures under natural disposability. We used Model (5.12) along with Eq. (5.13), assuming the window index analysis by DEA-EA. Meanwhile, Table 5.7 summarizes *UI* measures under managerial disposability. We used Model (5.14) along with Eq. (5.15), assuming the window index analysis in DEA-EA.

Comparing between Tables 5.6 and 5.7, we find that all unified indexes (*UI*) in Table 5.6 exhibit less than unity, so implying no significant technology progress in the US electric power generation. Meanwhile, some index numbers in Table 5.7 exhibit more than unity. The annual average of these unified indexes are close to or more than unity. This result implies that the US electric power industry has technology improvement on its environmental protection during the observed periods.

Figure 5.2 visually summarizes an annual change of the six measures, all of which we obtain from the last row of Tables 5.2, 5.3, 5.4, 5.5, 5.6 and 5.7. For visual convenience, Fig. 5.2, changing the names of efficiency and index measures, implies important features, some of which we summarize as follows:

First, the two cross-sectional analyses (i.e., CSN and CSM) used a data set in all periods from 1995 to 2007. Both unified efficiency measures (UEN_{kt}^{I} and UEM_{kt}^{I}) are determined by the following equations:

CSN: Cross-Sectional and Natural Disposability (UEN_{kt}^{I}): Measured by (5.5) and
CSM: Cross-Sectional and Managerial Disposability (UEM_{kt}^{I}): Measured by (5.7).

Table 5.2 Unified efficiencies: cross sectional and natural disposability (CSN)

DMU	1995	1996	1997	1998	1999	2000	2001	2002	2003	2004	2005	2006	2007
1	0.738	0.783	0.821	1.000	0.858	0.898	0.933	0.876	0.953	0.935	1.000	0.797	0.936
2	0.767	1.000	0.906	1.000	1.000	1.000	1.000	0.890	1.000	1.000	0.948	0.932	1.000
3	0.925	1.000	1.000	1.000	1.000	0.941	0.902	0.892	1.000	0.903	0.850	0.934	0.902
4	1.000	1.000	0.719	0.673	0.670	1.000	0.880	0.850	0.803	0.878	0.875	0.825	1.000
5	0.780	0.785	0.709	0.727	0.804	0.830	0.803	0.784	0.735	0.727	0.729	0.759	0.726
6	0.788	0.778	0.772	0.786	0.812	0.801	0.916	0.908	0.888	0.923	0.830	1.000	1.000
7	0.683	0.757	0.772	0.748	0.768	0.729	0.671	0.740	0.724	1.000	0.761	0.834	0.782
8	0.966	0.806	1.000	0.852	0.858	1.000	1.000	1.000	1.000	1.000	0.911	1.000	1.000
9	0.747	0.757	0.904	1.000	0.968	1.000	0.843	0.597	0.668	0.746	0.767	0.800	0.800
10	1.000	0.721	0.682	0.759	0.694	0.709	0.732	0.775	0.795	0.880	0.891	0.812	1.000
Avg	0.839	0.839	0.829	0.854	0.843	0.891	0.868	0.831	0.857	0.899	0.856	0.869	0.915

Table 5.3 Unified efficiencies: cross sectional and managerial disposability (CSM)

DMU	1995	1996	1997	1998	1999	2000	2001	2002	2003	2004	2005	2006	2007
1	0.795	0.833	0.874	1.000	0.897	0.930	0.970	0.923	1.000	0.986	1.000	1.000	1.000
2	0.698	0.702	0.697	0.724	0.739	0.720	0.768	0.765	0.976	1.000	0.925	0.942	0.940
3	0.866	0.956	0.931	0.980	0.934	0.872	0.876	0.823	0.821	0.837	0.845	0.903	1.000
4	0.553	0.614	0.604	0.599	0.618	0.703	1.000	0.876	0.796	0.941	0.979	0.873	1.000
5	0.573	0.566	0.570	0.582	0.664	0.693	0.695	0.699	0.740	0.712	0.694	0.727	0.710
6	0.653	0.642	0.669	0.666	0.646	0.686	0.717	0.690	0.716	0.739	0.744	0.802	1.000
7	0.869	0.855	1.000	0.861	1.000	1.000	1.000	0.806	0.878	1.000	0.888	1.000	1.000
8	0.683	0.655	0.670	0.673	0.683	0.732	0.738	0.786	0.747	0.705	0.703	0.744	0.745
9	0.572	0.571	0.603	0.608	0.639	0.640	0.649	0.568	0.612	0.655	0.666	0.695	0.686
10	0.933	0.714	0.712	0.682	0.675	0.677	0.722	1.000	0.829	0.864	0.895	0.888	1.000
Avg	0.720	0.711	0.733	0.737	0.750	0.765	0.813	0.794	0.812	0.844	0.834	0.857	0.908

Table 5.4 Unified efficiency: window analysis and natural disposability (WAN)

DMU	1999	2000	2001	2002	2003	2004	2005	2006	2007
1	0.862	0.901	0.937	0.884	1.000	0.984	1.000	0.846	0.973
2	1.000	1.000	1.000	0.948	1.000	1.000	0.951	0.936	1.000
3	1.000	0.962	0.924	1.000	1.000	0.959	0.888	1.000	0.961
4	0.766	1.000	1.000	1.000	0.843	0.881	0.892	0.837	1.000
5	0.958	0.838	0.803	0.784	0.789	0.767	0.785	0.837	0.769
6	0.909	0.900	1.000	0.944	0.915	0.923	1.000	1.000	1.000
7	1.000	1.000	0.744	0.841	0.750	1.000	0.762	1.000	0.782
8	0.983	1.000	1.000	1.000	1.000	1.000	1.000	1.000	1.000
9	1.000	1.000	0.873	0.620	0.718	0.762	0.776	0.813	0.810
10	0.861	0.864	0.852	0.907	0.960	1.000	1.000	0.927	1.000
Avg	0.934	0.946	0.913	0.893	0.898	0.928	0.905	0.920	0.930

Table 5.5 Unified efficiency: window analysis and managerial disposability (WAM)

DMU	1999	2000	2001	2002	2003	2004	2005	2006	2007
1	1.000	1.000	1.000	1.000	1.000	1.000	1.000	1.000	1.000
2	0.790	0.792	0.837	0.850	1.000	1.000	0.968	1.000	0.940
3	0.986	0.975	1.000	0.888	0.896	0.918	0.913	1.000	1.000
4	1.000	1.000	1.000	1.000	0.955	1.000	1.000	0.932	1.000
5	0.664	0.695	0.701	0.705	0.780	0.733	0.705	0.738	0.713
6	0.664	0.737	0.740	0.722	0.732	0.759	0.788	1.000	1.000
7	1.000	1.000	1.000	0.918	1.000	1.000	1.000	1.000	1.000
8	0.683	0.735	0.745	1.000	0.769	0.725	0.716	0.755	0.757
9	0.667	0.656	0.681	0.613	0.619	0.663	0.671	0.709	0.688
10	0.886	0.899	1.000	1.000	1.000	1.000	1.000	1.000	1.000
Avg	0.834	0.849	0.870	0.870	0.875	0.880	0.876	0.913	0.910

We find that the unified efficiency measures have improved their degrees under both natural and managerial disposability concepts. This implies that electric power plants have gradually improved their generation and environment activities.

Second, the two window analyses (i.e., WAN and WAM) have used 5 annual periods to make a window and annually shifted the length.

WAN: Window Analysis and Natural Disposability $\left(UEN_{kt}^{W}\right)$: Measured by (5.9) and

WAM: Window Analysis and Managerial Disposability (UEM_{kt}^{W}): Measured by (5.11).

We find that the window analyses slightly show an increasing trend in WAN and WAM.

Table 5.6 Unified index: window analysis and natural disposability (I-WAN)

	2000	2001	2002	2003	2004	2005	2006	2007
1	0.916	0.954	0.942	0.981	1.032	0.993	0.865	1.094
2	0.532	0.538	0.542	0.590	0.590	0.576	0.576	0.576
3	0.551	0.548	0.540	0.541	0.549	0.547	0.547	0.553
4	0.512	0.538	0.542	0.536	0.544	0.544	0.535	0.550
5	0.513	0.514	0.515	0.519	0.514	0.511	0.513	0.513
6	0.530	0.532	0.529	0.532	0.533	0.538	0.543	0.547
7	0.587	0.568	0.587	0.599	0.638	0.598	0.640	0.609
8	0.521	0.522	0.529	0.522	0.517	0.517	0.521	0.519
9	0.523	0.528	0.515	0.522	0.526	0.530	0.539	0.531
10	0.547	0.562	0.581	0.603	0.625	0.621	0.613	0.681
Avg	0.573	0.580	0.582	0.595	0.607	0.598	0.589	0.617

Table 5.7 Unified index: window analysis and managerial disposability (I-WAM)

	2000	2001	2002	2003	2004	2005	2006	2007
1	0.977	1.078	1.020	1.122	1.085	1.038	1.110	1.170
2	0.873	0.932	0.964	1.112	1.064	0.975	1.001	0.976
3	0.986	0.985	0.918	0.934	0.967	0.982	1.072	1.039
4	1.229	1.684	1.023	1.035	1.005	1.062	0.935	1.166
5	1.119	1.017	1.010	1.421	1.114	1.026	0.959	0.948
6	1.011	0.948	0.825	0.820	0.833	0.903	0.942	0.989
7	1.560	0.972	0.996	1.008	1.069	1.021	1.203	1.087
8	0.838	0.854	0.862	0.825	0.829	0.792	0.794	0.809
9	0.833	0.858	0.755	0.758	0.775	0.771	0.826	0.730
10	0.918	1.015	1.624	1.147	1.131	1.050	0.994	1.336
Avg	1.034	1.034	1.000	1.018	0.987	0.962	0.984	1.025

Finally, the two window index analyses (i.e., I-WAN and I-WAM) are specified as follows; I-WAN: Unified Indexes: Window Analysis and Natural disposability (UIN_{kt}): Measured by (5.13) and I-WAM: Unified Indexes: Window Analysis and Managerial disposability (UIM_{kt}): Measured by (5.15). They exhibit a major difference between their magnitudes. The I-WAN exists about 0.6 in the magnitude while the I-WAM exhibits about 1.0 in the magnitude. This implies that electric power plants could not achieve generation technology but attain environmental technology.

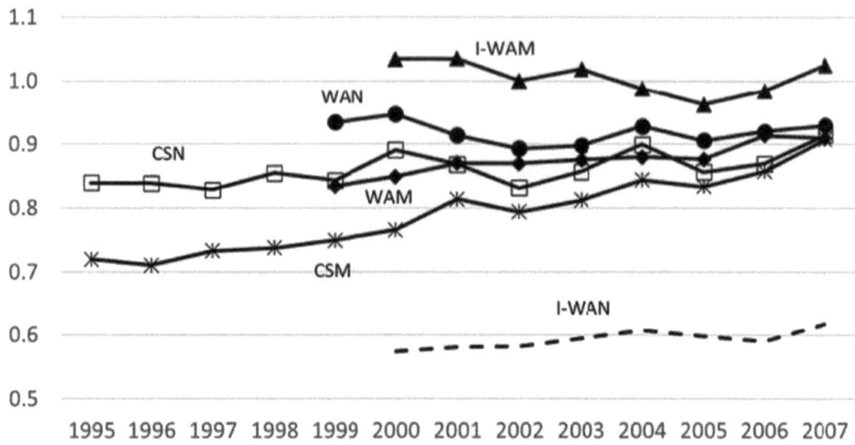

Fig. 5.2 Unified efficiency and index from 1995 to 2007. *Note* (a) The horizontal axis indicates an annual period and the vertical axis indicates the degree of unified efficiency and index. (b) The abbreviations are summarized as follows: CSN Cross-Sectional and Natural Disposability, CSM Cross-Sectional and Managerial Disposability, WAN Window Analysis and Natural Disposability, WAM Window Analysis and Managerial Disposability, I-WAN Unified Indexes Window Analysis and Natural disposability and I-WAM Unified Indexes: Window Analysis and Managerial disposability

5.5 Discussion

As an extension of Chap. 4, this chapter discussed a new use of DEA-EA in a time horizon, so serving as a method for SDGs. Chapter 4 discussed ESG assessment, but not discussing the approach for SDGs (except for goal setting) in a time horizon. The data sets on environmental protection have often a structure of time series. DEA-EA may indicate a technology progress on desirable and undesirable outputs for ESG enhancement. We focus upon the intermediate model among the three models discussed in Chap. 4. To capture an efficiency shift, this chapter proposed a new type of window analysis-based schemes for environmental assessment of SDGs.

This study applied the proposed DEA-EA to a data set on US coal-fired power plants during 1995–2007. The application finds that managers of the coal-fired power plants have gradually paid attention to environmental protections under CAA. Consequently, their performance under managerial disposability has increased in the observed periods. This may indicate the importance of CAA and strict implementation for US environmental protection. It is necessary to extend the scope of CAA for controlling the amount of CO_2 emission because current regulation has a limited policy influence on the source of global warming and climate change in our modern society.

Appendix

See Tables 5.8 and 5.9.

Table 5.8 Adjusted data set (DMUs 1–5)

Company	Year	Net generation (MWh)	Average number of employees (number)	Total cost of plant ($)	Total non-fuel O&M ($)	Fuel consumption (1000 ton)	SO_2 (ton)	NO_x (ton)	CO_2 (ton)
1	1995	0.09776	0.23788	0.06577	0.09717	0.11108	0.05818	0.13559	0.08062
1	1996	0.10234	0.23788	0.06634	0.11593	0.11816	0.05762	0.11820	0.07795
1	1997	0.10313	0.23788	0.07826	0.10905	0.12056	0.06504	0.05966	0.09072
1	1998	0.12626	0.21409	0.07751	0.10928	0.13487	0.05856	0.05646	0.08883
1	1999	0.10360	0.22004	0.07763	0.11228	0.12105	0.06246	0.06002	0.08030
1	2000	0.12166	0.22004	0.09313	0.11443	0.14766	0.06985	0.06507	0.08904
1	2001	0.12170	0.23788	0.09604	0.12048	0.14857	0.06315	0.06089	0.08905
1	2002	0.10974	0.21409	0.09885	0.12673	0.14062	0.06396	0.05888	0.08510
1	2003	0.11261	0.20220	0.11096	0.15006	0.14290	0.06149	0.05121	0.08042
1	2004	0.10374	0.20220	0.11560	0.17742	0.13377	0.05730	0.04860	0.07591
1	2005	0.11713	0.21409	0.10973	0.20628	0.13594	0.06435	0.05256	0.08233
1	2006	0.08337	0.18435	0.11600	0.26333	0.10796	0.05797	0.04720	0.07323
1	2007	0.09029	0.21409	0.11802	0.23642	0.12187	0.05002	0.04244	0.06566
2	1995	0.77943	1.09424	0.64322	0.66770	0.73675	0.40306	1.40955	0.76634
2	1996	1.00672	1.06450	0.66067	0.65269	0.90290	0.50410	1.73419	0.94317
2	1997	1.02073	0.98719	0.69058	0.72669	0.94383	0.55627	1.20312	1.02517
2	1998	1.09386	0.95151	0.68318	0.65395	0.99581	0.56259	1.21291	1.05603
2	1999	1.03139	0.95151	0.74023	0.74565	0.94478	0.56595	0.89376	0.99065
2	2000	1.04544	0.88015	0.76182	0.78317	0.93237	0.58436	0.85944	1.06217
2	2001	1.05829	1.04071	0.77132	0.85719	0.97943	0.54921	0.73304	1.02917
2	2002	0.95476	1.04071	0.78226	0.84219	0.93575	0.48706	0.68085	0.93217

(continued)

Table 5.8 (continued)

Company	Year	Net generation (MWh)	Average number of employees (number)	Total cost of plant ($)	Total non-fuel O&M ($)	Fuel consumption (1000 ton)	SO_2 (ton)	NO_x (ton)	CO_2 (ton)
2	2003	1.02758	0.81473	1.03808	1.15019	0.94922	0.18095	0.75114	1.07073
2	2004	1.09403	0.81473	1.08177	1.20025	1.00781	0.19676	0.70492	1.05395
2	2005	1.10125	0.89204	1.08522	1.20425	1.04833	0.21553	0.77609	1.11926
2	2006	1.05319	0.89799	1.10167	1.43052	1.02609	0.21720	0.73315	1.07079
2	2007	1.05089	0.87420	1.11531	1.42717	0.94492	0.21617	0.73969	1.06921
3	1995	0.88588	0.66011	0.80854	0.48259	1.09154	0.41915	0.45253	0.92679
3	1996	0.95107	0.67795	0.81707	0.48846	1.19587	0.39374	0.39009	0.98700
3	1997	0.97431	0.63038	0.82049	0.52055	1.21561	0.37661	0.45090	1.03340
3	1998	0.97706	0.61848	0.82480	0.56039	1.23647	0.38904	0.47957	0.96798
3	1999	1.00496	0.62443	0.82712	0.55367	1.26704	0.41817	0.50867	0.97743
3	2000	0.93010	0.58875	0.87861	0.49867	1.17183	0.43835	0.50142	0.95791
3	2001	0.97591	0.70769	0.89732	0.60582	1.24259	0.48563	0.49169	1.01700
3	2002	1.03432	0.68390	0.90272	0.53503	1.30125	0.51198	0.63301	1.11478
3	2003	1.07107	0.60659	0.92168	0.51602	1.32100	0.49543	0.65472	1.17522
3	2004	0.94727	0.60659	0.95831	0.85330	1.17946	0.42579	0.55050	1.04404
3	2005	0.94522	0.70769	0.97083	0.88732	1.18124	0.41031	0.57276	1.02656
3	2006	1.07413	0.75526	0.97234	0.75147	1.33732	0.42286	0.60436	1.09289
3	2007	0.98011	0.82068	0.99917	0.96362	1.24816	0.38475	0.53678	0.98488
4	1995	2.50051	1.98628	2.77988	1.77267	2.21329	2.78165	4.13037	3.27803
4	1996	2.55419	1.92086	2.79505	1.48990	2.32392	2.92714	3.65046	2.54342
4	1997	2.33532	2.16468	2.80778	1.86213	2.16749	3.12844	3.02240	2.41117

(continued)

Table 5.8 (continued)

Company	Year	Net generation (MWh)	Average number of employees (number)	Total cost of plant ($)	Total non-fuel O&M ($)	Fuel consumption (1000 ton)	SO_2 (ton)	NO_x (ton)	CO_2 (ton)
4	1998	2.18796	2.11116	2.84869	2.03670	2.03913	3.27859	2.69540	2.30013
4	1999	1.99335	2.05169	3.06185	2.11110	1.83498	2.91845	2.24891	2.03598
4	2000	2.35904	1.97438	3.07043	2.13060	2.08690	1.46809	2.59193	2.25130
4	2001	2.02561	1.97438	3.12966	2.46715	1.85494	0.41020	2.14448	2.02139
4	2002	1.87085	1.74245	3.27192	2.85018	1.75812	0.35409	2.13124	2.00292
4	2003	1.89492	1.74245	3.30402	2.67338	1.79835	0.40249	2.15887	2.19293
4	2004	2.00198	2.30146	3.34816	2.93646	1.92056	0.36363	2.05143	2.12614
4	2005	1.85705	2.30146	3.41488	3.03038	1.78440	0.34699	1.71408	1.96847
4	2006	2.07448	2.28957	3.51972	3.50847	1.98789	0.42663	2.20691	2.30280
4	2007	1.89560	2.31930	3.80060	3.57568	1.80775	0.30228	1.80533	2.04995
5	1995	2.05674	2.45608	0.99684	1.04344	2.10741	2.79301	4.42791	1.95048
5	1996	2.14342	2.40851	1.00198	1.14249	2.22155	3.18446	4.55941	2.02991
5	1997	1.94667	2.33120	1.02847	1.16699	1.95091	2.85257	4.29683	1.80430
5	1998	1.96862	2.33715	1.04340	1.18820	1.97256	2.72245	3.91308	1.80353
5	1999	1.87873	2.31930	1.07176	1.19651	2.01552	1.60783	2.37972	1.74142
5	2000	1.84272	2.26578	1.08062	1.37176	1.96210	1.30268	2.29084	1.70075
5	2001	1.76805	2.24199	1.09090	1.29346	1.85914	1.19541	2.24419	1.63135
5	2002	1.72612	2.21226	1.09370	1.51702	1.85994	1.16591	2.10035	1.61442
5	2003	1.58698	2.20037	1.57564	1.66204	1.75513	0.99975	1.57280	1.43323
5	2004	1.82446	2.20631	1.60705	1.77636	2.03095	1.62189	1.62953	1.61436
5	2005	1.97763	2.21226	1.62823	2.44029	2.03248	2.27883	1.62540	1.74369

(continued)

Table 5.8 (continued)

Company	Year	Net generation (MWh)	Average number of employees (number)	Total cost of plant ($)	Total non-fuel O&M ($)	Fuel consumption (1000 ton)	SO_2 (ton)	NO_x (ton)	CO_2 (ton)
5	2006	2.01014	2.23605	1.64334	2.83223	2.16255	1.99536	1.55647	1.72541
5	2007	1.82753	2.20631	1.66856	2.89330	1.97556	2.04153	1.46968	1.58590

Table 5.9 Adjusted data set (DMUs 6–10)

Company	Year	Net generation (MWh)	Average number of employees (number)	Total cost of plant ($)	Total non-fuel O&M ($)	Fuel consumption (1000 ton)	SO_2 (ton)	NO_x (ton)	CO_2 (ton)
6	1995	0.61363	0.76715	0.54824	0.44098	0.58527	1.18641	0.41302	0.61986
6	1996	0.65242	0.76121	0.55057	0.44727	0.62710	1.16835	0.44463	0.70565
6	1997	0.65988	0.74337	0.55295	0.56269	0.63869	1.12102	0.41138	0.68056
6	1998	0.74568	0.71363	0.56046	0.67476	0.71400	1.21983	0.47818	0.76968
6	1999	0.81396	0.68984	0.56273	0.48344	0.77699	1.36102	0.56763	0.86158
6	2000	0.77225	0.71363	0.60999	0.83317	0.73843	1.23039	0.46233	0.77455
6	2001	0.86745	0.89204	0.61755	0.76944	0.81581	1.31411	0.48312	0.80427
6	2002	0.81541	0.72553	0.62861	0.60821	0.75410	1.44277	0.47665	0.78909
6	2003	0.85019	0.69579	0.63762	0.60227	0.80596	1.55721	0.45644	0.77446
6	2004	0.88106	0.69579	0.66119	0.52654	0.84928	1.36692	0.44823	0.79582
6	2005	0.75984	0.73742	0.82135	1.08940	0.74690	1.50635	0.32751	0.74407
6	2006	0.83716	0.77905	0.82395	1.12238	0.80907	1.41464	0.31158	0.77176
6	2007	0.83343	0.77905	1.36089	1.04391	0.80781	1.10499	0.30685	0.75015
7	1995	0.64452	1.54026	0.79595	1.35478	0.62656	0.19062	1.85684	0.69059
7	1996	0.58642	0.76121	0.80756	1.34656	0.57563	0.11706	1.67002	0.62699
7	1997	0.61052	0.73147	0.81188	1.33294	0.60956	0.11584	1.64548	0.65333
7	1998	0.60965	0.70174	0.83323	1.36691	0.61363	0.12836	1.68747	0.64976
7	1999	0.62740	1.69488	0.84254	1.27454	0.62412	0.11640	1.80843	0.68892
7	2000	0.62125	1.69488	0.87417	1.39304	0.60711	0.15704	1.49631	0.63931
7	2001	0.58502	1.69488	0.88542	1.24554	0.58419	0.18546	1.33730	0.67427
7	2002	0.62337	0.61253	0.89148	1.19634	0.61495	0.15926	1.17697	0.65647

(continued)

Table 5.9 (continued)

Company	Year	Net generation (MWh)	Average number of employees (number)	Total cost of plant ($)	Total non-fuel O&M ($)	Fuel consumption (1000 ton)	SO_2 (ton)	NO_x (ton)	CO_2 (ton)
7	2003	0.50710	0.62443	0.92251	1.52798	0.49066	0.13870	0.95802	0.54432
7	2004	0.68234	0.64227	1.09830	1.36005	0.64457	0.11015	0.99881	0.75609
7	2005	0.59452	0.70769	1.10681	1.55357	0.55196	0.14408	0.88591	0.65558
7	2006	0.47203	0.64227	1.11000	1.65707	0.42473	0.10099	0.74397	0.51345
7	2007	0.51915	0.68984	1.19224	1.90425	0.47371	0.13166	0.72704	0.56608
8	1995	1.30555	0.80284	0.58349	0.49345	1.26879	2.78281	0.73643	1.27486
8	1996	1.10023	0.79094	0.59721	0.72568	1.07642	2.16251	0.71344	1.11546
8	1997	1.43361	0.77310	0.61070	0.49451	1.37611	3.32062	0.84167	1.40235
8	1998	1.22735	0.68984	0.63007	0.64210	1.20750	2.71470	0.71457	1.21175
8	1999	1.27883	0.91583	0.63705	0.68366	1.24896	2.54756	0.72878	1.26020
8	2000	1.41907	0.81473	0.65390	0.63610	1.37081	2.00641	0.74119	1.32225
8	2001	1.43088	0.83257	0.70652	0.55145	1.38185	1.79558	0.73741	1.35304
8	2002	1.27364	0.77905	0.71811	0.69366	1.23918	1.69761	0.55845	1.11983
8	2003	1.39809	0.75526	0.72293	0.67976	1.34150	2.04392	0.69275	1.27038
8	2004	1.46475	0.75526	0.73474	0.79834	1.44131	2.16093	0.86498	1.37785
8	2005	1.40373	0.79094	0.87118	0.87294	1.34231	2.36988	0.83079	1.26644
8	2006	1.33847	0.75526	1.02112	0.70129	1.25715	2.53873	0.65829	1.15269
8	2007	1.49521	0.71363	0.98647	0.88968	1.39952	2.77101	0.73272	1.28905
9	1995	0.58260	0.76715	0.43687	0.53549	0.52073	1.57592	0.49371	0.70343
9	1996	0.59025	0.60659	0.45315	0.48930	0.52427	1.53946	0.50700	0.72017
9	1997	0.51545	0.68390	0.47105	0.46475	0.43895	1.42986	0.41550	0.54675

(continued)

Table 5.9 (continued)

Company	Year	Net generation (MWh)	Average number of employees (number)	Total cost of plant ($)	Total non-fuel O&M ($)	Fuel consumption (1000 ton)	SO_2 (ton)	NO_x (ton)	CO_2 (ton)
9	1998	0.63791	0.64227	0.48625	0.48824	0.53280	1.54384	0.52353	0.65792
9	1999	0.65969	0.86231	0.49955	0.49925	0.56860	1.52240	0.49746	0.62202
9	2000	0.74106	0.78500	0.51507	0.56092	0.62843	1.80113	0.53996	0.69874
9	2001	0.65404	0.80284	0.53013	0.54516	0.59608	1.45020	0.47878	0.60903
9	2002	0.49630	0.71958	0.56675	0.49756	0.49617	1.45801	0.44069	0.60938
9	2003	0.59262	0.66011	0.59524	0.55467	0.58310	1.62814	0.45941	0.62250
9	2004	0.70403	0.68984	0.59892	0.58214	0.68369	1.91240	0.45263	0.67692
9	2005	0.63350	0.67795	0.61587	0.58794	0.60392	1.72966	0.38125	0.61308
9	2006	0.55420	0.67795	0.62259	0.66319	0.52437	1.55117	0.30457	0.51178
9	2007	0.67383	0.57685	0.67768	0.73870	0.63392	1.83116	0.38627	0.62275
10	1995	0.46494	0.60064	0.66781	0.45290	0.46309	0.09896	0.43944	0.51371
10	1996	0.47908	0.64227	0.67452	0.49050	0.48928	0.21664	0.48221	0.56980
10	1997	0.46004	0.63632	0.71929	0.56291	0.46828	0.21223	0.47756	0.54833
10	1998	0.59702	0.64822	0.72323	0.56311	0.58067	0.29272	0.59095	0.69650
10	1999	0.57675	0.64227	0.72498	0.72137	0.55954	0.34581	0.55112	0.64328
10	2000	0.59498	0.60659	0.73745	0.64811	0.58353	0.35826	0.56237	0.64355
10	2001	0.54056	0.60064	0.73686	0.62744	0.54060	0.29898	0.47007	0.54165
10	2002	0.53228	0.60064	0.75798	1.61321	0.52453	0.21729	0.45400	0.52930
10	2003	0.54930	0.59469	0.95527	0.73262	0.60100	0.17845	0.33798	0.60151
10	2004	0.57607	0.59469	0.96644	0.79971	0.58657	0.17051	0.23980	0.66064
10	2005	0.57614	0.60064	0.97945	0.86054	0.58883	0.16823	0.24224	0.62068

(continued)

Table 5.9 (continued)

Company	Year	Net generation (MWh)	Average number of employees (number)	Total cost of plant ($)	Total non-fuel O&M ($)	Fuel consumption (1000 ton)	SO_2 (ton)	NO_x (ton)	CO_2 (ton)
10	2006	0.51230	0.60064	0.94087	0.89829	0.52933	0.18307	0.23083	0.57691
10	2007	0.57903	0.53522	1.10379	0.77506	0.58166	0.11223	0.17543	0.64957

References

Goto, M., & Sueyoshi, T. (2016). Electricity market reform in Japan after Fukushima: Implications for climate change policy and energy market developments Economics of Energy & Environmental. *Policy, 5*, 15–30.

Goto, M., & Sueyoshi, T. (2020). Sustainable performance and impact of corporate social performance for Japanese manufacturing companies. *Sustainable Development, 28*, 844–856.

Sueyoshi, T., & Goto, M. (2013). Returns to scale vs. damages to scale in data envelopment analysis: An impact of U.S. clean air act on coal-fired power plants. *Omega, 41*, 164–175.

Sueyoshi, T., & Goto, T. (2018). *Environmental assessment on energy and sustainability by data envelopment analysis*. Wiley.

Sueyoshi, T., & Goto, M. (2019). Intermediate approach for sustainability enhancement and scale related measures in environmental assessment. *European Journal of Operational Research, 276*, 744–756.

Sueyoshi, T., Liu, X., & Li, A. (2020). Evaluating the performance of Chinese fossil fuel power plants by data environment analysis: an application of three intermediate approaches in a time horizon. *Journal of Cleaner Production, 277*, 1–14.

Sueyoshi, T., & Yuan, Y. (2017). Social sustainability measured by intermediate approach for DEA environmental assessment: Chinese regional planning for economic development and pollution prevention. *Energy Economics, 66*, 154–166.

Sueyoshi, T., Yuan, Y., Li, A. D., & Wang, D. (2017). Methodological comparison among radial, non-radial and intermediate approaches for DEA environmental assessment. *Energy Economics, 67*, 439–453.

Xie, J., Liang, Z., Zhang, X., & Zhu, L. (2019). Efficiency evaluation of thermal power plants in China based on the weighted Russell directional distance method. *Journal of Cleaner Production, 222*, 573–583.

Zhang, Y. J., & Chen, M. L. (2018). Evaluating the dynamic performance of energy portfolios: Empirical evidence from the DEA directional distance function. *European Journal of Operational Research, 269*, 64–78.

Zhou, P., Ang, B. W., & Poh, K. L. (2008). A survey of data envelopment analysis in energy and environmental studies. *European Journal of Operational Research, 189*, 1–18.

Chapter 6
A Frontier Shift on Unified Index Over Time: Malmquist Index for SDGs Enhancement

Abstract This chapter discusses a use of DEA-EA to measure a frontier shift over time. As discussed in Chap. 5, most of data sets on energy and environment have usually a time series structure. The use of DEA-EA needs to incorporate a computational process which can measure the change of a shift on SDGs. In applying DEA-EA over time, we need to examine each factor component whose sum produces the shift of an efficiency frontier among different periods. A unique feature of the proposed assessment proposed in this chapter is that it incorporates a framework of "Malmquist index" to examine the frontier shift among different periods. The frontier shift indicates a technology progress and/or a managerial effort for SDGs enhancement during observed periods. The computational process is different from that of Chap. 5 which measures a change of unified efficiency or index measures. Meanwhile, this chapter measures a frontier change, not such an efficiency/index change, among different periods. To attain the measurement, we conceptually separate a proposed unified index due to the frontier shift into six subcomponents. Then, we further divide them into twelve different subcomponents (= 6 subcomponents $\times$ 2 disposability concepts) under natural or managerial disposability. Thus, this chapter provides a new type of "SDGs decomposition" due to the frontier shift among different periods.

Keywords Time series · Malmquist index · Production technology · Ecological technology

6.1 Introduction

As an extension of Chap. 5, this chapter will explore a new approach to measure the level of SDGs. The proposed computational process is very different from the three approaches in Chap. 5 which have examined a change of unified efficiency/index measures. This chapter measures a frontier change, not such a change of unified efficiency/index, among different observed periods. Along with measuring the frontier shift, we propose a new type of "SDGs decomposition" among different periods.

T. Sueyoshi and M. Goto, *Environment and Sustainability for ESG and SDGs*,
https://doi.org/10.1007/978-981-96-2464-5_6

To prepare the decomposition, we first depend upon "Malmquist index" whose components produce the shift of an efficiency frontier among different periods. In this chapter, we conceptually separate a proposed unified index due to the frontier shift into six subcomponents. Then, we further divide them into twelve different subcomponents (= 6 subcomponents × 2 disposability concepts) under natural or managerial disposability. Thus, this chapter provides a new type of SDGs decomposition due to the frontier shift among different periods. We also explore two cases on an occurrence of a frontier crossover or no occurrence in this chapter.

As an illustrative example, we apply the proposed decomposition approach to the measurement on SDGs at the level of Japanese prefectures. This application documents how we may develop a sustainable society by examining the level of SDGs.

The remainder of this chapter has the following structure: Sect. 6.2 reviews Malmquist index measurement that serves as a conceptual basis for DEA-based time series analysis. Section 6.3 discusses how to unify desirable and undesirable outputs under natural or managerial disposability. This section also conceptually considers an occurrence of frontier crossover and no occurrence. Section 6.4 describes formulations under natural disposability. Section 6.5 shifts our interest to those under managerial disposability. Section 6.6 applies the proposed approach to the Japanese prefectures. Section 6.7 summarizes this chapter.

6.2 Malmquist Index

Two groups of research were closely related to DEA-EA in a time horizon. One of the two groups was due to Malmquist (1953). His study documented how to measure production indexes between different areas. The other production economists, including Bjurek (1996), Bjurek and Hjalmarsson (1995) and Grifell-Tatje and Lovel (1995), applied Malmquist index to DEA-based time series analysis. Here, the original Malmquist index did not consider the concept of managerial disposability, because previous research did not serious attention to the existence of undesirable outputs at the middle of the twentieth century (Malmquist, 1953).

The Malmquist index had a methodological strength and its drawback. A strength was that when the Malmquist index may separate it into subcomponents. Consequently, we could measure both a shift of an efficiency frontier and an influence of each subcomponent of the shift. That was a contribution, indeed. In contrast, the index measurement had a drawback. The measurement depended upon an assumption that production activity was characterized by a functional form. Furthermore, production technology always shifted an efficiency frontier toward better performance in observed periods. Unfortunately, many assessments did not satisfy such underlying assumptions. In some case, we often observe that an efficiency frontier shift may not occur or the frontier retreats itself in the worst case.

In addition to the economic concerns, management scientists (e.g., Bowlin, 1987) were interested in "DEA window analysis". See Chap. 5 that describes the two types of window analysis (for window efficiency and index). The analysis examined how much an efficiency score changed its magnitude by shifting a combination of adjacent periods, often referred to as a "window". For example, Thore et al (1994) and Goto and Tsutsui (1998) combined between window analysis and Malmquist index measurement. The combined measure was referred to as "Malmquist productivity index". An important assumption of the window analysis implied an analytical capability that an efficiency frontier did not retreat. Even though a crossover occurred among efficiency frontiers, the window analysis pooled all observations for a few consecutive periods into a window where we identified a new efficiency frontier. Consequently, a group of efficiency scores was smoothed over time on which we determined these efficiency scores by comparing these performances with a newly established efficiency frontier within the window. That was a contribution. A drawback of the window analysis was that it lacked an analytical scheme to decompose an efficiency change into subcomponents, as found in Malmquist index measurement.[1] See, for example, Sueyoshi and Aoki (2001) and Sueyoshi and Goto (2001) that have discussed a new type of combination between the Malmquist index measurement and the window analysis.

6.3 A Frontier Shift in a Time Horizon

6.3.1 No Occurrence of Frontier Crossover

We start with four figures which describe how to incorporate natural and managerial disposability concepts into the framework of Malmquist index. The four figures visually serve as an analytical basis for computing twelve subcomponents, all of which originate from Malmquist index under the two disposability concepts. The proposed decomposition cannot be founded in the previous studies because we consider the decomposition under managerial disposability.

Figure 6.1 depicts a frontier shift from the $t - 1$ th period to the t th period under natural disposability in which DMUs attempt to enhance their operational performance as the first priority and their environmental performance as the second priority. For our visual convenience, Fig. 6.1 considers a simple case of a single input (x) and two desirable outputs (g_1 and g_2). An undesirable output is assumed to be same on all DMUs, so dropping the influence on the frontier shift. The visual description is easily extendable to multiple inputs and desirable outputs, as discussed later, in the formulations of DEA-EA.

[1] We use the term "efficiency" when a performance measure exists between 0% (full inefficiency) and 100% (full efficiency). Such an analytical feature indicates the benefit of efficiency requirement. Meanwhile, we use the other term "index" to express a measure that may be more than unity (100%), hereafter. When the index is more than unity, it indicates a possible occurrence of a frontier shift due to a technology development and/or a managerial effort. In contrast, an opposite case (i.e., a frontier retreat) can be found if it is equal to or less than unity.

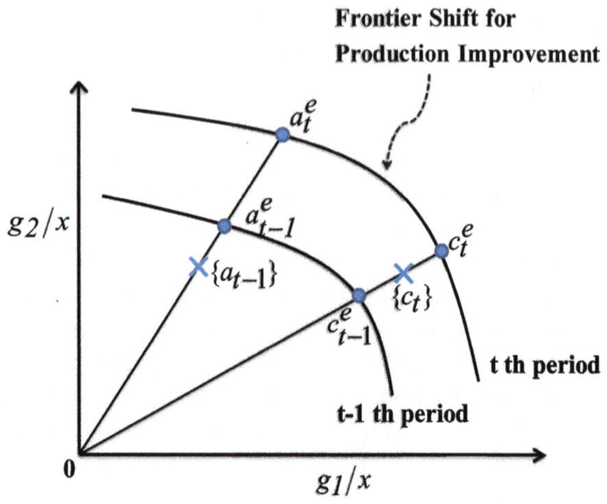

Fig. 6.1 A frontier shift under natural disposability. *Note* (a) An efficiency frontier shifts toward an increase in desirable outputs without any frontier crossover between the two periods. The natural disposability implies that the first priority is operational performance and the second priority is environmental performance. The figure assumes that an undesirable output is same on all DMUs, so dropping an influence on a frontier shift. (b) The figure assumes that DEA-EA does not suffer from an occurrence of multiple projections and multiple reference sets. (c) A unique projection onto the two efficiency frontiers is for our visual convenience. We fully understand that a real projection in DEA-EA is more complicated than the one depicted in the figure. (d) The parenthesis { } indicates the performance of an observed DMU. The other without it indicates the projected performance of the DMU on analytically generated efficient frontier. (e) Figure 6.1 modifies the original work prepared by Sueyoshi and Goto (2018) for a description on SDGs

In Fig. 6.1, $\{a_{t-1}\}$ stands for the observed performance of a DMU at the $t-1$ th period and $\{c_t\}$ indicates the performance at the t th period. The symbol (0) stands for an origin in the figure. A frontier shift occurs toward the north-east direction under an assumption that a technology progress on desirable outputs (g) occur between the two periods. The north-east direction is due to performance betterment under natural disposability. Figure 6.1 assumes that the amount of undesirable outputs (b) is the same between the two periods.

The DMU $\{a_{t-1}\}$ projects the performance to a_{t-1}^e on an efficiency frontier in the $t-1$ th period and a_t^e on that the t th period, respectively, where the superscript (e) implies an efficiency frontier onto which the observed performance is projected. In the two cases, we assume a unique projection and a unique reference set in the two periods, as visually described in Fig. 6.1. Under the same assumption, the performance of DMU $\{c_t\}$ projects the performance to c_{t-1}^e on the efficiency frontier of the $t-1$ th period and c_t^e on that of the t th period, respectively.

A geometric mean, which we often measure the average of the two line segments ($a_t^e - a_{t-1}^e$ and $c_t^e - c_{t-1}^e$), indicates the degree of a frontier shift between the $t-1$ th and t th periods. The geometric mean, indicating "Malmquist index", has the following subcomponents:

$$IN_{t-1}^{t} = \sqrt{\frac{0a_t^e}{0a_{t-1}^e}\frac{0c_t^e}{0c_{t-1}^e}} = \sqrt{\frac{\frac{0a_t^e}{0a_{t-1}}\frac{0c_t^e}{0c_t}}{\frac{0a_{t-1}^e}{0a_{t-1}}\frac{0c_{t-1}^e}{0c_t}}}, \tag{6.1}$$

where IN_{t-1}^{t} stands for the Malmquist Index between the $t - 1$ th and t th periods under natural disposability. Equation (6.1) indicates the degree of index, but the above abbreviation drops M because it does not consider the change due to managerial disposability. Later, we use M to express the disposability.

Changing our description from natural disposability to managerial disposability, Fig. 6.2 depicts a frontier shift from the $t - 1$ th period to the t th period in which each DMU attempts to enhance environmental performance as the first priority and the operational performance as the second priority. For our visual description, Fig. 6.2 considers a single input (x) and two undesirable outputs (b_1 and b_2). We assume that all the DMUs produce a same amount of a desirable output (g), so that the figure drops them. In Fig. 6.2, $\{d_{t-1}\}$ stands for the observed performance of a DMU in the $t - 1$ th period. Meanwhile, $\{q_t\}$ indicates that of the DMU in the t th period. A frontier shift occurs toward the south-west direction under an assumption that an eco-technology progress (e.g. clean coal technology for electricity generation) on undesirable outputs occur between the two periods. The south-west direction is due to managerial disposability.

The DMU $\{d_{t-1}\}$ projects the performance to d_{t-1}^e on the efficiency frontier for the $t - 1$ th period and d_t^e on that of the t th period, respectively, in Fig. 6.2. Meanwhile, the DMU $\{q_t\}$ projects the performance to q_{t-1}^e on the efficiency frontier of the $t - 1$ th period and q_t^e on that of the t th period, respectively. The Malmquist index, which measures the geometric mean of the two line segments ($d_{t-1}^e - d_t^e$ and $q_{t-1}^e - q_t^e$),

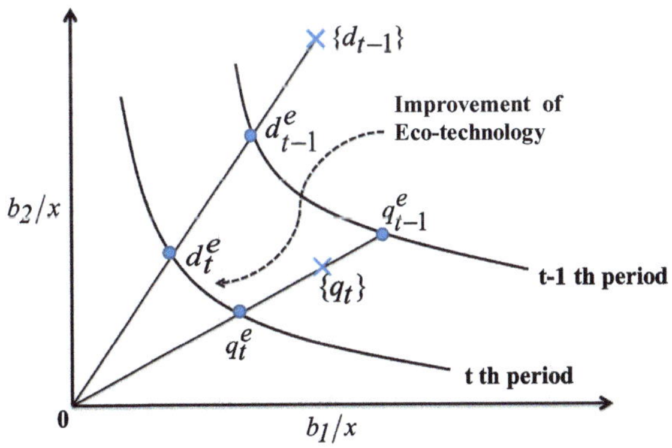

Fig. 6.2 Frontier shift under managerial disposability. *Note* (a) An efficiency frontier shifts toward a decrease in undesirable outputs without any frontier crossover between the two periods. The managerial disposability implies that the first priority is environmental performance and the second priority is operational performance. The figure assumes that desirable outputs are same on all DMUs, so dropping an influence on the frontier shift of production technology. (b) See the note of Fig. 6.1. (c) We modify the work prepared by Sueyoshi and Goto (2018)

has the following subcomponents:

$$IM_{t-1}^{t} = \sqrt{\frac{0d_{t-1}^{e}}{0d_{t}^{e}}\frac{0q_{t-1}^{e}}{0q_{t}^{e}}} = \sqrt{\frac{\frac{0d_{t-1}^{e}}{0d_{t-1}}}{\frac{0d_{t}^{e}}{0d_{t-1}}}\frac{\frac{0q_{t-1}^{e}}{0q_{t}}}{\frac{0q_{t}^{e}}{0q_{t}}}}, \quad (6.2)$$

where IM_{t-1}^{t} stands for the Malmquist index between the $t - 1$ th and t th periods under managerial disposability.

6.3.2 An Occurrence of Frontier Crossover

Figure 6.3, corresponding to Fig. 6.1, depicts a possible occurrence of the frontier crossover between the $t - 1$ th and t th periods. The observed performances of DMUs in Fig. 6.3 are measured under natural disposability. In Fig. 6.3, an efficiency frontier retreats between the two periods. As a result, we need to combine the two frontiers to shape a new efficiency frontier, or the dotted line in Fig. 6.3. To attain the status of efficiency, DMUs $\{a_{t-1}\}$ and $\{c_t\}$ need to shift their locations to $a_{t-1\&t}^{e}$ and $c_{t-1\&t}^{e}$ on the newly shaped efficiency frontier.

The geometric mean measures the average of the two line segments ($a_{t-1\&t}^{e} - a_{t-1}^{e}$ and $c_{t-1\&t}^{e} - c_{t}^{e}$) which indicates the degree of a frontier shift between the $t - 1$ th and t th periods. The geometric mean in this case has the following equation:

$$INC_{t-1}^{t} = \sqrt{\frac{0a_{t-1\&t}^{e}}{0a_{t-1}^{e}}\frac{0c_{t-1\&t}^{e}}{0c_{t}^{e}}} = \sqrt{\frac{\frac{0a_{t-1\&t}^{e}}{0a_{t-1}}}{\frac{0a_{t-1}^{e}}{0a_{t-1}}}\frac{\frac{0c_{t-1\&t}^{e}}{0c_{t}}}{\frac{0c_{t}^{e}}{0c_{t}}}}, \quad (6.3)$$

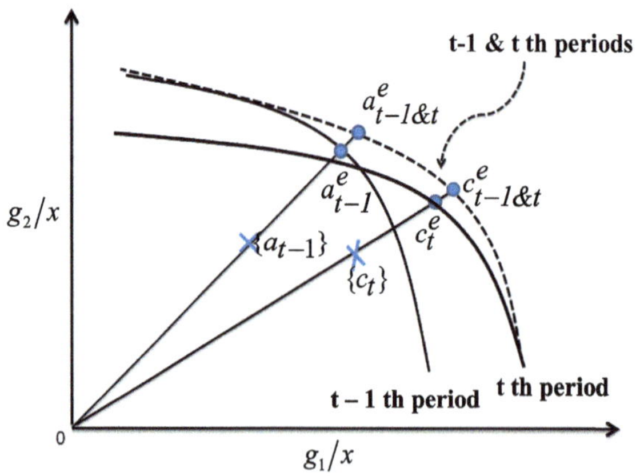

Fig. 6.3 Frontier crossover between two periods under natural disposability. *Note* (a) See the note of Fig. 6.1. (b) The dotted line for an upper curve indicates a frontier for the $t - 1$ and t th periods. (c) We modify the work prepared by Sueyoshi and Goto (2018)

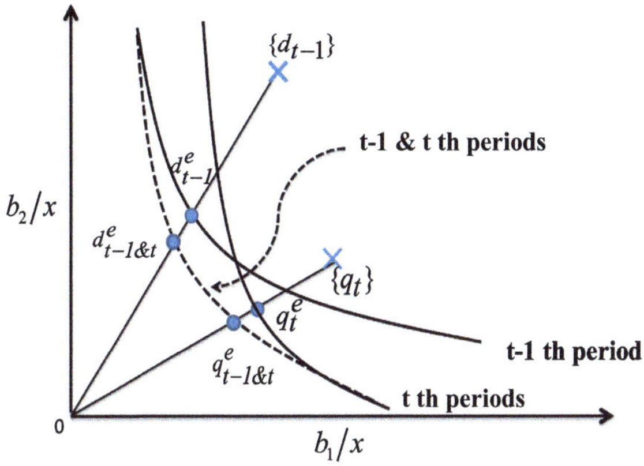

Fig. 6.4 Frontier crossover between two periods under managerial disposability. *Note* (a) See the note of Fig. 6.2. (b) The dotted line for a bottom curve indicates a frontier for the $t-1$ and t th periods. (c) We modify the work prepared by Sueyoshi and Goto (2018)

where INC^t_{t-1} stands for the Malmquist index between the $t-1$ th and t th periods under natural disposability, considering a possible occurrence of the frontier crossover (C) between the two periods.

In a similar manner, Fig. 6.4, corresponding to Fig. 6.2, visually describes a frontier crossover between the $t-1$ and t th periods. In the figure, DMUs $\{d_{t-1}\}$ and $\{q_t\}$ need to shift their locations to the projected points, $d^e_{t-1\&t}$ and $q^e_{t-1\&t}$, on the newly shaped efficiency frontier, or the dotted line for the enhancement of their environmental performance.

The geometric mean in this case measures the average of the two line segments ($d^e_{t-1} - d^e_{t-1\&t}$ and $q^e_t - q^e_{t-1\&t}$) which indicates the degree of a frontier shift between the $t-1$ and t th periods. The geometric mean has the following subcomponents:

$$IMC^t_{t-1} = \sqrt{\frac{0d^e_{t-1}}{0d^e_{t-1\&t}} \frac{0q^e_t}{0q^e_{t-1\&t}}} = \sqrt{\frac{\frac{0d^e_{t-1}}{0d_{t-1}}}{\frac{0d^e_{t-1\&t}}{0d_{t-1}}} \frac{\frac{0q^e_t}{0q_t}}{\frac{0q^e_{t-1\&t}}{0q_t}}}, \tag{6.4}$$

where IMC^t_{t-1} stands for the Malmquist index between the $t-1$ th and the t th periods under managerial disposability, considering a possible occurrence of the frontier crossover (C) between the two periods.

Here, it is important to note the three concerns. First, the performance of all DMUs at the t th period depends upon only that of the $t-1$ th and t th periods, not the other periods, as depicted in Figs. 6.3 and 6.4. Such a relationship is due to our visual convenience. However, it is not difficult for us to increase the number of periods in the proposed formulations. We can deal with an occurrence of the frontier crossover not only between the adjacent ($t-1$ th and t th) periods but also among all other period combinations. Second, Eqs. (6.3) and (6.4) have an analytical benefit, compared with Eqs. (6.1) and (6.2). We can measure the four components related to a frontier shift by Eqs. (6.3) and (6.4) even if a frontier crossover occurs between two periods. Meanwhile, Eqs. (6.1) and (6.2) do not incorporate such an occurrence of the frontier crossover. Finally, we conceptually separate the SDGs measurement into 4 cases [= 2 disposability concepts (natural and managerial) × 2 occurrence possibilities of frontier crossover (frontier crossover and no crossover)]. No previous study has investigated the research direction in DEA and DEA-EA. An exception may be found in Sueyoshi and Goto (2018).

6.4 Formulations for Natural Disposability

The nomenclatures for the Malmquist indexes (IN_{t-1}^{t} and INC_{t-1}^{t}) under Natural (N) disposability period to the $t-1$ th period,

$IUEN_{t-1\to t-1\&t}^{R}$: Inter-temporal Unified Efficiency from the $t-1$ th period to the $t-1$ & t th periods and.
$IUEN_{t\to t-1\&t}^{R}$: Inter-temporal Unified Efficiency from the t th period to the $t-1$ & t th periods.

All efficiency and index measures are determined by radial (R) measurement under natural (N) disposability and constant RTS. R is listed as a superscript and the other R indicates data ranges in this chapter.

6.4.1 No Occurrence of Frontier Crossover

To measure the Malmquist Index (I) under natural disposability in a time horizon ($t = 2, \ldots, T$), we consider n DMUs ($j = 1, \ldots, n$) whose operational and environmental achievements are relatively compared with others in their performance assessment. The performance comparison among multiple periods needs to add subscripts (t) to J so that J_t stands for all DMUs in the t th period.

Returning to Fig. 6.1, which depicts a frontier shift with a technology progress, the Malmquist index between the two periods becomes as follows:

$$IN_{t-1}^{t} = \sqrt{\frac{0a_t^e}{0a_{t-1}^e}\,\frac{0c_t^e}{0c_{t-1}^e}} = \sqrt{\frac{\frac{0a_t^e}{0a_{t-1}}\,\frac{0c_t^e}{0c_t}}{\frac{0a_{t-1}^e}{0a_{t-1}}\,\frac{0c_{t-1}^e}{0c_t}}} = \sqrt{\frac{\frac{0a_{t-1}}{0a_{t-1}^e}\,\frac{0c_t}{0c_{t-1}^e}}{\frac{0a_{t-1}}{0a_t^e}\,\frac{0c_t}{0c_t^e}}}$$

$$\Rightarrow IN_{t-1}^{t} = \sqrt{\frac{UEN_{t-1}^{R}}{IUIN_{t-1\to t}^{R}}\,\frac{IUIN_{t\to t-1}^{R}}{UEN_{t}^{R}}} \tag{6.5}$$

where UEN_{t-1}^{R} and UEN_{t}^{R} are two efficiency measures that belong to a range between zero (full inefficiency) and one (full efficiency). Meanwhile, $IUIN_{t\to t-1}^{R}$ and $IUIN_{t-1\to t}^{R}$ may become larger or smaller than unity between the two periods, so indicating an index (I) measure.

These measures have the four DEA formulations, each of which has following specifications: as the first measure, we determine the degree of UEN_t^R on the k th DMU in the t th period by the following model under natural disposability as well as constant RTS and DTS:

$$
\begin{aligned}
& Maximize\ \xi_{kt} + \varepsilon_s \left[\sum_{i=1}^{m} R_i^x d_i^{x-} + \sum_{r=1}^{s} R_r^g d_r^g + \sum_{f=1}^{h} R_f^b d_f^b \right] \\
& s.t. \quad \sum_{j \in J_t} x_{ijt} \lambda_{jt} + d_i^{x-} = x_{ikt} \ (k \in J_t \ \& \ i = 1, \ldots, m), \\
& \qquad \sum_{j \in J_t} g_{rjt} \lambda_{jt} - d_r^g - \xi_{kt} g_{rkt} = g_{rkt} \quad (k \in J_t \ \& \ r = 1, \ldots, s), \\
& \qquad \sum_{j \in J_t} b_{fjt} \lambda_{jt} + d_f^b + \xi_{kt} b_{fkt} = b_{fkt} \quad (k \in J_t \ \& f = 1, \ldots, h), \\
& \qquad \lambda_{jt} \geq 0 \quad (j = 1, \ldots, n \ and \ t = 2, \ldots, T), \\
& \qquad \xi_{kt} : URS, d_i^{x-} \geq 0 \quad (i = 1, \ldots, m), \\
& \qquad d_r^g \geq 0 \quad (r = 1, \ldots, s) \ \& \ d_f^b \geq 0 \quad (f = 1, \ldots, h),
\end{aligned}
\tag{6.6}
$$

where x_{ijt} is an observed value of the i th input on the j th DMU at the t th period, g_{rjt} is an observed value of the r th desirable output on the j th DMU at the t th period, b_{fjt} is an observed value of the f th undesirable output on the j th DMU at the t th period, d_i^{x-} $(i = 1, \ldots, m)$, d_r^g $(r = 1, \ldots, s)$ and d_f^b $(f = 1, \ldots, h)$ are all slack variables related to inputs, desirable outputs and undesirable outputs, respectively. $\lambda_{jt} = (\lambda_{1t}, \ldots, \lambda_{nt})^{Tr}$ is a column vector of unknown variables (multipliers), often referred to as "structural" or "intensity" variables which connect among production factors. An unknown scalar value (ξ_{kt}), which is URS (unrestricted), stands for an inefficiency measure. The inefficiency measure corresponds to a distance between an efficiency frontier and an observed vector of desirable and undesirable outputs, as depicted in Fig. 6.1. A scalar value (ε_s), incorporated into Model (6.6), stands for a very small number to indicate the relative importance between the inefficiency score and the total amount of slacks. This chapter sets $\varepsilon_s = 0.0001$ for our computation. The selection is subjective. It may be possible for us to set $\varepsilon_s = 0$, but we do not recommend the selection.

We determine the data range adjustments in Model (6.6) by the upper and lower bounds of production factors. These upper and lower bounds of data ranges have the following specification:

$$R_i^x = (m+s+h)^{-1} \left(\max \left\{ x_{ij} \ \middle| j \in J_{t-1} \cup \mathrm{J_t} \right\} - \min \left\{ x_{ij} \ \middle| j \in J_{t-1} \cup \mathrm{J_t} \right\} \right)^{-1}$$

$$R_r^g = (m+s+h)^{-1} \left(\max \left\{ g_{rj} \ \middle| j \in J_{t-1} \cup \mathrm{J_t} \right\} - \min \left\{ g_{rj} \ \middle| j \in J_{t-1} \cup \mathrm{J_t} \right\} \right)^{-1} \text{ and}$$

$$R_f^b = (m+s+h)^{-1} \left(\max \left\{ b_{fj} \ \middle| j \in J_{t-1} \cup \mathrm{J_t} \right\} - \min \left\{ b_{fj} \ \middle| j \in J_{t-1} \cup \mathrm{J_t} \right\} \right)^{-1}.$$

Here, $\cup$ stands for a union set and $J_{t-1} \cup J_t$ stands for all DMUs in the $t-1$ th and the t th periods.

The proposed computation consists of the four sub-processes. As the first measure, we determine the degree of UEN_t^R on the k th DMU in the t th period by the following equation:

$$UEN_t^R = 1 - \left[\xi_{kt}^* + \varepsilon_s\left(\sum_{i=1}^{m} R_i^x d_i^{x-*} + \sum_{r=1}^{s} R_r^g d_r^{g*} + \sum_{f=1}^{h} R_f^b d_f^{b*}\right)\right], \tag{6.7}$$

where the inefficiency score and all slack variables are on the optimality of Model (6.6). The equation within the parenthesis, obtained from the optimality of Model (6.6), indicates the level of unified inefficiency under natural disposability. The unified efficiency is obtained by subtracting the level of unified inefficiency from unity. The degree of UEN_t^R on the k th DMU is always less than unity, indicating an existence of some level of inefficiency, or equal unity for the status of full efficiency.

As the second measure, we determine the degree of UEN_{t-1}^R regarding the k th DMU in the $t-1$ th period by replacing t by $t-1$ in Model (6.6). Then, the degree, measured by Eq. (6.7) becomes as follows:

$$UEN_{t-1}^R = 1 - \left[\xi_{kt-1}^* + \varepsilon_s\left(\sum_{i=1}^{m} R_i^x d_i^{x-*} + \sum_{r=1}^{s} R_r^g d_r^{g*} + \sum_{f=1}^{h} R_f^b d_f^{b*}\right)\right], \tag{6.8}$$

where the inefficient score and slacks are on the optimality of Model (6.6) after replacing t by $t-1$ in the formulation. Equation (6.8) duplicates (6.7) by changing the period t to $t-1$.

As the third measure, we determine the degree of $IUIN_{t-1\to t}^R$ of the k th DMU from the $t-1$ th period to the t th period by applying the following model:

$$\begin{aligned}
&\text{Maximize } \xi_{kt-1} + \varepsilon_s[\sum_{i=1}^{m} R_i^x d_i^{x-} + \sum_{r=1}^{s} R_r^g d_r^g + \sum_{f=1}^{h} R_f^b d_f^b] \\
&s.t. \quad \sum_{j\in J_t} x_{ijt}\lambda_{jt} + d_i^{x-} = x_{ikt-1} (k \in J_{t-1} \ \&\ i = 1,\ldots,m), \\
&\qquad \sum_{j\in J_t} g_{rjt}\lambda_{jt} - d_r^g - \xi_{kt-1}g_{rkt-1} = g_{rkt-1} \quad (k \in J_{t-1} \ \&\ r = 1,\ldots,s), \\
&\qquad \sum_{j\in J_t} b_{fjt}\lambda_{jt} + d_f^b + \xi_{kt-1}b_{fkt-1} = b_{fkt-1} \quad (k \in J_{t-1} \ \&\ f = 1,\ldots,h), \\
&\qquad \lambda_{jt} \ge 0 \quad (j = 1,\ldots,n \ \&\ t = 2,\ldots,T), \\
&\qquad \xi_{kt-1} : URS,\ d_i^{x-} \ge 0 \quad (i = 1,\ldots,m), \\
&\qquad d_r^g \ge 0 \quad (r = 1,\ldots,s) \ \&\ d_f^b \ge 0 \quad (f 1,\ldots,h),
\end{aligned} \tag{6.9}$$

where an efficiency frontier consists of DMUs in the t th period and a DMU to be examined is selected from a group of DUMs in the $t-1$ th period. We measure the degree of the index by Eq. (6.7) where the inefficiency measure and all slack variables are on the optimality of Model (6.9).

As the last measure, we determine the degree of $IUIN^R_{t\to t-1}$ regarding the k th DMU, shifting from the t th period to the $t-1$ th period, by applying the following model:

$$\begin{aligned}
&Maximize\ \xi_{kt}+\varepsilon_s\left[\sum_{i=1}^{m}R_i^x d_i^{x-}+\sum_{r=1}^{s}R_r^g d_r^g+\sum_{f=1}^{h}R_f^b d_f^b\right]\\
&s.t.\quad \sum_{j\in J_{t-1}} x_{ijt-1}\lambda_{jt-1}+d_i^{x-}=x_{ikt}\quad (k\in J_t\ \&\ i=1,\ldots,m),\\
&\qquad \sum_{j\in J_{t-1}} g_{rjt-1}\lambda_{jt-1}-d_r^g-\xi_{kt}g_{rkt}=g_{rkt}\quad (k\in J_t\ \&\ r=1,\ldots,s),\\
&\qquad \sum_{j\in J_{t-1}} b_{fjt-1}\lambda_{jt-1}+d_f^b+\xi_{kt}b_{fkt}=b_{fkt}\quad (k\in J_t\ \&\ f=1,\ldots,h),\\
&\qquad \lambda_{jt-1}\geq 0\ (j=1,\ldots,n\ \&\ t=2,\ldots,T),\ \xi_{kt}:URS,\ d_i^{x-}\geq 0\quad (i=1,\ldots,m),\\
&\qquad d_r^g\geq 0\quad (r=1,\ldots,s)\ \&\ d_f^b\geq 0\quad (f=1,\ldots,h),
\end{aligned}\tag{6.10}$$

where an efficiency frontier consists of DMUs in the $t-1$ th period and a DMU to be examined is selected from a group of DUMs in the t th period. We measure the degree of the index by Eq. (6.8) where the inefficiency measure and all slack variables are on the optimality of Model (6.10).

The whole computation processes for this decomposition (no frontier crossover under natural disposability) are summarized as follows:

(a) UEN_t^R: Solve Model (6.6) and apply Eq. (6.7).
(b) UEN_{t-1}^R: Change t by $t-1$ in Model (6.6). Solve the reorganized Model (6.6) and apply Eq. (6.8).
(c) $IUIN^R_{t-1\to t}$: Solve Model (6.9) and apply Eq. (6.7).
(d) $IUIN^R_{t\to t-1}$: Solve Model (6.10) and apply Eq. (6.8).

6.4.2 An Occurrence of Frontier Crossover

Returning to Fig. 6.3, we express the conceptual framework for Eq. (6.3) under natural disposability by the following measures in the existence of a frontier crossover:

$$\begin{aligned}
INC_{t-1}^t&=\sqrt{\frac{0a^e_{t-1\&t}}{0a^e_{t-1}}\frac{0c^e_{t-1\&t}}{0c^e_t}}\\
&=\sqrt{\frac{\frac{0a^e_{t-1\&t}}{0a_{t-1}}}{\frac{0a^e_{t-1}}{0a_{t-1}}}\frac{\frac{0c^e_{t-1\&t}}{0c_t}}{\frac{0c^e_t}{0c_t}}}=\sqrt{\frac{\frac{0a_{t-1}}{0a^e_{t-1}}}{\frac{0a_{t-1}}{0a^e_{t-1\&t}}}\frac{\frac{0c_t}{0c^e_t}}{\frac{0c_t}{0c^e_{t-1\&t}}}}\\
\Rightarrow INC_{t-1}^t&=\sqrt{\frac{UEN^R_{t-1}}{IUEN^R_{t-1\to t-1\&t}}\frac{UEN^R_t}{IUEN^R_{t\to t-1\&t}}},
\end{aligned}\tag{6.11}$$

where INC_{t-1}^{t} has four subcomponents, all of which measure a frontier shift between the two periods (i.e., UEN_{t-1}^{R}, UEN_{t}^{R}, $IUEN_{t-1\to t-1\&t}^{R}$ and $IUEN_{t\to t-1\&t}^{R}$). Among the four subcomponents, we have already discussed the measurement of UEN_{t-1}^{R} and UEN_{t}^{R}, , so focusing upon the remaining measures ($IUEN_{t-1\to t-1\&t}^{R}$ and $IUEN_{t\to t-1\&t}^{R}$) hereafter.

In the case of a frontier crossover, the proposed computation has the four sub-processes. Note that we have already finished the computation of UEN_{t-1}^{R} and UEN_{t}^{R}. So, there are the remaining two computational tasks. One of the two computations is that we determine the degree of $IUEN_{t-1\to t-1\&t}^{R}$ on the k th DMU between the two periods by applying the following model:

$$\begin{aligned}
&Maximize\ \xi_{kt-1}+\varepsilon_s\left[\sum_{i=1}^{m}R_i^x d_i^{x-}+\sum_{r=1}^{s}R_r^g d_r^g+\sum_{f=1}^{h}R_f^b d_f^b\right]\\
&s.t.\quad \sum_{j\in J_{t-1\&t}} x_{ijt-1\&t}\lambda_{jt-1\&t}+d_i^{x-}=x_{ikt-1}\ (k\in J_{t-1}\ \&\ i=1,\ldots,m),\\
&\qquad \sum_{j\in J_{t-1\&t}} g_{rjt-1\&t}\lambda_{jt-1\&t}-d_r^g-\xi_{kt-1}g_{rkt-1}=g_{rkt-1}\ (k\in J_{t-1}\ \&\ r=1,\ldots,s),\\
&\qquad \sum_{j\in J_{t-1\&t}} b_{fjt-1\&t}\lambda_{jt-1\&t}+d_f^b+\xi_{kt-1}b_{fkt-1}=b_{fkt-1}\ (k\in J_{t-1}\ \&f=1,\ldots,h),\\
&\qquad \lambda_{jt-1\&t}\ge 0\ (j=1,\ldots,n\&\ t=2,\ldots,T),\ \xi_{kt-1}:URS,\ d_i^{x-}\ge 0\ \ (i=1,\ldots,m),\\
&\qquad d_r^g\ge 0\ (r=1,\ldots,s)\ \&\ d_f^b\ge 0\ \ (f=1,\ldots,h),
\end{aligned}\tag{6.12}$$

where an efficiency frontier consists of DMUs in the $t-1$ & t th periods and a DMU to be examined by Model (6.12) is selected from a group of DUMs in the $t-1$ th period. We determine the degree of $IUEN_{t-1\to t-1\&t}^{R}$ on the k th DMU by Eq. (6.8) where the inefficiency measure and all slack variables are on the optimality of Model (6.12).

The other computation is that we determine the degree of $IUEN_{t\to t-1\&t}^{R}$ on the k th DMU between the two periods by applying the following model:

$$\begin{aligned}
&Maximize\ \xi_{kt}+\varepsilon_s\left[\sum_{i=1}^{m}R_i^x d_i^{x-}+\sum_{r=1}^{s}R_r^g d_r^g+\sum_{f=1}^{h}R_f^b d_f^b\right]\\
&s.t.\quad \sum_{j\in J_{t-1\&t}} x_{ijt-1\&t}\lambda_{jt-1\&t}+d_i^{x-}=x_{ikt}\ (k\in J_t\ \&\ i=1,\ldots,m),\\
&\qquad \sum_{j\in J_{t-1\&t}} g_{rjt-1\&t}\lambda_{jt-1\&t}\ -d_r^g\ -\xi_{kt}g_{rkt}=g_{rkt}\ (k\in J_t\ \&\ r=1,\ldots,s),\\
&\qquad \sum_{j\in J_{t-1\&t}} b_{fjt-1\&t}\lambda_{jt-1\&t}+d_f^b+\xi_{kt}b_{fkt}=b_{fkt}\ (k\in J_t\ \&f=1,\ldots,h),\\
&\qquad \lambda_{jt-1\&t}\ge 0\ (j=1,\ldots,n\ \&;\ t=2,\ldots,T),\ \ \xi_{kt}:URS,\ d_i^{x-}\ge 0\ (i=1,\ldots,m),\\
&\qquad d_r^g\ge 0\ \ (r=1,\ldots,s)\ \&\ d_f^b\ge 0\ \ (f=1,\ldots,h),
\end{aligned}\tag{6.13}$$

where an efficiency frontier consists of DMUs in the $t-1$ & t th periods and a DMU to be examined is selected from DUMs in the t th period. We determine the degree of $IUEN_{t\to t-1\&t}^{R}$ regarding the k th DMU in the t th period by Eq. (6.7) where the inefficiency measure and all slack variables are on the optimality of Model (6.13).

The whole computation processes in this decomposition (frontier crossover under natural disposability) are summarized as follows:

(a) UEN_t^R: Solve Model (6.6) and apply Eq. (6.7).
(b) UEN_{t-1}^R: Change t by $t-1$ in Model (6.6). Solve the reorganized Model (6.6) and apply Eq. (6.8).
(c) $IUEN_{t-1 \to t-1\&t}^R$: Solve Model (6.12) and apply Eq. (6.8).
(d) $IUEN_{t \to t-1\&t}^R$: Solve Model (6.13) and apply Eq. (6.7).

Here, we describe two differences between index and efficiency measures. One of the two differences is that a frontier crossover incorporated in Models (6.12) and (6.13) always produce efficiency scores, not indexes, where they belong to a range between 0 (full inefficiency) and 1 (full efficiency). Such a feature cannot be found in Models (6.9) and (6.10). The other difference is that IN_{t-1}^t may be more than, equal to, or less than unity, but INC_{t-1}^t is more than or equal to unity and it cannot be less than unity.

If a DMU exhibits unity in INC_{t-1}^t, then it indicates that there is a frontier crossover between the $t-1$ th and t th periods and the achievement of the DMU locates on the three efficiency frontiers for the $t-1$ th, t th and the combined $t-1$ & t th periods. In other words, there is no technological progress between the two periods. In contrast, if a DMU exhibits more than unity in INC_{t-1}^t, then it indicates that the efficiency frontier of the t th period locates differently from that of the $t-1$ th period, as depicted in Fig. 6.3. Thus, it is possible for us to identify whether the DMU has an operational improvement (e,g., due to technological progress) or an operational retreat (e.g., due to poor business condition) between the two periods by examining INC_{t-1}^t.

Finally, it is important to note that our description here is based upon the assumption that a data set to be examined does not contain an outlier because it drastically changes the location of an efficiency frontier.

6.5 Formulations Under Managerial Disposability

To describe the six components regarding IM_{t-1}^t and IMC_{t-1}^t, we specify their descriptions in the following manner:

UEM_{t-1}^R: Unified Efficiency in the $t-1$ th period,
UEM_t^R: Unified Efficiency in the t th period,
$IUIM_{t-1 \to t}^R$: Inter-temporal Unified Index from the $t-1$ th period to the t th period,
$IUIM_{t \to t-1}^R$: Inter-temporal Unified Index from the t th period to the $t-1$ th period,
$IUEM_{t-1 \to t-1\&t}^R$: Inter-temporal Unified Efficiency from the $t-1$ th period to the $t-1$ & t th periods and.

$IUEM^{R}_{t\to t-1\&t}$: Inter-temporal Unified Efficiency from the t th period to the $t-1$ & t th periods.

The superscript R stands for radial measurement under Managerial (M) disposability with constant DTS determines all efficiency and index measures.

6.5.1 No Occurrence of Frontier Crossover

The conceptual framework on Eq. (6.2), IM^{t}_{t-1}, under managerial disposability has the following subcomponents as depicted in Fig. 6.2:

$$IM^{t}_{t-1} = \sqrt{\frac{0d^{e}_{t-1}}{0d^{e}_{t}}\frac{0q^{e}_{t-1}}{0q^{e}_{t}}} = \sqrt{\frac{\frac{0d^{e}_{t-1}}{0d_{t-1}}\ \frac{0q^{e}_{t-1}}{0q_{t}}}{\frac{0d^{e}_{t}}{0d_{t-1}}\ \frac{0q^{e}_{t}}{0q_{t}}}}$$

$$\Rightarrow IM^{t}_{t-1} = \sqrt{\frac{UEM^{R}_{t-1}}{IUIM^{R}_{t-1\to t}}\frac{IUIM^{R}_{t\to t-1}}{UEM^{R}_{t}}} \tag{6.14}$$

As formulated in Eq. (6.14), IM^{t}_{t-1}, has four subcomponents under constant DTS.

As the first measure, we determine the degree of UEM^{R}_{t} on the k th DMU in the t th period by the following model:

$$\begin{aligned}
&Maximize\ \xi_{kt} + \varepsilon_s\left[\sum_{i=1}^{m} R^{x}_{i} d^{x+}_{i} + \sum_{r=1}^{s} R^{g}_{r} d^{g}_{r} + \sum_{f=1}^{h} R^{b}_{f} d^{b}_{f}\right]\\
&s.t.\quad \sum_{j\in J_t} x_{ijt}\lambda_{jt} - d^{x+}_{i} = x_{ikt}\ (k \in J_t\ \&\ i = 1, \ldots, m),\\
&\qquad \sum_{j\in J_t} g_{rjt}\lambda_{jt} - d^{g}_{r} - \xi_{kt} g_{rkt} = g_{rkt}\ (k \in J_t\ \&\ r = 1, \ldots, s),\\
&\qquad \sum_{j\in J_t} b_{fjt}\lambda_{jt} + d^{b}_{f} + \xi_{kt} b_{fkt} = b_{fkt}\quad (k \in J_t\ \&\ f = 1, \ldots, h),\\
&\qquad \lambda_{jt} \ge 0\ (j = 1, \ldots, n\ \&\ t = 2, \ldots, T),\ \xi_{kt} : URS,\ d^{x+}_{i} \ge 0\ (i = 1, \ldots, m),\\
&\qquad d^{g}_{r} \ge 0\ (r = 1, \ldots, s)\ \&\ d^{b}_{f} \ge 0\ (f = 1, \ldots, h).
\end{aligned} \tag{6.15}$$

Here, we replace d^{x-}_{i} by d^{x+}_{i} to change natural disposability to managerial disposability in Eq. (6.15).

We determine the degree of UEM^{R}_{t} on the k th DMU in the t th period by the following equation:

$$UEM^{R}_{t} = 1 - \left[\xi^{*}_{kt} + \varepsilon_s\left(\sum_{i=1}^{m} R^{x}_{i} d^{x+*}_{i} + \sum_{r=1}^{s} R^{g}_{r} d^{g*}_{r} + \sum_{f=1}^{h} R^{b}_{f} d^{b*}_{f}\right)\right], \tag{6.16}$$

where the inefficiency score and all slack variables are on the optimality of Model (6.15). The equation within the parenthesis, obtained from the optimality of Model

(6.15), indicates the level of unified inefficiency under managerial disposability. We obtain the unified efficiency by subtracting the level of inefficiency from unity. Thus, the unified efficiency always belongs to the range between 0 (full inefficiency) and 1 (full efficiency).

As the second measure, we determine the degree of UEM^R_{t-1} on the k th DMU at the $t-1$ th period by replacing t by $t-1$ in Model (6.15). Equation (6.16) measures the degree of UEM^R_{t-1} after replacing t by $t-1$ in Model (6.15). Thus, the degree of UEM^R_{t-1} becomes as follows:

$$UEM^R_{t-1} = 1 - \left[\xi^*_{kt-1} + \varepsilon_s \left(\sum_{i=1}^{m} R^x_i d^{x+*}_i + \sum_{r=1}^{s} R^g_r d^{g*}_r + \sum_{f=1}^{h} R^b_f d^{b*}_f \right) \right], \quad (6.17)$$

As the third measure, we determine the degree of $IUIM^R_{t-1\to t}$ on the k th DMU from the $t-1$ th period to the t th period by the following model:

$$\begin{aligned}
&\text{Maximize } \xi_{kt-1} + \varepsilon_s \left[\sum_{i=1}^{m} R^x_i d^{x+}_i + \sum_{r=1}^{s} R^g_r d^g_r + \sum_{f=1}^{h} R^b_f d^b_f \right] \\
&\text{s.t. } \sum_{j \in J_t} x_{ijt}\lambda_{jt} - d^{x+}_i = x_{ikt-1} \ (k \in J_{t-1} \ \& \ i = 1, \ldots, m), \\
&\quad \sum_{j \in J_t} g_{rjt}\lambda_{jt} - d^g_r - \xi_{kt-1} g_{rkt-1} = g_{rkt-1} \ (k \in J_{t-1} \ \& \ r = 1, \ldots, s), \\
&\quad \sum_{j \in J_t} b_{fjt}\lambda_{jt} + d^b_f + \xi_{kt-1} b_{fkt-1} = b_{fkt-1} \ (k \in J_{t-1} \ \& f = 1, \ldots, h), \\
&\quad \lambda_{jt} \geq 0 \ \ (j = 1, \ldots, n \ \& \ t = 1, \ldots, T), \ \ \xi_{kt-1} : \text{URS}, \ d^{x+}_i \geq 0 \ \ (i = 1, \ldots, m), \\
&\quad d^g_r \geq 0 \ \ (r = 1, \ldots, s) \ \& \ d^b_f \geq 0 \ \ (f = 1, \ldots, h),
\end{aligned} \quad (6.18)$$

where an efficiency frontier consists of DMUs in the t th periods and a DMU to be examined is selected from DUMs in the $t-1$ th period. We measure the degree of $IUIM^R_{t-1\to t}$ on the k th DMU by the following equation:

$$UEM^R_{t-1\to t} = 1 - \left[\xi^*_{kt-1} + \varepsilon_s \left(\sum_{i=1}^{m} R^x_i d^{x+*}_i + \sum_{r=1}^{s} R^g_r d^{g*}_r + \sum_{f-1}^{h} R^b_f d^{b*}_f \right) \right], \quad (6.19)$$

where the inefficiency measure and all slack variables are on the optimality of Model (6.18).

As the last measure, we determine the degree of $IUIM^R_{t\to t-1}$ of the k th DMU from the t th period to the $t-1$ th period becomes as follows:

$$
\begin{aligned}
&Maximize\ \xi_{kt} + \varepsilon_s\left[\sum_{i=1}^{m} R_i^x d_i^{x+} + \sum_{r=1}^{s} R_r^g d_r^g + \sum_{f=1}^{h} R_f^b d_f^b\right] \\
&s.t. \quad \sum_{j\in J_{t-1}} x_{ijt-1}\lambda_{jt-1} - d_i^{x+} = x_{ikt} (k \in J_t\ \&\ i = 1, \ldots, m), \\
&\qquad \sum_{j\in J_{t-1}} g_{rjt-1}\lambda_{jt-1} - d_r^g - \xi g_{rkt} = g_{rkt}\ (k \in J_t\ \&\ r = 1, \ldots, s), \\
&\qquad \sum_{j\in J_{t-1}} b_{fjt-1}\lambda_{jt-1} + d_f^b + \xi b_{fkt} = b_{fkt}\ (k \in J_t\ \& f = 1, \ldots, h), \\
&\qquad \lambda_{jt-1} \ge 0\ (j = 1, \ldots, n\ \&\ t = 2, \ldots, T), \xi : URS, d_i^{x+} \ge 0\ (i = 1, \ldots, m), \\
&\qquad d_r^g \ge 0\ (r = 1, \ldots, s)\ \&\ d_f^b \ge 0 \quad (f = 1, \ldots, h),
\end{aligned}
\tag{6.20}
$$

where an efficiency frontier consists of DMUs in the $t-1$ th period and a DMU to be examined is selected from a group of DUMs in the t th period. We determine the degree of $IUIM_{t\to t-1}^{R}$ on the k th DMU between the two periods by

$$
IUIM_{t\to t-1}^{R} = 1 - \left[\xi_{kt}^{*} + \varepsilon_s\left(\sum_{i=1}^{m} R_i^x d_i^{x+*} + \sum_{r=1}^{s} R_r^g d_r^{g*} + \sum_{f=1}^{h} R_f^b d_f^{b*}\right)\right], \tag{6.21}
$$

where the inefficiency measure and all slack variables are on the optimality of Model (6.20).

The whole computation processes in this case (no frontier crossover under managerial disposability) are summarized as follows:

(a) UEM_{t}^{R}: Solve Model (6.15) and apply Eq. (6.16).
(b) UEM_{t-1}^{R}: Change t by $t-1$ in Model (6.15). Solve the reorganized Model (6.15) and apply Eq. (6.17).
(c) $IUEM_{t-1\to t-1\&t}^{R}$: Solve Model (6.18) and apply Eq. (6.19).
(d) $IUEM_{t\to t-1\&t}^{R}$: Solve Model (6.20) and apply Eq. (6.21).

6.5.2 An Occurrence of Frontier Crossover

By shifting our description to the case of a frontier crossover, the conceptual framework on Eq. (6.4), IMC_{t-1}^{t}, under managerial disposability, has the following unified measures as depicted in Fig. 6.4:

$$
\begin{aligned}
IMC_{t-1}^{t} &= \sqrt{\frac{0d_{t-1}^{e}}{0d_{t-1\&t}^{e}}\frac{0q_{t}^{e}}{0q_{t-1\&t}^{e}}} = \sqrt{\frac{\frac{0d_{t-1}^{e}}{0d_{t-1}}}{\frac{0d_{t-1\&t}^{e}}{0d_{t-1}}}\frac{\frac{0q_{t}^{e}}{0q_{t}}}{\frac{0q_{t-1\&t}^{e}}{0q_{t}}}} \\
\Rightarrow IMC_{t-1}^{t} &= \sqrt{\frac{UEM_{t-1}^{R}}{IUEM_{t-1\to t-1\&t}^{R}}\frac{UEM_{t}^{R}}{IUEM_{t\to t-1\&t}^{R}}}.
\end{aligned}
\tag{6.22}
$$

Model (6.15) measures the degree of UEM_{t-1}^{R} and that of UEM_{t}^{R}. The first measurement needs to replace the t th by the $t-1$ th period in the model. The two measures are determined by Eqs. (6.17) and (6.16), respectively.

The remaining task is to determine the two components ($IUEM_{t-1\to t-1\&t}^{R}$ and $IUEM_{t\to t-1\&t}^{R}$) in Eq. (6.22). One of the two components needs to determine the degree of $IUEM_{t-1\to t-1\&t}^{R}$ of k th DMU in the $t-1$ th period by the following model:

$$\begin{aligned}
&\text{Maximize } \xi_{kt-1} + \varepsilon_s\left[\sum_{i=1}^{m} R_i^x d_i^{x+} + \sum_{r=1}^{s} R_r^g d_r^g + \sum_{f=1}^{h} R_f^b d_f^b\right] \\
&s.t. \quad \sum_{j\in J_{t-1\&t}} x_{ijt-1\&t}\lambda_{jt-1\&t} - d_i^{x+} = x_{ikt-1} (k \in J_{t-1}\ \&\ i = 1,\ldots,m), \\
&\qquad \sum_{j\in J_{t-1\&t}} g_{rjt-1\&t}\lambda_{jt-1\&t} - d_r^g - \xi_{kt-1} g_{rkt-1} = g_{rkt-1} \quad (k \in J_{t-1}\ \&\ r = 1,\ldots,s), \\
&\qquad \sum_{j\in J_{t-1\&t}} b_{fjt-1\&t}\lambda_{jt-1\&t} + d_f^b + \xi_{kt-1} b_{fkt-1} = b_{fkt-1} \quad (k \in J_{t-1}\ \& f = 1,\ldots,h), \\
&\qquad \lambda_{jt-1\&t} \geq 0 \quad (j = 1,\ldots,n\ \&\ t = 2,\ldots,T), \xi_{kt-1} : URS, d_i^{x+} \geq 0 \quad (i = 1,\ldots,m), \\
&\qquad d_r^g \geq 0 \quad (r = 1,\ldots,s), \text{ and } d_f^b \geq 0 \quad (f = 1,\ldots,h),
\end{aligned} \tag{6.23}$$

where an efficiency frontier consists of DMUs in the $t-1$ & t th periods and a DMU to be examined is selected from DUMs in the $t-1$ th period. We measures the degree of $IUEM_{t-1\to t-1\&t}^{R}$ on the k th DMU by the following equation:

$$IUEM_{t-1\to t-1\&t}^{R} = 1 - \left[\xi_{kt-1}^{*} + \varepsilon_s\left(\sum_{i=1}^{m} R_i^x d_i^{x+*} + \sum_{r=1}^{s} R_r^g d_r^{g*} + \sum_{f=1}^{h} R_f^b d_f^{b*}\right)\right], \tag{6.24}$$

where the inefficiency score and all slack variables are on the optimality of Model (6.23).

The other component is to determine the degree of $IUEM_{t\to t-1\&t}^{R}$ of the k th DMU in the t th period by the following model:

$$\begin{aligned}
&\text{Maximize } \xi_{kt} + \varepsilon_s\left[\sum_{i=1}^{m} R_i^x d_i^{x+} + \sum_{r=1}^{s} R_r^g d_r^g + \sum_{f=1}^{h} R_f^b d_f^b\right] \\
&s.t. \quad \sum_{j\in J_{t-1\&t}} x_{ijt-1\&t}\lambda_{jt-1\&t} - d_i^{x+} = x_{ikt} \ (k \in J_t\ \&\ i = 1,\ \ldots,m), \\
&\qquad \sum_{j\in J_{t-1\&t}} g_{rjt-1\&t}\lambda_{jt-1\&t} - d_r^g - \xi_{kt} g_{rkt} = g_{rkt} \ (k \in J_t\ \& r = 1,\ \ldots,s), \\
&\qquad \sum_{j\in J_{t-1\&t}} b_{fjt-1\&t}\lambda_{jt-1\&t} + d_f^b + \xi_{kt} b_{fkt} = b_{fkt} \ (k \in J_t\ \& f = 1,\ \ldots,h), \\
&\qquad \lambda_{jt-1\&t} \geq 0 \quad (j = 1,\ \ldots,n\ \&\ t = 2,\ \ldots,T), \ \ \xi_{kt} : URS, d_i^{x+} \geq 0 \ (i = 1,\ \ldots,m), \\
&\qquad d_r^g \geq 0 \ (r = 1,\ \ldots,s)\ \&\ d_f^b \geq 0 \ (f = 1,\ \ldots,h),
\end{aligned} \tag{6.25}$$

where an efficiency frontier consists of DMUs in the $t-1\&t$ th periods and a DMU to be examined is selected from a group of DUMs in the t th period. We determine the degree of $IUEM_{t\to t-1\&t}^{R}$.

$$IUEM^{R}_{t \to t-1\&t} = 1 - \left[\xi^{*}_{kt} + \varepsilon_s \left(\sum_{i=1}^{m} R^{x}_{i} d^{x+*}_{i} + \sum_{r=1}^{s} R^{g}_{r} d^{g*}_{r} + \sum_{f=1}^{h} R^{b}_{f} d^{b*}_{f} \right) \right], \tag{6.26}$$

where the inefficiency score and all slack variables are on the optimality of Model (6.25). As a result of incorporating an occurrence of a frontier shift, Models (6.23) and (6.25) can always produce an efficiency score on a range between 0 (full inefficiency) and 1 (full efficiency).

The whole computation processes in this case (frontier crossover under managerial disposability) are summarized as follows:

(a) UEM^{R}_{t}: Solve Model (6.15) and apply Eq. (6.16).
(b) UEM^{R}_{t-1}: Change t by $t-1$ in Model (6.15). Solve the reorganized Model (6.15) and apply Eq. (6.17).
(c) $IUEM^{R}_{t-1 \to t-1\&t}$: Solve Model (6.23) and apply Eq. (6.24).
(d) $IUEM^{R}_{t \to t-1\&t}$: Solve Model (6.25) and apply Eq. (6.26).

The Malmquist index measurement under natural or managerial disposability has the four important features to be discussed here. First, all the models are formulated under constant RTS or DTS. Variable RTS and DTS may produce an infeasible solution. Second, we assume that all DEA models can uniquely produce a DEA solution. However, the assumption is not always true because they may suffer from an occurrence of multiple solutions (e.g., multiple projections and multiple reference sets). If such a problem occurs, we need to incorporate SCSCs (Strong Complementary Slackness Conditions) to the proposed DEA models for a time horizon. Third, we consider only two periods ($t-1$ and t) in discussing the occurrence of a frontier crossover between the two periods. It is possible to extend the number of periods to more than three periods ($J_p \cup \cdots \cup J_{t-1} \cup J_t$), where the subscript ($p$) indicates a starting period of the time horizon. See Sueyoshi and Goto (2015). In the case of multiple (more than two) periods, the data ranges (R) are determined by the upper and lower bounds of production factors as follows:

$$\begin{aligned} R^{x}_{i} &= (m+s+h)^{-1} \left(\max\left\{ x_{ij} \middle| j \in J_p \cup \cdots \cup J_{t-1} \cup J_t \right\} \right. \\ &\quad \left. - \min\left\{ x_{ij} \middle| j \in J_p \cup \cdots \cup J_{t-1} \cup J_t \right\} \right)^{-1} \\ R^{g}_{r} &= (m+s+h)^{-1} \left(\max\left\{ g_{rj} \middle| j \in J_p \cup \cdots \cup J_{t-1} \cup J_t \right\} \right. \\ &\quad \left. - \min\left\{ g_{rj} \middle| j \in J_p \cup \cdots \cup J_{t-1} \cup J_t \right\} \right)^{-1} \text{ and} \\ R^{b}_{f} &= (m+s+h)^{-1} \left(\max\left\{ b_{fj} \middle| j \in J_p \cup \cdots \cup J_{t-1} \cup J_t \right\} \right. \\ &\quad \left. - \min\left\{ b_{fj} \middle| j \in J_p \cup \cdots \cup J_{t-1} \cup J_t \right\} \right)^{-1}. \end{aligned}$$

Finally, many production economists have used a directional distance function to express the analytical structure for inefficiency measurement. We do not follow such a conventional way of measurement because of a difficulty in mathematically describing a frontier crossover between different periods and different technology developments. Furthermore, the use of conventional distance functions has implicitly assumed a unique solution on DEA-EA. In contrast, we formulate DEA-EA models as linear programming, so that these models may have a possible occurrence of multiple solutions in the primal and dual models.

6.6 An Illustrative Example

Table 6.1 summarizes descriptive statistics of an illustrative example. A desirable output is a gross prefectural product (unit: million Yen). An undesirable output is an amount of CO_2 emission (unit: t-CO_2). There are three inputs. The first input is final energy consumption (unit: Tera joule), the second input is capital stock (real-term, million Yen) and the third input is the number of workers. The observed periods were from 2007 to 2018.

6.6.1 Under Natural Disposability

We consider two cases for the natural disposability: (a) no frontier crossover and (b) frontier crossover. Malmquist index measures do not consider an occurrence of crossover in the first case. Table 6.2 summarizes the computational results under no occurrence. Meanwhile, in the case of crossover, Table 6.3 summarizes Malmquist index measures. Both index measures mainly show an annual shift in production technology, so exhibiting a progress in production technology. If the index measure is more than unity, we can confirm technology progress on production process. If it is less than unity, we observe an opposite case from the index. For example, the DMU group had 1.1199 in 2008 and 1.0696 in 2009. The group showed the indexes that are less than unity in the remaining years (2010–2018), so not exhibiting a major production progress. See the last row of Table 6.2. This observation may depend upon a DMU (Prefecture: Japanese administrative unit like a state in the United States). For example, Tokyo (DMU 14: a capital of Japan) exhibited more than unity (1.0002) on average (2008–2018). Although it was not a major, but Tokyo showed a technology progress on production. See the last column of Table 6.2.

Table 6.3 summarized that DMUs have exhibited more than unity on them. This result simply implies that all DMUs (Japanese prefectures) have showed a considerable progress on production under a possible occurrence of frontier progress. See the last raw and the last column of Table 6.3.

Comparing Table 6.2 with Table 6.3, we find that the consideration of frontier crossover increases our capability to identify a progress on production technology. This indicates the importance of considering the frontier crossover in DEA-EA.

Table 6.1 Descriptive statistics on 20 Japanese prefectures

		2007	2008	2009	2010	2011	2012	2013	2014	2015	2016	2017	2018
Gross prefectural product	Avg	14,950	14,489	13,794	13,931	14,057	13,968	14,247	14,368	14,850	14,944	15,232	15,391
	Max	105,331	103,815	97,557	97,911	100,277	99,824	101,235	101,769	104,495	105,127	105,965	107,042
	Min	3383	3264	3030	3212	3201	3042	3101	3034	3266	3212	3352	3460
	S.D	22,804	22,498	21,099	21,208	21,740	21,602	21,888	21,979	22,577	22,728	22,926	23,154
CO_2 emissions	Avg	11,401	11,101	9834	10,370	9735	10,290	11,265	11,104	10,705	10,497	10,482	10,562
	Max	55,450	51,592	47,890	53,301	47,795	50,015	52,997	53,702	49,258	47,216	45,611	46,690
	Min	980	1023	758	900	784	950	986	951	931	950	985	992
	S.D	13,672	12,935	11,774	12,927	12,103	12,188	13,201	13,203	12,333	11,872	11,546	11,947
Finalc energy consumption	Avg	339	320	321	327	318	319	322	312	308	292	295	291
	Max	1541	1435	1438	1487	1325	1356	1410	1409	1313	1317	1310	1273
	Min	54	54	56	58	55	54	53	49	48	46	47	46
	S.D	393	366	368	373	353	353	365	359	349	336	341	329
Capital stock	Avg	33,793	33,827	33,631	33,445	33,095	33,100	33,192	33,444	33,735	33,972	34,302	34,602
	Max	191,838	193,516	193,716	193,760	194,639	194,446	194,774	196,482	197,854	198,791	200,336	202,495
	Min	8307	8321	8275	8351	8626	8898	9064	9081	9124	9215	9337	9428
	S.D	41,358	41,678	41,682	41,650	41,924	41,834	41,865	42,191	42,464	42,638	42,945	43,365
Number of workers	Avg	1690	1699	1700	1696	1683	1685	1687	1694	1694	1700	1711	1723
	Max	9151	9378	9590	9536	9488	9498	9538	9677	9698	9792	9942	10,083
	Min	422	419	418	420	421	419	418	416	417	410	409	407
	S.D	1988	2037	2086	2084	2076	2078	2086	2114	2117	2140	2175	2206

Note All DMUs are twenty Japanese prefectures (corresponding to "States" in the United States). They are (1) Hokkaido, (2) Aomori, (3) Iwate, (4) Miyagi, (5) Akita, (6) Yamagata, (7) Fukushima, (8) Ibaraki, (9) Tochigi, (10) Gunma, (11) Saitama, (12) Chiba, (13) Tokyo, (14) Kanagawa, (15) Niigata, (16) Toyama, (17) Ishikawa, (18) Fukui, (19) Yamanashi and (20) Nagano. They locate at the north areas from Tokyo which is the capital of Japan

Table 6.2 Malmquist index under natural disposability: no frontier crossover

DMU	2008	2009	2010	2011	2012	2013	2014	2015	2016	2017	2018	Avg
1	1.0997	1.0166	0.9963	0.9901	1.0045	0.9399	0.9433	0.9252	0.9868	0.9548	0.9725	0.9845
2	1.2977	1.0327	1.0034	1.0584	1.0054	1.0553	0.9198	0.8588	0.9919	1.0569	1.0347	1.0286
3	1.1444	1.0436	0.9913	0.7415	0.9580	0.9809	0.9990	0.9981	1.0309	1.0197	1.0390	0.9951
4	1.1445	1.0689	0.9608	0.7872	0.9338	0.9906	0.9769	0.9809	1.0251	1.0244	0.9913	0.9895
5	1.2725	1.0268	0.9360	0.9510	1.0127	0.9910	1.0147	0.9973	0.9808	0.9156	1.0221	1.0110
6	1.2168	1.0715	0.9284	1.0226	0.9664	0.9353	1.0378	0.9631	0.9643	0.9329	1.0306	1.0063
7	1.1550	1.0680	0.9900	0.9341	0.9193	0.9050	0.9933	1.0281	1.0261	0.9912	0.9931	1.0003
8	1.0541	1.0632	0.9359	0.9216	1.0335	1.0067	0.9691	0.9484	0.9985	0.9415	0.9803	0.9866
9	1.1326	1.0213	0.9515	1.0174	1.0070	0.8984	0.9946	0.9250	1.0014	0.9715	1.0093	0.9936
10	1.0635	1.0387	0.9517	1.0122	0.9781	0.9362	0.9719	0.9523	1.0043	0.9735	1.0028	0.9896
11	1.0326	1.0320	0.9744	0.9698	1.0311	0.9804	1.0093	0.9719	0.9960	0.9706	1.0037	0.9975
12	1.0387	1.0260	1.0078	1.0183	1.0154	0.9255	1.0123	0.9786	1.0064	0.9735	0.9928	0.9996
13	1.0055	1.0570	0.9994	0.9591	1.0211	1.0233	0.9976	1.0092	0.9251	0.9991	1.0010	0.9998
14	1.0404	1.1081	0.9398	0.9863	1.0166	0.9881	1.0033	0.9512	0.9898	0.9843	0.9944	1.0002
15	1.1776	1.0272	0.9628	0.9936	0.9941	0.9400	0.9981	0.9326	0.9658	0.9482	0.9756	0.9923
16	1.1370	1.1647	0.9044	0.9826	1.0189	0.9895	0.9392	0.9559	1.0269	0.9601	0.9508	1.0027
17	1.1016	1.1841	1.0073	1.0515	0.9723	0.8880	0.9356	0.9032	0.9936	0.9678	0.9525	0.9961
18	1.0676	1.0612	0.9817	1.0417	1.2019	0.9621	1.0523	0.8420	1.0441	0.9112	0.9403	1.0096
19	1.0828	1.0367	0.9692	1.0438	1.1303	0.9812	0.9730	0.9138	0.9253	0.9308	0.9396	0.9933

(continued)

Table 6.2 (continued)

DMU	2008	2009	2010	2011	2012	2013	2014	2015	2016	2017	2018	Avg
20	1.1329	1.0433	0.9539	0.9826	1.0336	0.9722	0.9711	0.9231	0.9970	0.9867	0.9771	0.9976
Avg	1.1199	1.0596	0.9673	0.9733	1.0127	0.9645	0.9856	0.9479	0.9940	0.9707	0.9902	0.9987

Note (a) We compute the degree of Malmquist index by Eq. (6.5). DMUs stand for 20 Japanese prefectures. (b) (1) Hokkaido, (2) Aomori, (3) Iwate, (4) Miyagi, (5) Akita, (6) Yamagata, (7) Fukushima, (8) Ibaraki, (9) Tochigi, (10) Gunma, (11) Saitama, (12) Chiba, (13) Tokyo, (14) Kanagawa, (15) Niigata, (16) Toyama, (17) Ishikawa, (18) Fukui, (19) Yamanashi and (20) Nagano

Table 6.3 Malmquist index under natural disposability: frontier crossover

DMU	2008	2009	2010	2011	2012	2013	2014	2015	2016	2017	2018	Avg
1	1.0710	1.1257	1.0114	1.0381	1.0075	1.0133	1.0105	1.0287	1.0038	1.0071	1.0036	1.0292
2	1.0544	1.1289	1.0057	1.0346	1.0112	1.0198	1.0178	1.0496	1.0062	1.0131	1.0072	1.0317
3	1.0410	1.1020	1.0046	1.0276	1.0031	1.0110	1.0030	1.0174	1.0012	1.0002	1.0006	1.0192
4	1.0397	1.1023	1.0046	1.0264	1.0031	1.0110	1.0030	1.0172	1.0011	1.0002	1.0037	1.0193
5	1.0503	1.1195	1.0053	1.0293	1.0052	1.0185	1.0053	1.0312	1.0021	1.0003	1.0058	1.0248
6	1.0300	1.0801	1.0037	1.0199	1.0036	1.0129	1.0035	1.0203	1.0013	1.0002	1.0005	1.0160
7	1.0492	1.1170	1.0107	1.0353	1.0035	1.0124	1.0030	1.0172	1.0048	1.0070	1.0037	1.0240
8	1.0415	1.0843	1.0080	1.0237	1.0043	1.0076	1.0068	1.0185	1.0026	1.0046	1.0024	1.0186
9	1.0244	1.0615	1.0029	1.0161	1.0031	1.0110	1.0026	1.0150	1.0009	1.0049	1.0026	1.0132
10	1.0227	1.0592	1.0028	1.0155	1.0028	1.0100	1.0024	1.0140	1.0009	1.0001	1.0004	1.0119
11	1.0173	1.0454	1.0022	1.0125	1.0023	1.0082	1.0023	1.0130	1.0008	1.0001	1.0004	1.0095
12	1.0203	1.0523	1.0025	1.0152	1.0030	1.0105	1.0027	1.0155	1.0010	1.0002	1.0005	1.0112
13	1.0000	1.0166	1.0000	1.0000	1.0000	1.0000	1.0000	1.0000	1.0000	1.0000	1.0000	1.0015
14	1.0162	1.0483	1.0024	1.0124	1.0023	1.0082	1.0023	1.0131	1.0008	1.0001	1.0004	1.0097
15	1.0869	1.1510	1.0133	1.0427	1.0084	1.0149	1.0127	1.0350	1.0046	1.0085	1.0044	1.0348
16	1.0265	1.0808	1.0038	1.0195	1.0058	1.0103	1.0085	1.0233	1.0035	1.0064	1.0032	1.0174
17	1.0525	1.1157	1.0135	1.0299	1.0078	1.0162	1.0118	1.0323	1.0042	1.0080	1.0040	1.0269
18	1.0426	1.0860	1.0082	1.0262	1.0073	1.0128	1.0121	1.0334	1.0042	1.0073	1.0035	1.0221
19	1.0264	1.0221	1.0000	1.0192	1.0074	1.0161	1.0055	1.0197	1.0035	1.0063	1.0030	1.0118

(continued)

Table 6.3 (continued)

DMU	2008	2009	2010	2011	2012	2013	2014	2015	2016	2017	2018	Avg
20	1.0257	1.0667	1.0032	1.0175	1.0033	1.0118	1.0030	1.0176	1.0011	1.0002	1.0005	1.0137
Avg	1.0369	1.0833	1.0054	1.0231	1.0048	1.0118	1.0059	1.0216	1.0024	1.0037	1.0025	1.0183

Note (a) We compute the degree of Malmquist index by Eq. (6.10). DMUs stand for 20 Japanese prefectures. (b) (1) Hokkaido, (2) Aomori, (3) Iwate, (4) Miyagi, (5) Akita, (6) Yamagata, (7) Fukushima, (8) Ibaraki, (9) Tochigi, (10) Gunma, (11) Saitama, (12) Chiba, (13) Tokyo, (14) Kanagawa, (15) Niigata, (16) Toyama, (17) Ishikawa, (18) Fukui, (19) Yamanashi and (20) Nagano

6.6.2 *Under Managerial Disposability*

Shifting from natural to managerial disposability, we consider two cases for managerial disposability: (a) no frontier crossover and (b) frontier crossover. Table 6.4 summarizes Malmquist index measures with no frontier crossover. Meanwhile, Table 6.5 summarizes Malmquist index measures with a possible occurrence of frontier crossover.

Table 6.4 exhibits that the Malmquist index measures have showed 0.8733 in 2009 and more than in the other annual periods (2008, 2010–2018) under the managerial disposability. The results indicate that there was a technology progress in their environmental protection activities. See the last raw of Table 6.4. This observation may be applicable to Table 6.5. The table summarizes the Malmquist index measure with a possible occurrence of frontier crossover. An important finding by comparing between Tables 6.4 and 6.5 is that the total average (1.0547) of Table 6.5 is larger than that (1.0139) of Table 6.4. This indicates that the incorporation of a possible occurrence of frontier crossover may be more sensitive than the case of no crossover. This finding implies that we need to consider a time lag in technology transfer. See Chap. 8 which discuss how to incorporate a time lag into DEA.

Figure 6.5 visually summarizes the change of Malmquist indexes under four cases. It is interesting to note that they have differences in their magnitudes at the initial stage but such differences are gradually converging along with the annual periods because DMUs (Japanese local units) can share knowledge with each other. Such information share is important for their technology developments on operation and environmental protection. Thus, we need to consider an occurrence of "convergence" in DEA-EA. See Chap. 7 that discusses the convergence issue of efficiency and index measures related to DEA-EA. The convergence is closely related to the investigation on a possible pass towards SDGs enhancement.

6.7 Discussion

This chapter discussed a new use of SDGs decomposition in a time horizon because most of data sets on energy and environment usually have a time series structure. In applying the SDGs assessment to such a time series data, we need to examine multiple components that produce a shift of an efficiency frontier over time. A unique feature of the proposed assessment is that it incorporates a framework of "Malmquist index" to examine the frontier shift among multiple periods. The frontier shift indicates a technology progress and/or managerial improvement during the observed periods. The computational process is different from Chapter 5 in which we have discussed a change of unified efficiency measures. Meanwhile, we measured a frontier change, not the efficiency changes, in this chapter.

Table 6.4 Malmquist index under managerial disposability: no frontier crossover

DMU	2008	2009	2010	2011	2012	2013	2014	2015	2016	2017	2018	Avg
1	1.0054	0.9241	0.9795	1.0066	0.9873	1.1743	0.9959	0.9773	1.0317	0.9913	1.0346	1.0098
2	1.0775	0.8504	1.0397	0.9204	1.1785	1.0743	0.9744	1.0273	0.9865	1.0316	1.0155	1.0160
3	1.0448	0.9299	1.0243	0.6718	1.4880	1.1607	1.0290	0.9504	1.0252	1.0720	0.9631	1.0327
4	0.9790	0.7324	1.1404	0.8924	1.2796	1.0233	0.9609	1.0004	1.0359	1.0566	0.9203	1.0019
5	1.1127	0.8780	0.8587	1.2695	0.9818	1.1537	1.0063	1.0422	0.9795	1.0487	0.9794	1.0282
6	0.9853	0.8748	1.0625	0.9871	1.1746	0.9306	1.0602	1.1034	1.0007	1.0029	0.9839	1.0151
7	1.0365	0.8798	0.9896	0.8087	1.1266	1.1767	0.9859	1.0122	1.0825	1.0511	0.9461	1.0087
8	1.0413	0.9146	1.0045	1.0233	0.7711	1.3020	1.0805	0.9649	1.0529	0.9669	1.0366	1.0144
9	0.9981	0.9152	0.9932	0.9112	1.0830	1.0929	0.9984	1.0841	1.0021	0.9427	1.0243	1.0041
10	0.9923	0.9427	1.0014	0.9203	1.1392	1.1354	0.9943	1.0078	1.0145	1.0712	0.9232	1.0129
11	1.1345	0.8276	1.0038	0.9600	1.0832	1.1094	1.0153	0.9671	1.0649	0.9607	0.9941	1.0110
12	0.9993	0.9261	1.0767	1.0060	1.0228	1.0188	1.0138	0.9846	0.9556	0.9709	1.0534	1.0026
13	1.0832	1.0061	1.0168	0.8191	1.1245	1.1395	0.9842	0.9380	1.0740	0.9830	0.9952	1.0149
14	1.0691	0.7830	1.1699	0.9864	1.1767	0.9190	1.0331	0.9516	1.0189	0.9571	1.1123	1.0161
15	0.9986	0.9316	0.9592	1.0129	1.0945	1.0327	1.0290	1.0446	0.9663	1.0589	0.9632	1.0083
16	0.9501	0.8947	0.8454	1.0676	1.3109	1.0414	0.9821	1.0625	1.0851	1.0349	0.9029	1.0161
17	1.0794	0.8724	0.8609	1.1012	1.1652	0.9955	1.2332	0.9204	1.1687	1.0082	0.8935	1.0272
18	1.0082	0.8722	0.8991	1.0986	1.0587	1.0804	1.0427	1.1302	1.0416	1.0231	0.9281	1.0166
19	1.0353	0.7474	1.1329	0.9051	1.2393	1.0564	1.0375	1.0076	1.0567	1.0215	1.0241	1.0240

(continued)

Table 6.4 (continued)

DMU	2008	2009	2010	2011	2012	2013	2014	2015	2016	2017	2018	Avg
20	0.9033	0.7640	1.1500	1.0323	1.0786	1.0311	1.0419	0.9600	1.0432	1.0270	0.9480	0.9981
Avg	1.0267	0.8733	1.0104	0.9700	1.1282	1.0824	1.0249	1.0068	1.0343	1.0140	0.9821	1.0139

Note (a) We compute the degree of Malmquist index by Eq. (6.13). DMUs stand for 20 Japanese prefectures. (b) (1) Hokkaido, (2) Aomori, (3) Iwate, (4) Miyagi, (5) Akita, (6) Yamagata, (7) Fukushima, (8) Ibaraki, (9) Tochigi, (10) Gunma, (11) Saitama, (12) Chiba, (13) Tokyo, (14) Kanagawa, (15) Niigata, (16) Toyama, (17) Ishikawa, (18) Fukui, (19) Yamanashi and (20) Nagano

Table 6.5 Malmquist index under managerial disposability: frontier crossover

DMU	2008	2009	2010	2011	2012	2013	2014	2015	2016	2017	2018	Avg
1	1.0600	1.1646	1.0679	1.0556	1.0851	1.0631	1.0205	1.0442	1.0469	1.0141	1.0277	1.0591
2	1.0600	1.1627	1.0679	1.0556	1.0851	1.0630	1.0205	1.0442	1.0468	1.0141	1.0277	1.0589
3	1.0600	1.1455	1.0591	1.0602	1.0851	1.0661	1.0171	1.0449	1.0504	1.0120	1.0239	1.0568
4	1.0600	1.1647	1.0679	1.0556	1.0851	1.0630	1.0205	1.0442	1.0468	1.0141	1.0277	1.0591
5	1.0600	1.1508	1.0679	1.0556	1.0851	1.0630	1.0198	1.0442	1.0468	1.0133	1.0273	1.0576
6	1.0600	1.1350	1.0536	1.0645	1.0851	1.0664	1.0169	1.0450	1.0551	1.0117	1.0219	1.0559
7	1.0600	1.1072	1.0447	1.0821	1.0851	1.0721	1.0148	1.0462	1.0635	1.0110	1.0184	1.0550
8	1.0600	1.1646	1.0679	1.0557	1.0851	1.0631	1.0205	1.0442	1.0469	1.0141	1.0277	1.0591
9	1.0600	1.1143	1.0412	1.0860	1.0851	1.0735	1.0143	1.0465	1.0648	1.0112	1.0183	1.0559
10	1.0600	1.1166	1.0445	1.0787	1.0851	1.0723	1.0145	1.0463	1.0600	1.0103	1.0179	1.0551
11	1.0600	1.0950	1.0406	1.0847	1.0851	1.0744	1.0134	1.0469	1.0636	1.0114	1.0191	1.0540
12	1.0600	1.1646	1.0679	1.0557	1.0851	1.0631	1.0205	1.0442	1.0469	1.0141	1.0277	1.0591
13	1.0219	1.0000	1.0040	1.0684	1.0363	1.0409	1.0025	1.0141	1.0000	1.0045	1.0009	1.0176
14	1.0600	1.1646	1.0679	1.0557	1.0851	1.0631	1.0205	1.0442	1.0469	1.0141	1.0277	1.0591
15	1.0600	1.1458	1.0604	1.0582	1.0851	1.0630	1.0196	1.0442	1.0481	1.0132	1.0269	1.0568
16	1.0600	1.1454	1.0638	1.0556	1.0851	1.0640	1.0190	1.0442	1.0521	1.0126	1.0245	1.0569
17	1.0600	1.1069	1.0509	1.0662	1.0851	1.0675	1.0140	1.0463	1.0600	1.0117	1.0206	1.0536
18	1.0600	1.1095	1.0500	1.0734	1.0851	1.0662	1.0178	1.0447	1.0563	1.0114	1.0211	1.0541
19	1.0600	1.1275	1.0551	1.0556	1.0851	1.0630	1.0171	1.0441	1.0599	1.0119	1.0206	1.0545

(continued)

Table 6.5 (continued)

DMU	2008	2009	2010	2011	2012	2013	2014	2015	2016	2017	2018	Avg
20	1.0600	1.1357	1.0609	1.0577	1.0851	1.0634	1.0185	1.0442	1.0468	1.0130	1.0264	1.0556
Avg	1.0581	1.1311	1.0552	1.0640	1.0827	1.0647	1.0171	1.0433	1.0504	1.0122	1.0227	1.0547

Note (a) We compute the degree of Malmquist index by Eq. (6.18). DMUs stand for 20 Japanese prefectures. (b) (1) Hokkaido, (2) Aomori, (3) Iwate, (4) Miyagi, (5) Akita, (6) Yamagata, (7) Fukushima, (8) Ibaraki, (9) Tochigi, (10) Gunma, (11) Saitama, (12) Chiba, (13) Tokyo, (14) Kanagawa, (15) Niigata, (16) Toyama, (17) Ishikawa, (18) Fukui, (19) Yamanashi and (20) Nagano

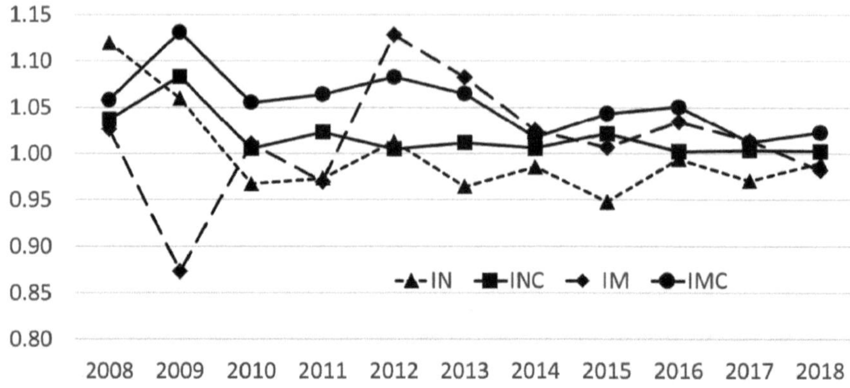

Fig. 6.5 Malmquist index measures under four cases. *Note* (a) Four conditions are due to 2 disability concepts × 2 crossover situations. (b) IN: Malmquist Index under Natural disposability with no crossover, INC: Malmquist Index under Natural disposability with crossover, IM: Malmquist Index under Managerial disposability with no crossover and IMC: Malmquist Index under Managerial disposability with frontier crossover

To attain the research objective, we conceptually separate the frontier shift index into six subcomponents, which are further divided into twelve different subcomponents (= 6 subcomponents × 2 disposability concepts) under natural or managerial disposability. The proposed measurement considers a possible occurrence of frontier crossover among different periods because technology diffusion usually has a time lag. The finding in this chapter will be further discussed in Chap. 7 that discusses the importance of convergence in DEA-EA. We will also explore a new DEA approach, based upon the finding, for a time lag in Chap. 8. Thus, the proposed frontier shift measurement becomes a useful methodology for the enhancement of SDGs.

References

Bjurek, H. (1996). The Malmquist total factor productivity index. *Scandinavian Journal of Economics, 98*, 303–3013.

Bjurek, H., & Hjalmarsson, L. (1995). Productivity in multiple output public services: A quadratic frontier function and the Malmquist index approach. *Journal of Public Economics, 56*, 447–460.

Bowlin, W. F. (1987). Evaluating the efficiency of US air force real-property maintenance activities. *Journal of the Operational Research Society, 38*, 127–135.

Goto, M., & Tsutsui, M. (1998). Comparison of productive and cost efficiencies among Japanese and US electric utilities. *Omega, 26*, 177–194.

Grifell-Tatje, E., & Lovel, C. A. K. (1995). A note on the Malmquist productivity index. *Economic Letters, 47*, 167–175.

Malmquist, S. (1953). Index number and indifferences surfaces. *Trabajos De Estatistica, 4*, 209–2042.

Sueyoshi, T., & Aoki, S. (2001). A use of a nonparametric statistic for DEA frontier shift: The Kruskal and Wallis rank test. *Omega, 29*, 1–18.

Sueyoshi, T., & Goto, M. (2001). Slack-adjusted DEA for time series analysis: Performance measurement of Japanese electric power generation industry in 1984–1993. *European Journal of Operational Research, 133*, 232–259.

Sueyoshi, T., & Goto, M. (2018). *Environmental Assessment on Energy and Sustainability by Data Envelopment Analysis*. John Wiley & Sons.

Thore, S., Kozmetsky, G., & Phillips, F. (1994). DEA of financial statements data: The US computer industry. *Journal of Productivity Analysis, 5*, 229–248.

Chapter 7
Club Convergence Among OECD Nations Under Managerial Disposability

Abstract Environmental protection is important for all nations, as discussed in Chap. 2. In preparing a policy to combat the climate change, so enhancing the level of ESG and SDGs, we use a new approach whose assessment is useful for promoting both sustainable development and green growth economy. The approach also assesses a technological progress over time, focusing upon pollution reduction. The methodology used in the approach is DEA-EA discussed in Chaps. 5 and 6. In this chapter, we apply DEA-EA to 37 OECD countries during 1995–2014, examine performance differences among country groups, and then discuss their convergences to multiple subgroups in a long run. Such convergence indicates an invariant status of their SDGs performances. As an extension of a previous study (Sueyoshi and Wang, Journal of Cleaner Production 250:1–13, 2020), which has compared between OECD and Non-OECD nations, this study focuses upon only OECD and examine whether we can find club (core group) convergences among the member nations. The DEA-EA, used in this chapter, examines whether OECD can provide member nations with an opportunity to improve the status of their green technology along with their economic growths. The underlying concepts incorporated into DEA-EA are *UEM* (Unified Efficiency) and *UIM* (Unified Index), both are under managerial disposability. The *UIM* finds a technology shift more clearly than the *UEM*. The *UEM* incorporates SDGs in a time horizon and the *UIM* extends it more clearly from a technology shift on environmental protection. Our empirical results indicate that there is the overall convergence of OECD nations in *UEM*, but we cannot find it in *UIM*. They are classified into two clubs in the *UIM* convergence assessment. The results indicate that there are uneven economic and environmental progresses between the two (higher and lower) member groups. The disparity implies that OECD membership does not guarantee uniform green growth and sustainable development for their developments for SDGs. We also find that "renewable and nuclear" energy shares are important for maintaining the higher group within OECD because both are energy sources with zero carbon emission.

Keywords OECD · Sustainable development · Convergence · Unified efficiency

T. Sueyoshi and M. Goto, *Environment and Sustainability for ESG and SDGs*,
https://doi.org/10.1007/978-981-96-2464-5_7

7.1 Introduction

Chapters 5 and 6 have discussed DEA-EA over time to understand an annual change of SDGs. However, the time span was limited within their research scope. This chapter extends the time span by considering an existence of "convergence" in a long run. In this chapter, the convergence implies whether we may find an existence of several core groups by examining their trends in a data set. Such different groups usually provide us with useful implications in a data domain.

Before describing the convergence, we need to mention the importance of our illustrative example discussed in this chapter. That is, UN (United Nations) adopted the 2030 Agenda for Sustainable Development in 2015, so providing a shared blueprint for peace and prosperity for people and the planet. At the heart, the UN includes the 17 SDGs which request an urgent call for action on all countries for global partnership as discussed in Chap. 2. In particular, Goal 13 of the SDGs: Climate Action discusses "Take urgent action to combat climate change and its impacts". The request contains "implement the UNFCCC (United Nations Framework Convention on Climate Change)", and "promote mechanisms to raise capacity for planning and management.[1] In a similar trend", the OECD (Organization for Economic Co-operation and Development)[2] also proposes an important strategy for green growth among member nations. The proposed new approach includes the measurement of group performance of OECD countries from their green growth developments in a long run because it is expected that the organization provides member nations with reliable data sets and policy suggestions for their green developments.

Here, considering a general trend of SDGs in OECD, this chapter examines, as an illustrative example, whether the member nations converge for sustainability development to make group development by which they may share their knowledge and educate each other in a form of international cooperation and technology shift. We examine an underlying influence of energy sector transition on the status of sustainable development in these countries. We also describe the effectiveness of unified index for future planning and assessment on sustainable development. Thus, this chapter is interested in group convergence among OECD nations so that we may examine whether the international cooperation exists on SDGs in a long run.

The remainder of this chapter has the following structure: Sect. 7.2 summarizes previous research related to the convergence issue. Section 7.3 describes underlying concepts along with null hypotheses to be examined. Section 7.4 describes the analytical frameworks used for this empirical study. Section 7.5 discusses a data set on OECD and summarizes empirical results. Section 7.6 concludes this research along with future research tasks. The appendix describes a computational algorithm and a nonparametric test used in this chapter.

---

[1] See Chap. 2 for a description on both ESG and SDGs.

[2] Http://www.oecd.org/greengrowth/whatisgreengrowthandhowcanithelpdeliversustainabledevelopment.htm

7.2 Previous Studies

Previous studies on group convergence have the following five research categories: First, studies on early efficiency and convergence examined whether the productivity and efficiency of OECD nations converged among countries over time. Here, the "convergence" implied that some nations attained a similar industrial path in international competition. This might be rephrased by whether SDGs had a similar developing path among different nations. For example, Dowrick and Nguyen (1989) belonged to this research group by examining whether a systematic tendency existed at an income level and converged within OECD nations between 1950 and 1985.

Second, the convergence (or a core group trend) was a dominant and stable research direction in previous studies that used with various methodologies. DEA, combined with the Malmquist index, was one of such popular methods for measuring the shift of efficiency frontiers and its related decomposition analysis. See Chap. 6 on Malmquist index and related decomposition that incorporated natural and managerial disposability concepts. An example of this group included the research prepared by Färe et al. (1994). The study analyzed the productivity growth of 17 OECD countries during 1979–1988 using DEA and computed the Malmquist productivity indexes from DEA results. Other examples, that applied DEA and the Malmquist productivity index, included Margaritis et al. (2002), Maudos et al. (2010) and Ozbugday et al. (2020). Margaritis et al. (2002) analyzed trends in labor productivity and its underlying determinants in a panel of OECD countries from 1979 to 2002. Their results indicated that on average gaps in productivity or income levels were narrowing down although there was no evidence that entire OECD comprised a single convergence, or "club". Maudos et al. (2010) analyzed labor productivity convergence in OECD countries during 1975–1990 and showed that a technical change did not exist on the labor productivity convergence. Ozbugday et al. (2020) analyzed efficiency levels of long-term care for a subset of OECD countries and conducted component decompositions. Their studies obtained similar results to the other two empirical studies (Maudos et al., 2010; Ozbugday et al., 2020).

Third, we find an important research work in EU KLEMS project.[3] The study created a data base for several measures on economic growth, productivity, employment creation, capital formation and technological change at the industry level for all EU (European Union) member states from 1970 onwards. The project was related to 2003–2008 and funded by European Commission. It published a series of research efforts on productivity based on growth accounting methodology. The articles from the project included van Ark et al. (2008) as well as Inklaar and Timmer (2008) that introduced a data set that compared output, inputs and productivity at an industry level for a set of 30 OECD countries and discussed the productivity convergence across industries and countries.

[3] See a detail project description in http://www.euklems.net /index.html. EU KLEMS is an industry level, growth and productivity research project. EU KLEMS stands for EU level analysis of capital (K), labor (L), energy (E), materials (M) and service (S) inputs.

Fourth, the relationship between economic growth and environmental protection was consistent with the concept of OECD that discussed the importance of economic development and green growth. Some of those studies particularly focused upon energy use and economic development because the former was directly linked to various pollutions through CO_2 emissions from fossil fuels. For example, Wang et al. (2019) used a panel data of OECD countries' industrial sectors, and analyzed how the stringency of environmental regulation policies influenced green effort and productivity growth. Some other studies in this research group were also interested in the convergence of productivity and efficiency.

Fifth, the energy efficiency of OECD countries was a popular topic in previous studies, which examined whether the energy productivity converged among countries. They were interested in relationship between economic growth and environmental protection from energy conservation. The research group included Le Pen and Sevi (2010) and Liddle (2010) which revealed the convergence in energy productivity among OECD countries. Parker and Liddle (2017) analyzed energy productivity convergence for 33 OECD and non-OECD countries during 1971–2008. They identified four clubs for economy-wide energy productivity and six clubs for manufacturing energy productivity. In contrast to these findings on energy productivity convergence, Apergis and Christou (2016) found a lack of convergence among 26 OECD countries.

Comparing with the previous research works, we describe the following new research concerns: First, most of previous studies have used standard DEA models, so that they have not incorporated undesirable outputs (e.g., CO_2 emission). Meanwhile, we use DEA-EA that is a holistic approach to estimate the performance of many organizations by relatively comparing multiple factors (i.e., inputs, desirable and undesirable outputs). The DEA-EA can incorporate undesirable outputs in its analytical structure.

Second, there are two drawbacks of DEA-EA. One of the two drawbacks is that it cannot evaluate the performance of organizations in a steady state of a long run. To overcome the methodological difficulty, Sueyoshi and Wang (2020) has first combined DEA-EA with a convergence algorithm over time. We follow their research direction. The other drawback is that DEA-EA may produce many efficient DMUs. To handle the practical difficulty, the previous studies have used "sensitivity analysis" by dropping an efficient DMU and reevaluated it from the remaining DMU group. We do not follow the same analysis, rather incorporating the formulation for ESG into the DEA-EA formulations. Thus, the convergence process used in this chapter are different from the previous study (Sueyoshi & Wang, 2020).

Third, as an application of DEA-EA, we examine the unified (operational and environmental) efficiency and index of 37 OECD countries from 1995 to 2014. This assessment employs the four types of CO_2 emissions as multiple undesirable outputs, thus looking for the reduction of environmental factors in the proposed measures. This indicates that this study is part of research efforts toward SDGs, being different from the previous study (Sueyoshi & Wang, 2020) which has used only a single undesirable output (e.g., CO_2 emission).

Finally, this chapter incorporates a possible occurrence of frontier crossover between multiple efficiency frontiers over time and calculates an index measure by applying DEA-EA. See Chap. 6 on the frontier crossover. This study examines an overall trend of unified efficiency and index measures of OECD nations in a long run. Using the efficiency and the index, we examine whether there is converge(s) among the OECD member nations as a whole and/or some clubs comprising part of member nations. Thus, we can examine whether the OECD membership may enhance their industrial developments for SDGs.

7.3 Underlying Concepts

This chapter applies DEA-EA to a data set on OECD countries which contains a column vector of X with m inputs, a column vector of G with s desirable outputs and a column vector of B with h undesirable outputs. We focus upon the concept of "managerial disposability", because we are interested in environmental assessment as part of ESG and SGDs. See Sueyoshi and Goto (2012, 2018), along with Chap. 3, for a detail description on the relationship between the managerial disposability and ESG and SDGs.

The managerial disposability is a concept to measure the level of environmental sustainability. For an example, let us consider a coal-fired power plant. The plant may increase the amount of coal combustion to generate electricity. Here, even if the power plant increases the amount of coal combustion for electricity generation, the increase may produce the less amount of CO_2 emission by its managerial effort and/or engineering effort. The power company may consider a change of environmental regulation as a business opportunity. Under the managerial disposability, the investment for green technology may provide electric firms with such an opportunity to enhance not only green image but also economic success. We think that both economic prosperity and environmental protection by green technology are not mutually exclusive in modern business. Rather, both are necessary condition toward sustainable development and green growth, so implying the enhancement of ESG and SDGs. See Chap. 3.

This section describes several important underlying concepts to understand the managerial disposability.

Null-joint hypothesis: The first concept is the null-joint hypothesis between G (desirable outputs) and B (undesirable outputs). The hypothesis implies that components of B are "by-products" of G. In other words, B cannot exist without G. The concept is straightforward and realistic in discussing the production process and environment measured by DEA-EA. See Chap. 3. We incorporate the assumption between G and B into our formulations under managerial disposability.

Convergence: If a green growth rate depends on human and physical capital factors, the growth rate would be expected to slow down over a long run because of their diminishing marginal effects. However, there is another important factor: technology development. Here, we can easily imagine that different countries start their industrialization processes (paths) with different periods. Similarly, their green efforts start from different periods in their industrial developments, following their own unique backgrounds. Advanced industries have initiated their industrial processes at an early stage but have exhibited slow green developments. Less developed nations, meanwhile, have been paying attention to their economic achievements, not considering their efforts on pollution preventions. As a result, many nations have different industrial structures, technology advancements, and economic growth situations. See Sueyoshi and Goto (2018, Chap. 14).

The view on different industrializations, discussed above, often leads to the concept of "club convergence", so being an important part of SDGs. The concept implies that peer countries with similar industrial conditions for economic growth, energy efficiency, and green technology, may catch up each other and become comparable in a global market. However, they are usually not belonging to a large global group, pertaining to different conditions. If the club (i.e., a group of nation convergence) is true, variations in different policy targets may be effective for industrial developments. The concern is applicable to green technology and sustainable developments. Thus, we attempt to investigate the convergence issue, which is a path for development, by applying DEA-EA. This type of application measures the sustainable level for green growth to enhance the level of SDGs.

Here, this chapter specifies our research concerns by using the following hypotheses (H_0):

First H_0: There is no difference in their performance measures of nations.
Second H_0: There is no club convergence in their performance measures.
Third H_0: Energy sector transition for zero-carbon emissions does not influence the club convergence.

To examine the above null hypotheses, we attempt to statistically reject the first hypothesis. The alternative hypothesis indicates that OECD can provide members with an opportunity to learn each other and to access advanced green technology and economic development by their international cooperation, mutual understanding and technology shift. As a consequence, all OECD nations may promote their industrial structures and statuses toward similar economic and green technology, so reducing the amount of GHG emissions. However, as discussed above, the technology development may be different among member nations because they have different industrial structures and economic conditions. As a result, all member nations may have different technology structures so that their performance measures may be classified into several groups.

In the second null hypothesis, we attempt to statistically reject similar development processes by measuring the existence of "club convergence" among multiple groups. In this examination, we examine the two hypotheses by a statistical test (log t test) and a convergence test, both were first used by Sueyoshi and Wang (2020) who have applied them to DEA-EA measures. In a similar vein, Goto and Sueyoshi (2022) have followed after their work (Sueyoshi & Wang, 2020) from different perspectives on club convergence by using DEA-EA.

The third null hypothesis, directly related to ESG and SDGs, intends to reject an assumption that primary energy consumption from zero-carbon emission sources do not influence differences in the sustainable development of OECD countries. We attempt to identify which energy source produce convergence which separates all the nations into core trends (groups).

7.4 Approach

7.4.1 Computation Scheme

Figure 7.1 visually summarizes the whole computational process of DEA-EA to measure the club convergence. Figure 7.1 separates the whole computation process into three sub-processes. First, we sample a data set to which we apply DEA-EA. Models (7.2) and Model (7.4) produce *UEM* (Unified Efficiency under Managerial disposability) and *UIM* (Unified Index under Managerial disposability), respectively. Second, we apply the convergence algorithm to examine whether club (core) groups exist or not. Finally, we apply the rank sum test (K-W: Kruskal–Wallis) on efficiency and index measures in the club groups. Appendix 1 of this chapter discusses on the convergence algorithm and Appendix 2 describes the K-W rank sum test.

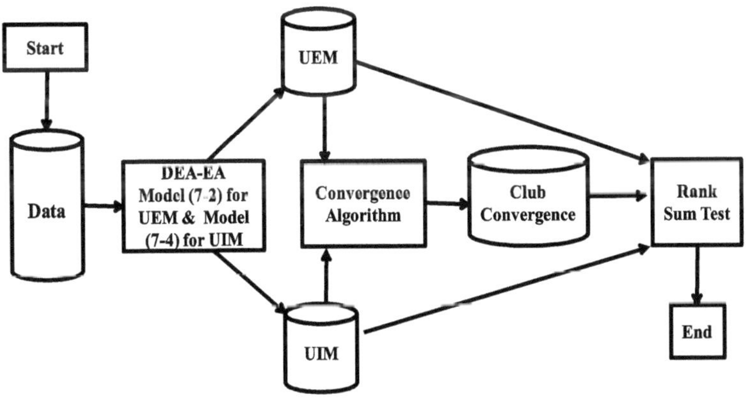

Fig. 7.1 Computational process. *Note* (a) The software for convergence is STATA/MP17.0, Statacorp, Lakeway Dr. College Stations TX 77845-4512, USA. (b) *UEM* stands for unified efficiency under managerial disposability. *UIM* stands for unified index under managerial disposability. Chapter 4 describes the concept of managerial disposability. (c) Appendix 1 summarizes the convergence algorithm. (d) Appendix 2 describes the rank sum test

7.4.2 Formulations

This section describes mathematical formulations to measure the degree of unified (operational and environmental) efficiency and its related index of DMUs (e.g., OECD nations). Each "country" corresponds to a DMU in DEA studies. We start specifying the following nomenclatures:

x_{ijt} is the i th input of the j th DMU at the t th period, g_{rjt} is the r th desirable output of the j th DMU at the t th period, b_{fjt} is the f th undesirable output of the j th DMU at the t th period, ξ_{kt} is an inefficiency score of the k th DMU at the t th period, d_{ikt}^{x} is an unknown slack variable of the i th input of the k th DMU at the t th period, d_{fkt}^{b} is an unknown slack variable of the f th undesirable output of the k th DMU at the t th period, λ_{jt} is an unknown column vector of intensity variables on the j th DMU at the t th period, ε_s is a prescribed very small number, R_i^x is a data range related to the i th input, R_f^b is a data range related to the f th undesirable output, and t is the observed t th period ($t = 1, \ldots, T$). All production factors (x_{ijt}, g_{rjt} and b_{fjt}) are strictly positive.

We use the following two types of data ranges (R) according to the upper and lower bounds on production factors:

$$R_i^x = (m+h)^{-1}\left(\max_{j\&t}\{x_{ijt}\} - \min_{j\&t}\{x_{ijt}\}|j = 1, \ldots, n \text{ and } t = 1, \ldots, T\}\right)^{-1} \quad \text{and}$$
$$R_f^b = (m+h)^{-1}\left(\max_{j\&t}\{b_{ijt}\} - \min_{j\&t}\{b_{ijt}\}|j = 1, \ldots, n \text{ and } t = 1, \ldots, T\}\right)^{-1}. \tag{7.1}$$

The use of the data ranges avoids an occurrence of zero in multipliers (i.e., dual variables). Such an occurrence implies that corresponding production factors (e.g.,X, G and B) are not fully utilized in the efficiency and index measures. We need to avoid such a difficulty in our empirical studies. The managerial disposability does not need the ranges for desirable outputs so that Eq. (7.1) drops R_r^g. See the objective function of Models (7.2) and (7.4).

Unified Efficiency under Managerial Disposability (*UEM*): We assume that there are n DMUs at the t th period to be examined and all of their production factors are strictly positive in a data domain. All DMUs are specified by $j = 1, \ldots, n$ in the proposed formulations. This chapter uses the following formulation to compute the *UEM* of the specific k th DMU, where k is a specific DMU to be examined from all n ones ($j = 1, \ldots, n$) under managerial disposability at the specific t th period:

$$
\begin{aligned}
& \textit{Maximize}\ \xi_{kt} + \varepsilon_s \left[\sum_{i=1}^{m} R_i^x d_{ikt}^{x+} + \sum_{f=1}^{h} R_f^b d_{fkt}^b \right] \\
& s.t. \quad \sum_{t=1}^{T} \sum_{j=1}^{n} x_{ijt}\lambda_{jt} - d_{ikt}^{x+} = x_{ikt} \quad (i = 1, \ldots, m \ \&\ \textit{specific}\ t = 1, \ldots, T), \\
& \qquad \sum_{t=1}^{T} \sum_{j=n}^{n} g_{rjt}\lambda_{jt} - \xi_{kt} g_{rkt} = g_{rkt} \quad (r = 1, \ldots, s \ \&\ \textit{specific}\ t = 1, \ldots, T), \\
& \qquad \sum_{t=1}^{T} \sum_{j=n}^{n} b_{fjt}\lambda_{jt} + d_{fkt}^b + \xi_{kt} b_{fkt} = b_{fkt} \quad (f = 1, \ldots, h \ \&\ \textit{specific}\ t = 1, \ldots, T), \\
& \qquad \lambda_{jt} \geq 0 \quad (j = 1, \ldots, n \ \&\ t = 1, \ldots, T),\ \xi_{kt} : URS, \\
& \qquad d_{ikt}^{x+} \geq 0 \quad (i = 1, \ldots, m \ \&\ \textit{specific}\ t = 1, \ldots, T)\ \& \\
& \qquad d_{fkt}^b \geq 0 \quad (f = 1, \ldots, h \ \&\ \textit{specific}\ t = 1, \ldots, T).
\end{aligned} \tag{7.2}
$$

Model (7.2) has the following eight unique features: First, Model (7.2) is a primal form of Model (4.44) which incorporates the minimization of undesirable outputs so that we may identify green investments. Model (7.2) also incorporates the maximization of desirable outputs to increase the status of economic prosperity. That is the important part of ESG. Model (7.2) incorporates all the periods in the form of a cross-sectional structure of Model (7.2). That follows the principle of SDGs, implying the sustainability in a long run. Second, the unknown vector $\lambda_{jt} = (\lambda_{11}, \ldots, \lambda_{nT})^{\mathrm{Tr}}$ is referred to as "structural" or "intensity" variable in the DEA terminology. Note that Tr is a vector transpose. They connect all the production factors (X, G and B) in each efficiency frontier. They are not parameters, rather being weights, connecting production factors. Third, the production and pollution possibility set of Model (7.2) assumes constant DTS (Damages to Scale: undesirable outputs increase proportionally due to a unit increase in inputs) because $\sum_{t=1}^{T} \sum_{j=1}^{n} b_{fjt}\lambda_{jt} = 1$ does not exist in the Model (7.2). It is possible to incorporate the equation to make it variable DTS. Fourth, Model (7.2) considers only single-sided input deviations ($d_{ikt}^{x+} = \sum_{t=1}^{T} \sum_{j=1}^{n} x_{ijt}\lambda_{jt} - x_{ikt} \geq 0$) on all input factors to attain the status of managerial disposability. As a result, the formulation increases the amount of X until they attain the efficiency frontiers. Model (7.2) specifies the upper bound of X by increasing X and reducing B as specified by $\sum_{t=1}^{T} \sum_{j=1}^{n} x_{ijt}\lambda_{jt}^{*} = x_{ikt} + d_{ikt}^{x+*} (i = 1, \ldots, m)$ and $\sum_{t=1}^{T} \sum_{j=1}^{n} b_{fjt}\lambda_{jt}^{*} = b_{fkt} - d_{fkt}^{b*} - \xi_{kt}^{*} b_{fkt} (f = 1, \ldots, h)$ on optimality, where the superscript (*) indicates optimality. Fifth, a scalar value (ξ_{kt}) stands for a unified "inefficiency" score that measures a distance to attain the two efficiency frontiers on G and B of the k th DMU at the tth period. Therefore, we need to measure the level of unified efficiency by subtracting it from unity. Sixth, a small scalar value (ε_s) indicates relative importance between the inefficiency measure and the total sum of slacks. We need to prescribe the small number in the range that the efficiency measure of all DMUs locates between zero (standing for full inefficiency) and unity (standing for full efficiency). For example, this study applies 0.0001 for ε_s in the computation of Model (7.2). Seventh, this type of measurement (i.e., a distance measure) belongs to the "Debreu-Farrell" criterion. Finally, the equations $\sum_{t=1}^{T} \sum_{j=1}^{n} g_{rjt}\lambda_{jt} - \xi_{kt} g_{rkt} = g_{rkt}$ on desirable outputs drop slacks related to G in order to incorporate a possible occurrence of technological progress in each DMU (e.g., OECD country in this chapter).

We measure a unified efficiency under managerial disposability (UEM) of the k th DMU at the tth period by the following equation:

$$UEM_{kt}^{*} = 1 - \left[\xi_{kt}^{*} + \varepsilon_{s}\left(\sum_{i=1}^{m} R_{i}^{x} d_{ikt}^{x+*} + \sum_{f=1}^{h} R_{f}^{b} d_{fkt}^{b*}\right)\right]. \tag{7.3}$$

Here, the inefficiency measure and all slack variables are on the optimality of Model (7.2). We obtain the degree of unified efficiency by subtracting the inefficiency from unity.

Unified Index under Managerial Disposability (UIM): Next, we measure the unified index (UIM) of the k th DMU at the t th period. To extend the efficiency measure to its corresponding index measure, we modify Model (7.2) as follows:

$$\begin{aligned}
&\textit{Maximize}\ \xi_{kt} + \varepsilon_{s}\left[\sum_{i=1}^{m} R_{i}^{x} d_{ikt}^{x+} + \sum_{f=1}^{h} R_{f}^{b} d_{fkt}^{b}\right] \\
&s.t. \quad \sum_{j=1}^{n} x_{ijt-1}\lambda_{jt-1} - d_{ikt}^{x+} = x_{ikt}\ (i = 1, \ldots, m\ \&\ \textit{specific}\ t = 2, \ldots, T), \\
&\qquad \sum_{j=n}^{n} g_{rjt-1}\lambda_{jt-1} - \xi_{kt} g_{rkt} = g_{rkt}\ (r = 1, \ldots, s\ \&\ \textit{specific}\ t = 2, \ldots, T), \\
&\qquad \sum_{j=n}^{n} b_{fjt-1}\lambda_{jt-1} + d_{fkt}^{b} + \xi_{kt} b_{fkt} = b_{fkt}\ (f = 1, \ldots, h\ \&\ \textit{specific}\ t = 2, \ldots, T), \\
&\qquad \lambda_{jt-1} \geq 0\ \ (j = 1, \ldots, n\ \&\ t = 2, \ldots, T),\ \xi_{kt} : URS(k : \textit{specific}\ t = 2, \ldots, T), \\
&\qquad d_{ikt}^{x+} \geq 0\ \ (i = 1, \ldots, m\ \&\ \textit{specific}\ t = 2, \ldots, T)\ \& \\
&\qquad d_{fkt}^{b} \geq 0\ \ (f = 1, \ldots, h\ \&\ \textit{specific}\ t = 2, \ldots, T),
\end{aligned} \tag{7.4}$$

The index measures the performance of the k th DMU in the specific t th period by comparing itself with the previous ($t - 1 = 1, \ldots, T - 1$) efficiency frontier.

Model (7.4) assumes that there is no overlap among efficiency frontiers in the production and pollution possibility set during multiple periods. Recently, many industrial nations pay attention to a technological progress for green growth so that we may accept the assumption. The assumption makes it possible to compare the performance of the k th DMU at t th period with those at the $t - 1$ period as formulated in Model (7.4). Furthermore, it is important to note that we can formulate and solve Model (7.4) more easily than its augmented form.

We measure the UIM of the k th DMU at the tth period by the following equation:

$$UIM_{kt}^{*} = 1 - \left[\xi_{kt}^{*} + \varepsilon_{s}\left(\sum_{i=1}^{m} R_{i}^{x} d_{ikt}^{x+*} + \sum_{f=1}^{h} R_{f}^{b} d_{fkt}^{b*}\right)\right]. \tag{7.5}$$

Here, the inefficiency measure and all slack variables are on the optimality of Model (7.4). We determine the degree of UIM by subtracting the level of inefficiency from unity as specified in Eq. (7.5). Unlike (7.3), Eq. (7.5) produces an index that may be larger than unity, showing an efficiency progress of the k th DMU from an efficiency frontier one period ago $(t-1)$.

7.5 Illustrative Examples

The following two articles provides readers with illustrative examples:

Sueyoshi, T., Wang, D. (2020) Rank dynamics and club convergence of sustainability development in countries around the world. Journal of Cleaner Production, 250: 1–13.

Goto, M., Sueyoshi, T. (2022) Sustainable development and convergence under energy sector transition in industrial nations: An application of DEA environmental assessment. Socio-Economic Planning Sciences 101316: 1–13.

7.5.1 Data

This chapter uses a data set, first obtained by Goto and Sueyoshi (2022), which consists of a desirable output, three inputs and four undesirable outputs regarding 37 OECD countries. The OECD was established in 1961 to promote the improvement of economic and social welfare around the world. The predecessor was established in 1948 by 16 European countries.

The OECD has been serving as a forum for information exchange and dialogue among industrialized countries so that they can share and find solutions to the world's economic, social, environmental and sustainability challenges as expressed by the spirit of ESG and SDGs. The OECD works with governments to contribute to economic growth, increased trade liberalization and support for developing countries. According to Trade Union Advisory Committee to the OECD, "becoming a member of the OECD is a complex procedure which goes beyond signing its founding convention. Countries wishing to become OECD members must demonstrate a "readiness" and a "commitment" to adhere to essentially two fundamental requirements: (a) democratic societies committed to rule of law and protection of human rights, and (b) open, transparent and free-market economies.

The data set was sampled from World Bank Open Data (https://data.worldbank.org/) for 1995 to 2014.[4] The research of Goto and Sueyoshi (2022) assembled it from

[4] The last year in our data base, which we can access for this study, was July 2021. The latest available year depends on the data series, e.g., a data on GDP was obtained through 2019, but energy use was only available through 2014 for Colombia, Latvia, and Lithuania, although the other nations has published the series through 2015. In addition, undesirable outputs (CO_2 emissions) were available through 2014 for France and Italy, while the other nations through 2016. To use a balanced panel data set for this study, our data set period was from 1995 to 2014.

the data source. Table 7.1 summarizes the descriptive statistics of the data set used in this study.

Following Färe et al. (1994), we consider real-term GDP as a desirable output, and capital and labor are used as inputs. We also use energy as an input, considering its use as a source of undesirable outputs (CO_2). We have four undesirable outputs. They are (a) the amounts of CO_2 emitted from solid fuel consumption (mainly coal), (b) that of liquid fuel consumption (mainly from petroleum-derived fuels), (c) that of gaseous fuel (mainly from natural gas) and (d) that of the other sources.[5]

7.5.2 *Results*

7.5.2.1 *UEM* and *UIM*

Using the data set in Table 7.1, we have obtained *UEM* and *UIM* estimates. We first consider general implications from these estimates and then apply a statistical test (i.e., a rank sum test) to them in this section. Table 7.2 has the following two findings:

One of the two findings is that Table 7.2, obtained from Goto and Sueyoshi (2022), summarizes the *UEM* estimates of OECD nations. These estimates, obtained after from Model (7.1), summarize Avg. (Average), Max. (Maximum), Min. (Minimum) and DoC (Degree of Change: the degree of a specific year divided by that of a base year). For example, we have calculated the *UEM* measure in 2014 divided by that of 1995 (the base year). The efficiency (*UEM*) is less than or equal to unity. The magnitude of DoC indicates an annual efficiency change during the observed periods (1995–2014). Note that both Sueyoshi and Wang (2020) and Goto and Sueyoshi (2022) have discussed time series analysis using DEA-EA.

The other finding is that the country average of *UEM* in each year (Table 7.2, the third row from the bottom) has ranged from 0.674 in 1998 to 0.815 in 2014, indicating the overall improvement in the unified efficiency of OECD nations during 1995–2014. The table lists averages, maximums, and minimums at the bottom. Along with the trend, we have found the gradual improvement although the maximum value of *UEM* is constant at unity. The total annual average of *UEM* for each country (Table 7.2: the second column from the right) ranged from the minimum at 0.478 of Korea to the maximum at 0.987 of Switzerland. Korea was the third on its DoC at 1.54 after Italy (1.60) and Ireland (1.59), all these countries presented stronger growth in unified efficiency during the period. The average of DoC (at the last column) ranged from 0.70 (Portugal) to 1.60 (Italy). Note that the magnitude of DoC has depended on the status of the starting period (1995) in this study. For example, the *UEM* of Portugal was unity in 1995, but it drastically decreased to 0.526 in 2004 and slightly recovered after the year to reach 0.698 in 2014. Meanwhile, Italy exhibited 0.524 in

[5] The last undesirable output is calculated from statistics as CO_2 emissions from the burning of fossil fuels and the manufacture of cement minus the former three undesirable outputs (CO_2 from solid, liquid, and gaseous fuels).

Table 7.1 Descriptive statistics

	Production factors							
	GDP	Capital	Labor	Energy	CO_2-solid	CO_2-liquid	CO_2-gas	CO_2-other
Countries	constant 2010 mio US$	constant 2010 mio US$	mio # Total	1000 kg of oil equivalent	kilo ton	kilo ton	kilo ton	kilo ton
Australia	981,540	243,682	10.5563	114,590,884	190,872	100,502	53,132	4464
Austria	360,295	85,822	4.0686	31,315,555	13,612	33,512	16,445	2134
Belgium	436,326	97,917	4.5637	56,728,753	20,564	52,246	31,581	3555
Canada	1,397,368	319,521	17.4552	259,445,873	102,364	239,667	176,591	10,337
Chile	181,293	35,424	7.0773	28,179,543	15,443	36,734	9656	2177
Colombia	242,385	48,341	19.9496	28,599,892	11,237	33,899	15,594	5829
Czech Republic	178,799	48,437	5.1931	43,021,084	77,873	19,737	16,888	2011
Denmark	307,508	59,467	2.8936	19,117,044	17,383	22,143	9311	1469
Estonia	17,704	4570	0.6834	5,328,834	13,298	1906	1460	251
Finland	225,013	51,232	2.6202	34,143,644	23,626	25,341	7835	645
France	2,460,415	540,778	28.4403	255,883,144	50,205	215,723	84,540	9813
Germany	3,237,013	656,937	41.0344	331,596,061	322,209	294,363	168,290	17,433
Greece	271,220	52,433	4.8976	27,094,768	33,161	43,282	4945	6211
Hungary	120,677	26,016	4.2329	25,514,577	13,443	16,669	22,878	1461
Iceland	12,183	2859	0.1761	3,918,723	324	1716	0	55
Ireland	192,378	42,782	2.0392	13,538,312	9,614	20,245	8287	1501
Israel	197,425	39,798	3.0780	19,889,742	27,235	27,798	4071	2703
Italy	2,078,879	420,363	24.0550	170,312,498	53,363	219,607	136,549	18,358

(continued)

Table 7.1 (continued)

	Production factors							
	GDP	Capital	Labor	Energy	CO_2-solid	CO_2-liquid	CO_2-gas	CO_2-other
Countries	constant 2010 mio US$	constant 2010 mio US$	mio # Total	1000 kg of oil equivalent	kilo ton	kilo ton	kilo ton	kilo ton
Japan	5,531,471	1,416,635	66.9732	495,090,545	397,608	601,207	175,104	34,967
Korea, Rep	911,132	294,119	24.0677	210,018,630	202,298	193,434	60,838	25,960
Latvia	21,590	5032	1.1033	4,374,778	466	4178	2775	197
Lithuania	32,289	6153	1.5955	8,412,182	779	7540	5219	400
Luxembourg	45,705	8363	0.2102	3,783,189	524	6649	2132	435
Mexico	968,461	201,791	43.5130	166,506,217	38,905	270,703	102,294	25,558
Netherlands	773,231	162,703	8.3932	78,167,835	28,241	67,972	80,379	1539
New Zealand	130,866	26,985	2.1324	17,305,687	5802	16,819	9282	698
Norway	395,306	81,763	2.4797	27,578,410	3316	26,628	11,299	1963
Poland	390,019	76,339	17.5877	95,456,755	223,947	55,688	26,181	7306
Portugal	221,718	48,256	5.3223	23,549,326	11,684	34,105	6339	3937
Slovak Republic	72,112	17,451	2.6305	17,816,133	16,522	7331	12,020	1690
Slovenia	41,903	10,066	0.9978	6,896,775	5624	7188	1869	541
Spain	1,262,106	300,028	20.5466	124,286,332	63,834	157,691	51,181	17,029
Sweden	439,352	98,879	4.7437	50,080,741	9705	37,741	2083	1221
Switzerland	526,180	123,705	4.2381	25,764,428	520	31,485	6006	2018
Turkey	657,638	156,433	23.2991	88,542,705	98,900	76,668	50,310	23,178
United Kingdom	2,290,991	386,701	30.5493	211,333,171	139,823	184,287	180,155	8977
United States	13,634,534	2,783,260	150.6189	2,218,174,001	1,946,218	2,236,054	1,232,131	51,547

Note (a) mio stands for million. # stands for a number. (b) *Data Source* Goto and Sueyoshi (2022)

Table 7.2 *UEM* from 1995 to 2014

Country	1995	1996	1997	1998	1999	2000	2001	2002	2003	2004	2005	2006	2007	2008	2009	2010	2011	2012	2013	2014	Avg	DoC
Australia	0.647	0.636	0.668	0.687	0.682	0.699	0.750	0.733	0.724	0.743	0.734	0.742	0.753	0.743	0.753	0.753	0.745	0.768	0.802	0.775	0.727	1.20
Austria	0.666	0.647	0.664	0.658	0.692	0.714	0.700	0.694	0.681	0.673	0.670	0.682	0.689	0.702	0.726	0.742	0.762	0.775	0.772	0.782	0.705	1.17
Belgium	0.512	0.493	0.507	0.520	0.543	0.573	0.561	0.595	0.579	0.596	0.604	0.625	0.656	0.646	0.657	0.644	0.650	0.687	0.686	0.687	0.601	1.34
Canada	0.457	0.460	0.457	0.445	0.460	0.472	0.481	0.496	0.489	0.496	0.514	0.512	0.535	0.556	0.568	0.578	0.598	0.600	0.615	0.608	0.520	1.33
Chile	0.862	0.816	0.620	0.574	0.594	0.589	0.618	0.614	0.635	0.632	0.619	0.621	0.539	0.627	0.635	0.644	0.628	0.632	0.635	0.666	0.640	0.77
Colombia	1.000	0.933	0.844	0.840	1.000	0.952	1.000	1.000	1.000	1.000	0.979	0.957	1.000	0.957	1.000	1.000	1.000	1.000	0.868	1.000	0.966	1.00
Czech Republic	0.659	0.661	0.661	0.640	0.664	0.683	0.696	0.711	0.699	0.685	0.693	0.707	0.695	0.710	0.746	0.784	0.773	0.807	0.829	0.807	0.715	1.22
Denmark	0.684	0.663	0.666	0.701	0.703	0.762	0.753	0.781	0.802	0.798	0.842	0.802	0.818	0.851	0.951	0.935	0.955	0.973	0.978	0.997	0.821	1.46
Estonia	1.000	1.000	0.872	0.675	0.639	1.000	0.681	0.683	0.678	0.685	0.709	0.769	0.803	0.784	0.969	0.908	0.881	0.895	0.959	1.000	0.829	1.00
Finland	0.704	0.656	0.683	0.673	0.688	0.741	0.765	0.745	0.721	0.737	0.766	0.748	0.783	0.797	0.828	0.819	0.819	0.845	0.901	0.841	0.763	1.19
France	0.713	0.698	0.726	0.724	0.739	0.770	0.753	0.769	0.774	0.773	0.781	0.787	0.808	0.825	0.845	0.876	0.877	0.901	0.911	0.934	0.799	1.31
Germany	0.628	0.628	0.624	0.628	0.651	0.672	0.582	0.701	0.723	0.743	0.759	0.763	0.819	0.801	0.808	0.826	0.836	0.840	0.840	0.855	0.741	1.36
Greece	0.830	0.789	0.751	0.646	0.590	0.540	0.536	0.535	0.530	0.539	0.524	0.530	0.535	0.520	0.539	0.560	0.570	0.563	0.583	0.607	0.591	0.73
Hungary	0.594	0.616	0.602	0.616	0.631	0.669	0.689	0.739	0.753	0.761	0.752	0.741	0.733	0.752	0.764	0.822	0.877	0.887	0.885	0.895	0.739	1.51
Iceland	1.000	0.897	0.983	0.920	1.000	0.845	0.875	0.811	0.843	0.857	0.946	1.000	1.000	1.000	0.982	0.976	1.000	1.000	1.000	1.000	0.947	1.00
Ireland	0.544	0.538	0.544	0.557	0.535	0.567	0.524	0.558	0.553	0.547	0.585	0.609	0.612	0.629	0.677	0.730	0.793	0.910	0.814	0.863	0.634	1.59
Israel	0.635	0.680	0.685	0.717	0.744	0.761	0.736	0.774	0.737	0.637	0.640	0.591	0.598	0.531	0.557	0.555	0.564	0.554	0.674	0.750	0.656	1.18
Italy	0.524	0.534	0.539	0.538	0.544	0.551	0.559	0.554	0.563	0.581	0.602	0.617	0.638	0.659	0.675	0.710	0.718	0.780	0.804	0.836	0.626	1.60
Japan	0.541	0.544	0.560	0.583	0.581	0.589	0.610	0.619	0.632	0.651	0.653	0.671	0.690	0.712	0.738	0.765	0.756	0.746	0.757	0.774	0.659	1.43
Korea, Rep	0.416	0.380	0.362	0.407	0.384	0.379	0.396	0.406	0.429	0.436	0.476	0.505	0.505	0.543	0.556	0.552	0.586	0.596	0.606	0.639	0.478	1.54
Latvia	1.000	1.000	0.722	0.764	1.000	1.000	1.000	1.000	0.964	1.000	1.000	1.000	1.000	1.000	0.956	0.849	0.875	0.990	0.977	1.000	0.955	1.00

(continued)

Table 7.2 (continued)

Country	1995	1996	1997	1998	1999	2000	2001	2002	2003	2004	2005	2006	2007	2008	2009	2010	2011	2012	2013	2014	Avg	DoC
Lithuania	1.000	1.000	0.964	1.000	1.000	1.000	1.000	0.897	0.938	0.869	0.788	0.691	0.735	0.744	0.861	0.734	0.723	0.717	0.693	0.708	0.853	0.71
Luxembourg	0.466	0.476	0.487	0.499	0.512	0.525	0.532	0.556	0.580	0.539	0.574	0.527	0.519	0.512	0.527	0.518	0.506	0.541	0.579	0.575	0.528	1.23
Mexico	0.596	0.532	0.544	0.528	0.542	0.510	0.472	0.450	0.425	0.453	0.433	0.434	0.427	0.447	0.465	0.467	0.480	0.500	0.524	0.515	0.487	0.87
Netherlands	0.759	0.776	0.797	0.815	0.823	0.849	0.843	0.863	0.889	0.896	0.899	0.896	1.000	0.923	0.963	0.976	0.972	1.000	0.982	0.956	0.894	1.26
New Zealand	0.833	0.824	0.841	0.841	0.822	0.826	0.875	0.867	0.816	0.835	0.844	0.853	0.817	0.746	0.896	0.852	0.895	0.882	0.841	0.870	0.844	1.04
Norway	0.658	0.635	0.613	0.614	0.620	0.628	0.631	0.663	0.644	0.657	0.676	0.688	0.669	0.639	0.650	0.672	0.681	0.682	0.711	0.728	0.658	1.11
Poland	1.000	0.863	0.736	0.669	0.670	0.661	0.685	0.711	0.685	0.652	0.661	0.623	0.616	0.612	0.646	0.635	0.629	0.661	0.711	0.722	0.692	0.72
Portugal	1.000	1.000	0.954	0.707	0.535	0.559	0.542	0.510	0.546	0.526	0.505	0.553	0.561	0.571	0.611	0.661	0.671	0.730	0.684	0.698	0.656	0.70
Slovak Republic	0.695	1.000	0.801	1.000	0.862	1.000	0.846	0.779	0.820	0.831	0.811	0.837	0.849	0.842	0.877	0.853	0.870	0.880	0.898	0.947	0.865	1.36
Slovenia	0.471	0.438	0.435	0.468	0.455	0.497	0.493	0.513	0.509	0.524	0.535	0.527	0.549	0.500	0.558	0.599	0.607	0.611	0.651	0.655	0.530	1.39
Spain	0.573	0.569	0.547	0.540	0.525	0.525	0.516	0.521	0.523	0.522	0.530	0.545	0.554	0.580	0.607	0.640	0.683	0.755	0.784	0.776	0.591	1.36
Sweden	0.725	0.720	0.760	0.770	0.798	0.825	0.815	0.780	0.814	0.839	0.862	0.900	0.933	0.918	1.000	0.953	0.950	0.975	0.979	1.000	0.866	1.38
Switzerland	0.950	0.957	0.996	1.000	1.000	0.979	0.967	0.987	1.000	0.985	0.966	0.991	1.000	1.000	1.000	0.973	0.997	1.000	0.996	1.000	0.987	1.05
Turkey	0.746	0.695	0.677	0.697	0.656	0.607	0.631	0.626	0.645	0.671	0.702	0.721	0.732	0.752	0.793	0.812	0.822	0.825	0.983	1.000	0.740	1.34
United Kingdom	0.674	0.683	0.719	0.727	0.730	0.758	0.770	0.797	0.813	0.818	0.824	0.843	0.870	0.891	0.924	0.928	0.964	0.983	1.000	1.000	0.836	1.48
United States	0.511	0.516	0.523	0.545	0.556	0.565	0.566	0.575	0.574	0.578	0.586	0.604	0.616	0.640	0.666	0.673	0.685	0.696	0.691	0.692	0.603	1.35
Avg	**0.710**	**0.701**	**0.679**	**0.674**	**0.680**	**0.698**	**0.690**	**0.692**	**0.695**	**0.696**	**0.704**	**0.708**	**0.720**	**0.721**	**0.756**	**0.756**	**0.767**	**0.789**	**0.800**	**0.815**	**0.723**	**1.197**
Max	**1.000**	**1.000**	**0.996**	**1.000**	**1.000**	**1.000**	**1.000**	**1.000**	**1.000**	**1.000**	**1.000**	**1.000**	**1.000**	**1.000**	**1.000**	**1.000**	**1.000**	**1.000**	**1.000**	**1.000**	**0.987**	**1.596**
Min	**0.416**	**0.380**	**0.362**	**0.407**	**0.384**	**0.379**	**0.396**	**0.406**	**0.425**	**0.436**	**0.433**	**0.434**	**0.427**	**0.447**	**0.465**	**0.467**	**0.480**	**0.500**	**0.524**	**0.515**	**0.478**	**0.698**

1995, which was lower than Portugal, but it continuously improved to reach 0.836 in 2014, so achieving a high level of DoC. Thus, the degree of DoC has explained how much each country attains the improvement on unified efficiency by preparing policy efforts on environmental protection and economic growth during the observed periods (e.g., 1995–2014).

Table 7.3, obtained from Goto and Sueyoshi (2022), presents the annual development of *UIM* of 37 OECD countries with averages, maximums, and minimums at the bottom. The values over unity indicates that each nation belongs to a status of technological advancement from the frontier of one period before. On the other hand, the values less than or equal to unity indicate that the nation is in a status of technological stagnation or retreat. The table indicates that some countries (e.g., Iceland, Sweden, and Switzerland) have exhibited index measures more than unity in most years. Meanwhile, other countries (e.g., Australia, Belgium, and Canada) have exhibited less than unity in their magnitudes during all years. Thus, there were variations among OECD countries in the status of technological advancement and retreat in the observed annual periods (1995–2014).

7.5.2.2 Group Performance in *UEM* and *UIM*

We classify 37 countries into four groups according to their annual periods when they have obtained OECD membership. The classification is because we use the timing of each nation's entry into OECD as a proxy variable to express their levels of membership maturity in economic, environmental and technological conditions. We comparatively examine the degree of *UEM* and that of *UIM* among the classified groups. They are the following four groups:

Group 1 consists of 20 original member countries. They have joined in OECD since 1961 as founding members. The first group contained Austria, Belgium, Denmark, France, Germany, Greece, Iceland, Ireland, Italy, Luxemburg, Netherland, Norway, Portugal, Spain, Sweden, Switzerland, Turkey, the United Kingdome, the United States, and Canada.

Group 2 includes four early member countries that have joined before 1980. They were Japan (1964), Finland (1969), Australia (1971), and New Zealand (1973). The annual periods, when these members have joined OECD, are very close to those of the original members.

Group 3 includes six mid-term member countries that have joined by the year 2000. They were Mexico (1994), Czech Republic (1995), Hungary (1996), Poland (1996), Korea (1996) and Slovak Republic (2000). This group's joining periods are very different from both Group 2 and Group 4.

Group 4 comprises seven new member countries that have joined after 2000. They were Chile (2010), Slovenia (2010), Israel (2010), Estonia (2010), Latvia (2016), Lithuania (2018), and Colombia (2020).

Table 7.3 *UIM* from 1996 to 2014

Country	1996	1997	1998	1999	2000	2001	2002	2003	2004	2005	2006	2007	2008	2009	2010	2011	2012	2013	2014	Avg
Australia	0.869	0.916	0.920	0.916	0.925	0.957	0.910	0.911	0.933	0.903	0.917	0.887	0.823	0.840	0.813	0.957	0.811	0.975	0.888	0.898
Austria	0.930	**1.000**	0.868	0.896	0.907	0.847	0.854	0.828	0.827	0.819	0.840	0.842	0.801	0.822	0.838	0.829	0.826	0.810	0.841	0.854
Belgium	0.742	0.753	0.752	0.794	0.826	0.774	0.782	0.769	0.825	0.835	0.849	0.844	0.764	0.742	0.740	0.723	0.746	0.732	0.721	0.774
Canada	0.834	0.815	0.755	0.777	0.756	0.713	0.723	0.703	0.721	0.726	0.689	0.665	0.650	0.663	0.633	0.670	0.662	0.660	0.626	0.707
Chile	0.868	0.808	0.771	0.868	0.745	0.737	0.709	0.754	0.758	0.739	0.751	0.768	0.900	**1.079**	0.911	0.905	0.939	0.956	**1.071**	0.844
Colombia	**1.020**	**1.020**	0.995	**1.054**	**1.031**	**1.073**	0.986	0.990	0.999	0.974	**1.028**	**1.042**	**1.023**	0.992	0.983	0.962	**1.006**	0.968	0.920	**1.003**
Czech Republic	0.922	**1.018**	0.982	**1.027**	0.940	**1.023**	0.966	**1.015**	0.982	**1.009**	**1.032**	0.974	0.974	0.981	0.879	0.904	0.936	0.964	0.883	0.969
Denmark	0.853	0.849	0.878	0.887	0.925	0.881	0.938	0.949	0.969	0.977	0.985	0.978	0.909	**1.030**	0.988	**1.007**	**1.013**	**1.000**	**1.033**	0.950
Estonia	**1.125**	**1.055**	**1.068**	0.994	**1.025**	0.894	**1.119**	0.888	**1.004**	0.911	0.928	0.984	**1.094**	**1.273**	0.946	**1.098**	**1.002**	**1.073**	**1.259**	**1.039**
Finland	**1.022**	**1.090**	0.976	**1.025**	**1.047**	**1.006**	**1.006**	0.963	**1.002**	**1.067**	0.958	0.958	0.947	**1.206**	0.929	0.891	0.915	0.955	0.862	0.991
France	0.963	0.984	0.949	0.964	0.991	0.929	0.944	0.970	0.964	0.965	0.960	0.941	0.913	0.958	0.943	0.957	0.980	0.960	**1.007**	0.960
Germany	0.868	0.851	0.843	0.869	0.897	0.858	0.877	0.910	0.926	0.937	0.944	0.987	0.910	0.928	0.899	0.906	0.895	0.880	0.882	0.898
Greece	0.975	0.931	0.828	0.809	0.719	0.684	0.691	0.721	0.707	0.669	0.658	0.647	0.583	0.625	0.652	0.632	0.620	0.652	0.669	0.709
Hungary	**1.025**	0.963	0.952	**1.016**	0.959	0.861	0.930	0.977	0.966	0.984	0.962	0.926	0.904	0.887	0.926	**1.263**	**1.001**	0.996	**1.157**	0.982
Iceland	**1.121**	**1.092**	**1.150**	**1.091**	0.932	**1.193**	**1.591**	**1.163**	**1.123**	**1.045**	**1.173**	**1.072**	**1.073**	**1.014**	0.959	**1.037**	**1.030**	2.000	0.971	**1.149**
Ireland	0.731	0.714	0.719	0.677	0.710	0.654	0.697	0.713	0.726	0.761	0.784	0.777	0.723	0.735	0.793	0.839	0.950	0.829	0.887	0.759
Israel	0.924	**1.008**	**1.041**	**1.032**	**1.021**	0.960	0.976	0.958	0.827	0.796	0.735	0.741	0.623	0.657	0.672	0.642	0.627	0.734	0.835	0.832
Italy	0.702	0.698	0.699	0.711	0.730	0.713	0.704	0.711	0.763	0.780	0.796	0.805	0.763	0.791	0.854	0.802	0.834	0.846	0.899	0.768
Japan	0.958	0.979	0.977	0.788	0.772	0.751	0.778	0.780	0.790	0.784	0.806	0.806	0.781	0.833	0.823	0.810	0.785	0.780	0.795	0.820
Korea, Rep	**1.028**	0.893	0.929	0.615	0.631	0.578	0.628	**1.005**	0.960	0.689	0.708	0.671	0.678	0.668	0.931	0.739	0.650	0.658	0.702	0.756
Latvia	0.974	**1.194**	0.970	2.000	**1.119**	**1.061**	**1.066**	0.973	0.847	**1.054**	**1.053**	**1.045**	**1.019**	0.987	0.923	0.900	0.863	**1.041**	**1.015**	**1.058**

(continued)

Table 7.3 (continued)

Country	1996	1997	1998	1999	2000	2001	2002	2003	2004	2005	2006	2007	2008	2009	2010	2011	2012	2013	2014	Avg
Lithuania	**1.004**	0.998	0.972	**1.082**	**1.080**	**1.286**	**1.011**	**1.049**	0.967	0.933	0.932	0.934	0.914	0.896	0.809	0.891	0.984	0.863	**1.011**	0.980
Luxembourg	0.632	0.635	0.649	0.653	0.655	0.625	0.660	0.641	0.589	0.654	0.604	0.621	0.552	0.573	0.601	0.537	0.594	0.602	0.598	0.615
Mexico	0.909	0.892	0.803	0.749	0.623	0.645	0.568	0.535	0.555	0.527	0.552	0.542	0.532	0.575	0.532	0.569	0.745	0.729	0.795	0.651
Netherlands	0.977	0.992	0.989	0.975	**1.018**	0.993	**1.049**	**1.020**	**1.019**	0.998	**1.025**	**1.079**	**1.012**	**1.067**	**1.070**	**1.006**	**1.023**	0.998	0.975	**1.015**
New Zealand	**1.018**	**1.147**	0.966	0.998	**1.021**	**1.071**	**1.023**	0.948	0.987	0.985	0.951	0.999	0.853	0.971	0.941	0.954	0.930	0.873	0.907	0.976
Norway	0.927	0.881	0.850	0.850	0.833	0.811	0.821	0.831	0.834	0.845	0.844	0.798	0.735	0.754	0.753	0.761	0.753	0.762	0.782	0.812
Poland	0.983	**1.033**	0.983	0.992	**1.006**	0.929	0.989	0.939	0.888	0.902	0.895	0.853	0.820	0.820	0.737	0.748	0.734	0.787	0.850	0.889
Portugal	**1.031**	0.955	0.882	0.738	0.723	0.673	0.645	0.697	0.659	0.630	0.685	0.692	0.658	0.692	0.737	0.731	0.795	0.730	0.816	0.746
Slovak Republic	0.735	**1.070**	**1.117**	**1.035**	**1.405**	0.909	0.948	**1.075**	0.993	**1.007**	**1.055**	**1.030**	0.993	**1.041**	0.979	0.975	0.957	0.985	**1.056**	**1.019**
Slovenia	0.649	0.642	0.689	0.673	0.715	0.673	0.713	0.713	0.729	0.720	0.704	0.701	0.606	0.656	0.647	0.675	0.684	0.814	0.744	0.692
Spain	0.760	0.754	0.754	0.739	0.734	0.691	0.717	0.704	0.699	0.690	0.704	0.700	0.675	0.706	0.752	0.747	0.817	0.850	0.868	0.740
Sweden	**1.053**	**1.112**	**1.028**	**1.107**	**1.148**	**1.036**	**1.019**	**1.049**	**1.046**	**1.111**	**1.134**	**1.135**	**1.055**	**1.093**	0.979	0.995	**1.003**	**1.008**	0.968	**1.057**
Switzerland	**1.052**	**1.023**	**1.013**	**1.017**	**1.022**	0.985	**1.032**	**1.010**	0.982	**1.001**	**1.022**	**1.029**	0.996	**1.021**	0.986	**1.058**	**1.022**	0.983	**1.095**	**1.019**
Turkey	0.818	0.850	0.908	0.869	0.804	0.777	0.778	0.793	0.825	0.849	**1.071**	0.906	0.881	0.926	0.970	0.849	0.982	0.876	0.988	0.880
United Kingdom	0.945	0.969	0.966	0.964	0.986	0.951	0.980	**1.005**	**1.003**	0.997	**1.019**	**1.027**	**1.020**	**1.053**	0.986	**1.050**	**1.057**	**1.034**	**1.027**	**1.002**
United States	0.773	0.791	0.794	0.822	0.811	0.782	0.783	0.793	0.775	0.767	0.791	0.830	0.816	0.936	0.804	0.740	0.747	0.717	0.703	0.788
Avg	**0.911**	**0.929**	**0.902**	**0.921**	**0.897**	**0.865**	**0.881**	**0.877**	**0.869**	**0.866**	**0.880**	**0.871**	**0.837**	**0.878**	**0.846**	**0.858**	**0.863**	**0.894**	**0.895**	**0.881**
Max	**1.125**	**1.194**	**1.150**	**2.000**	**1.405**	**1.286**	**1.591**	**1.163**	**1.123**	**1.111**	**1.173**	**1.135**	**1.094**	**1.273**	**1.070**	**1.263**	**1.057**	**2.000**	**1.259**	**1.149**
Min	**0.632**	**0.635**	**0.649**	**0.615**	**0.623**	**0.578**	**0.568**	**0.535**	**0.555**	**0.527**	**0.552**	**0.542**	**0.532**	**0.573**	**0.532**	**0.537**	**0.594**	**0.602**	**0.598**	**0.615**

Note The values over unity are marked by bold in the table, indicating that a nation belongs to a status of technological advancement from the frontier of one period ago

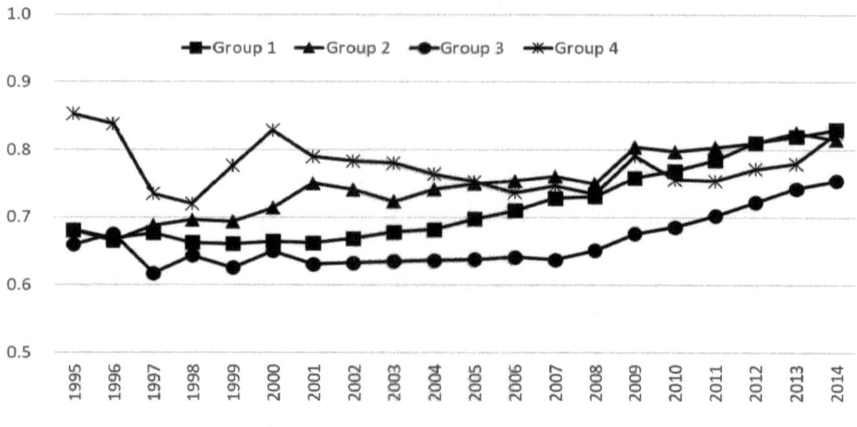

Fig. 7.2 Group averages in *UEM*

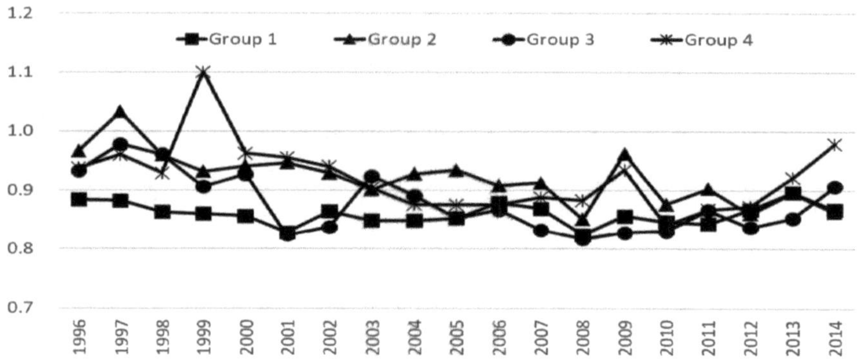

Fig. 7.3 Group averages in *UIM*

Figures 7.2 and 7.3 depict the average of *UEM* and that of *UIM* for each group, respectively.[6] Figure 7.2 indicates a gradually increasing trend of *UEM* for all groups except for Group 4. The group attained the highest in 1995, but it decreased after the year and ended at the level that the group was approximately same as Groups 1 and 2. Group 3 (mid-term member countries) continued to show the lowest efficiency over the annual periods, although it began to increase after 2007. Meanwhile, Fig. 7.3 exhibits a slightly decreasing trend on *UIM* toward 2008 for all groups. They turned to increase after 2008. Group 4 was the highest in 2014 among the four groups. However, the index was less than unity. This indicates that a technological progress for green growth was weak for all groups of OECD countries. Indeed, the group average of *UIM*, being over unity, appeared only in 1997 for Group 2 and in 1999 for Group 4. Thus, the OECD nations has limited achievement on pollution prevention in the observed annul periods.

[6] Tables 7.2 and 7.3 provide detailed values of Figs. 7.2 and 7.3, respectively.

K-W rank sum test on the first hypothesis: To statistically examine the first null hypothesis whether there are no differences among the four groups in *UEM* and *UIM*, we have used the K-W (Kruskal–Wallis) rank sum test on the measures. An important feature of the K-W test is that it is non-parametric for testing whether sample ranks originate from the same distribution or not. The research of Sueyoshi and Goto (2018) has provided both a detailed description on the H statistics (obtained from the K-W test) and a description regarding how to deal with many firms on a same rank. The test statistics was $H = 29.8$ for *UEM* and $H = 20.9$ for *UIM* after adjusting ties, indicating "both reject the first null hypothesis at the 1% level of significance". Thereby, there were differences among the four groups in the two measures over the observed periods.

Convergence test on the second hypothesis: We have statistically confirmed that the four groups are different in *UEM* and *UIM* by the K-W tests. The proceeding investigation is whether they have converged as a whole or in groups (clubs) over time. To test whether the whole or group convergence exists, we have used the method and its related theory proposed by Phillips and Sul (2007). Note that Sueyoshi and Wang (2020) have extended the method to handle the environmental concern by *UEM*. No study has previously applied the convergence algorithm to *UIM*. Since their previous study (Sueyoshi & Wang, 2020) has provided a detailed description on the test, we do not discuss it here, rather summarizing the computational process in Appendix 1 of this chapter.

We examine the convergence of the OECD countries in terms of *UEM* and *UIM*, using the club convergence algorithm. Tables 7.4 and 7.5 report club convergence results. By both *UEM* and *UIM*, we reject the null hypothesis of full convergence (i.e., convergence among all the countries) over 1990–2014 at the 1% level. Rather, the convergence analysis exhibits strong evidence in club convergence (i.e., convergence of countries into subgroups).

To examine the convergence issue further, we have performed the statistical (i.e., $\log t$) test to examine the second null hypothesis on convergence as a whole sample. The statistical test has rejected the null hypothesis by both measures (*UEM* and *UIM*) with a 1% significance level. Since the test has rejected the convergence for a whole sample, we have identified the existence of convergence clubs. The test found that there was one convergence club consisting of 34 countries for *UEM*, while the test also identified two convergence clubs for *UIM*, in which one group (Club 1) consisted of 24 countries[7] and the other group (Club 2) consisted of 13 countries[8]. Only three countries were not included in the convergence club for *UEM*: Israel, Luxembourg, and Mexico. The three countries remained lower efficiency over the periods; in particular, the latter two countries were the first and the second lowest in *UEM* in 2014 showing 0.575 and 0.515, respectively.

---

[7] The Club 1 group consists of Australia, Chile, Colombia, Czech Republic, Denmark, Estonia, Finland, France, Germany, Hungary, Iceland, Ireland, Italy, Latvia, Lithuania, Mexico, Netherlands, New Zealand, Slovak Republic, Spain, Sweden, Switzerland, Turkey, and United Kingdom.

[8] The Club 2 group consists of Austria, Belgium, Canada, Greece, Israel, Japan, the Republic of Korea, Luxembourg, Norway, Poland, Portugal, Slovenia, and the United States.

Table 7.4 *UEM* of four groups (convergence)

Country Group	Statistics	1995	1996	1997	1998	1999	2000	2001	2002	2003	2004	2005	2006	2007	2008	2009	2010	2011	2012	2013	2014
1	Avg	0.681	0.669	0.677	0.662	0.661	0.664	0.662	0.669	0.678	0.682	0.698	0.710	0.728	0.731	0.759	0.769	0.784	0.811	0.820	0.830
	Max	1.000	1.000	0.996	1.000	1.000	0.979	0.967	0.987	1.000	0.985	0.966	1.000	1.000	1.000	1.000	0.976	1.000	1.000	1.000	1.000
	Min	0.457	0.460	0.457	0.445	0.460	0.472	0.481	0.496	0.489	0.496	0.505	0.512	0.519	0.512	0.527	0.518	0.506	0.541	0.579	0.575
2	Avg	0.681	0.665	0.688	0.696	0.693	0.714	0.750	0.741	0.723	0.741	0.750	0.754	0.761	0.749	0.804	0.797	0.804	0.810	0.825	0.815
	Max	0.833	0.824	0.841	0.841	0.822	0.826	0.875	0.867	0.816	0.835	0.844	0.853	0.817	0.797	0.896	0.852	0.895	0.882	0.901	0.870
	Min	0.541	0.544	0.560	0.583	0.581	0.589	0.610	0.619	0.632	0.651	0.653	0.671	0.690	0.712	0.738	0.753	0.745	0.746	0.757	0.774
3	Avg	0.660	0.675	0.618	0.643	0.626	0.650	0.631	0.633	0.635	0.636	0.638	0.641	0.638	0.651	0.676	0.686	0.702	0.722	0.742	0.754
	Max	1.000	1.000	0.801	1.000	0.862	1.000	0.846	0.779	0.820	0.831	0.811	0.837	0.849	0.842	0.877	0.853	0.877	0.887	0.898	0.947
	Min	0.416	0.380	0.362	0.407	0.384	0.379	0.396	0.406	0.425	0.436	0.433	0.434	0.427	0.447	0.465	0.467	0.480	0.500	0.524	0.515
4	Avg	0.853	0.838	0.734	0.720	0.776	0.828	0.790	0.783	0.780	0.764	0.753	0.736	0.746	0.735	0.791	0.756	0.754	0.771	0.779	0.825
	Max	1.000	1.000	0.964	1.000	1.000	1.000	1.000	1.000	1.000	1.000	1.000	1.000	1.000	1.000	1.000	1.000	1.000	1.000	0.977	1.000
	Min	0.471	0.438	0.435	0.468	0.455	0.497	0.493	0.513	0.509	0.524	0.535	0.527	0.539	0.500	0.557	0.555	0.564	0.554	0.635	0.655
All	Avg	0.710	0.701	0.679	0.674	0.680	0.698	0.690	0.692	0.695	0.696	0.704	0.708	0.720	0.721	0.756	0.756	0.767	0.789	0.800	0.815
	Max	1.000	1.000	0.996	1.000	1.000	1.000	1.000	1.000	1.000	1.000	1.000	1.000	1.000	1.000	1.000	1.000	1.000	1.000	1.000	1.000
	Min	0.416	0.380	0.362	0.407	0.384	0.379	0.396	0.406	0.425	0.436	0.433	0.434	0.427	0.447	0.465	0.467	0.480	0.500	0.524	0.515

Table 7.5 *UIM* of four groups (convergence)

Country group	Statistics	1996	1997	1998	1999	2000	2001	2002	2003	2004	2005	2006	2007	2008	2009	2010	2011	2012	2013	2014
1	Avg	0.884	0.882	0.864	0.860	0.856	0.829	0.864	0.849	0.849	0.853	0.879	0.869	0.824	0.856	0.847	0.844	0.867	0.897	0.868
	Max	1.121	1.112	1.150	1.107	1.148	1.193	1.591	1.163	1.123	1.111	1.173	1.135	1.073	1.093	1.070	1.058	1.057	2.000	1.095
	Min	0.632	0.635	0.649	0.653	0.655	0.525	0.645	0.641	0.589	0.630	0.604	0.621	0.552	0.573	0.601	0.537	0.594	0.602	0.598
2	Avg	0.967	1.033	0.960	0.932	0.941	0.946	0.929	0.901	0.928	0.935	0.908	0.912	0.851	0.962	0.877	0.903	0.860	0.896	0.863
	Max	1.022	1.147	0.977	1.025	1.047	1.071	1.023	0.963	1.002	1.067	0.958	0.999	0.947	1.206	0.941	0.957	0.930	0.975	0.907
	Min	0.869	0.916	0.920	0.788	0.772	0.751	0.778	0.780	0.790	0.784	0.806	0.806	0.781	0.833	0.813	0.810	0.785	0.780	0.795
3	Avg	0.934	0.978	0.961	0.906	0.927	0.824	0.838	0.924	0.891	0.853	0.867	0.832	0.817	0.828	0.831	0.866	0.837	0.853	0.907
	Max	1.028	1.070	1.117	1.035	1.405	1.023	0.989	1.075	0.993	1.009	1.055	1.030	0.993	1.041	0.979	1.263	1.001	0.996	1.157
	Min	0.735	0.892	0.803	0.615	0.623	0.578	0.568	0.535	0.555	0.527	0.552	0.542	0.532	0.575	0.532	0.569	0.650	0.658	0.702
4	Avg	0.937	0.961	0.929	1.101	0.962	0.955	0.940	0.904	0.876	0.875	0.876	0.888	0.883	0.934	0.842	0.868	0.872	0.921	0.979
	Max	1.125	1.194	1.068	2.000	1.119	1.286	1.119	1.049	1.004	1.054	1.053	1.045	1.094	1.273	0.983	1.098	1.006	1.073	1.259
	Min	0.649	0.642	0.689	0.673	0.715	0.678	0.709	0.713	0.729	0.720	0.704	0.701	0.606	0.656	0.647	0.642	0.627	0.734	0.744
All	Avg	0.911	0.929	0.902	0.921	0.897	0.865	0.881	0.877	0.869	0.866	0.880	0.871	0.837	0.878	0.846	0.858	0.863	0.894	0.895
	Max	1.125	1.194	1.150	2.000	1.405	1.286	1.591	1.163	1.123	1.111	1.173	1.135	1.094	1.273	1.070	1.263	1.057	2.000	1.259
	Min	0.632	0.635	0.649	0.615	0.623	0.578	0.568	0.535	0.555	0.527	0.552	0.542	0.532	0.573	0.532	0.537	0.594	0.602	0.598

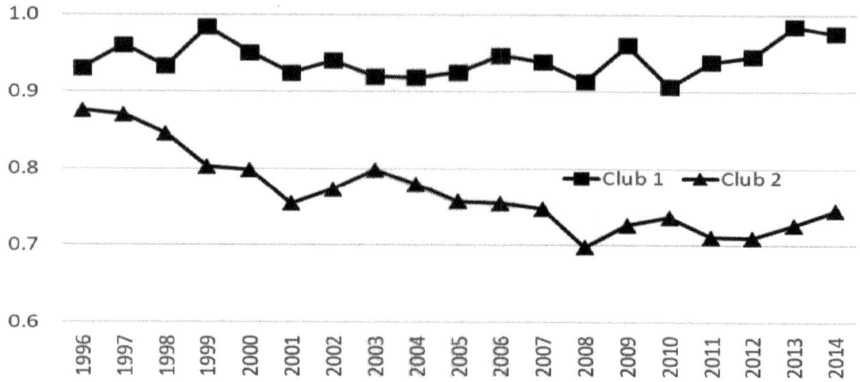

Fig. 7.4 Club averages in *UIM*

The result rejects overall convergence in the two efficiency measures, but supports the existence of convergence clubs in OECD countries. In particular, a difference in *UIM* existed between the two clubs, as depicted in Fig. 7.4. Club 1 slightly increased in the index, revealing that countries in the club were advancing in the unified index for sustainable development.

K-W rank sum test on the third hypothesis: To statistically examine the third null hypothesis on whether primary consumption from energy sources, which are not zero-carbon emission energy sources, produce differences in the status of sustainable developments. This study has applied the K-W rank sum test to compare between countries classified in Club 1 and those in Club 2 on *UIM*. This study does not examine *UEM* because we have already identified a single convergence club consisting of 34 countries with only three excepted countries. For the research purpose, we have performed the three tests between two clubs whether there are statistically significant differences on the primary energy consumption share from (a) nuclear, (b) renewables, and (c) zero-carbon emissions energy sources (nuclear and renewables). We have obtained the data on the primary energy consumption volumes from Our World in Data (https://ourworldindata.org/energy).

We have computed and summarized all shares by primary energy consumption volume from (a), (b) and (c) divided by the total volume of primary energy consumption, including fossil fuel energy sources such as oil and gas. Table 7.6 summarizes the average of these shares on the OECD nations from 1995 to 2014.

The null hypothesis for the tests is whether there are no differences in shares between the two converged clubs. The test statistics (H statistics) are (a) $H = 7.5$, (b) $H = 13.91$, (c) $H = 8.51$, after adjusting ties, indicating the null hypothesis is rejected for all three tests at the 1% significance level. Table 7.7 presents the shares in primary energy consumption of nuclear, renewables, and zero-carbon sources (nuclear and renewables) for each club as well as the test statistics of K-W tests.

The shares in Table 7.7 and Fig. 7.5 indicate that Club 1 (the higher *UIM* group (see footnote 7)] holds higher than Club 2 [the lower *UIM* group (see footnote 8)] in nuclear (8.57% for Club 1 vs. 5.63% for Club 2 on averages), renewables (14.17% for

Table 7.6 Average shares (%) in primary energy consumption and GDP (1995–2014)

Country	Nuclear	Renewables	Zero Carbon	GDP (2010 billion US$)
Australia	0.00	4.42	4.42	997
Austria	0.00	29.63	29.63	364
Belgium	16.54	1.61	18.16	441
Canada	6.46	27.74	34.20	1417
Chile	0.00	18.99	18.99	185
Colombia	0.00	29.76	29.76	245
Czech Republic	12.12	2.24	14.37	181
Denmark	0.00	10.79	10.79	310
Estonia	0.00	1.46	1.46	18
Finland	17.18	17.60	34.78	228
France	38.20	6.90	45.09	2484
Germany	10.13	5.66	15.79	3258
Greece	0.00	4.86	4.86	274
Hungary	13.76	1.42	15.18	122
Iceland	0.00	72.28	72.28	12
Ireland	0.00	4.11	4.11	197
Israel	0.00	0.15	0.15	201
Italy	0.00	8.76	8.76	2090
Japan	10.98	4.88	15.86	5556
Korea, Rep	13.02	0.57	13.59	930
Latvia	0.00	19.23	19.23	22
Lithuania	24.58	2.23	26.81	33
Luxembourg	0.00	1.29	1.29	47
Mexico	1.44	5.65	7.09	982
Netherlands	0.98	1.88	2.86	782
New Zealand	0.00	34.73	34.73	133
Norway	0.00	66.40	66.40	400
Poland	0.00	1.87	1.87	397
Portugal	0.00	16.58	16.58	224
Slovak Republic	20.00	6.33	26.33	73
Slovenia	17.85	13.24	31.09	43
Spain	9.96	10.26	20.23	1279
Sweden	28.70	33.62	62.33	445
Switzerland	20.43	28.23	48.66	531
Turkey	0.00	11.11	11.11	670
United Kingdom	8.26	2.50	10.76	2318
United States	8.30	4.83	13.13	13,814

Table 7.7 Shares of energy sources in total primary energy consumption and K-W rank sum test results

Country Group	Club 1				Club 2			
Shares (%) in Primary Energy Consumption and GDP (constant 2010 billion US$)	Nuclear	Renewables	Zero Carbon	GDP	Nuclear	Renewables	Zero Carbon	GDP
Avg	8.57	14.17	22.75	733	5.63	13.36	18.98	1854
Max	41.71	82.84	82.84	3639	20.03	71.13	71.13	16,243
Min	0.00	0.02	0.02	9	0.00	0.02	0.02	31
S.D	11.40	16.24	18.92	900	6.86	18.30	17.73	3765
K-W test	Nuclear		Renewables		Zero Carbon		GDP	
H statistics	7.50		13.91		8.51		8.69	
p value	0.0062		0.0002		0.0035		0.0032	

Note (a) Renewables include hydro, biofuel, solar, wind, and others. (b) All shares are computed by the primary energy consumption volume from nuclear, renewables or zero carbon divided by the total volume of primary energy consumption, which include fossil fuel energy sources such as oil and gas

Club 1 vs. 13.36% for Club 2 on averages), and zero-carbon energy sources (22.75% for Club 1 vs. 18.98% for Club 2 on averages) in primary energy consumption. Club 1 includes, e.g., Iceland (average *UIM* is 1.149), Latvia (1.058), Sweden (1.057), and Club 2 includes, e.g., the United States (0.788), Japan (0.820), and Norway (0.812). These differences are statistically significant, as shown in the lower panel (K-W Test) of Table 7.7.

Meanwhile, *UIM* also represents countries' capability for the economic growth. Average GDP of Club 1 countries (733 billion US$) are much smaller than that

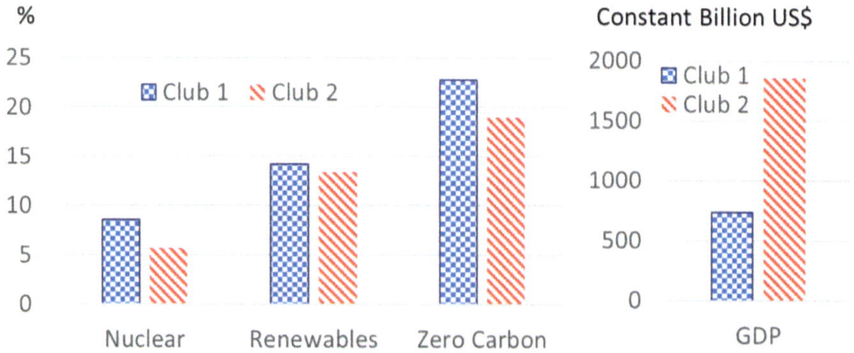

Fig. 7.5 Average shares of energy sources in total primary energy consumption and GDP

of Club 2 (1854 billion US$) as presented in Table 7.7. This indicates the larger economies/countries have historically prioritized economic growth than the development of green economy, therefore on average they have more opportunity to improve their growth strategy in a more balanced manner by integrating environmental and economic growth aspects.

It is important to note that energy sector transition from high carbon to low or zero-carbon sources may lead countries toward sustainable development, so directing toward SDGs enhancement. The new measures proposed in this chapter effectively capture the status and trend for sustainability of OECD countries. These measures are useful for macro-level planning and assessment for green growth economy and strategy for future SDGs development.

7.6 Discussion

This chapter proposed a new approach to measure unified efficiency and unified index over time. The assessments were useful for sustainable development and green growth enhancement. A unique feature of the proposed approach was that it incorporated both economic and environmental factors as required in ESG. The new approach also measured a technology progress, putting the priority on pollution reduction, in a time horizon. Such a pollution reduction over time is an important part of SDGs.

An illustrative example, obtained from Goto and Sueyoshi (2022), documented the unified efficiency and index measures of OECD member nations. Using their results, we examined differences among four pre-defined country groups and discussed the existence of club convergence during 1995–2014. The implication of this chapter will be reexamined with that of Chap. 8 (a technology shift in the US military industry).

The empirical study implies the following three policy suggestions: First, there was differences in the performance measures (*UEM* and *UIM*) on the OECD member nations. Second, there was a single convergence in their *UEM* measure and there were two club convergence clubs in their *UIM* measures. The results indicated that the OECD countries were classified into two convergence clubs (higher and lower groups) in their unified index (*UIM*). Usually, *UIM* measures may capture a technology change more sensitively than *UEM* measures. Finally, the energy sector transition for zero-carbon emissions influenced the club convergence. The countries in the two clubs exhibited statistically significant differences in the shares of primary energy sources from nuclear and renewable energies. The higher/lower shares of renewable energy corresponded to the status (higher/lower) of *UIM*. Therefore, the *UIM* measure is useful for planning and assessment for developing green growth economy, so being useful for the enhancement of SDGs.

The disparity became large over time, indicating that OECD's effort for green growth was limited in terms of sustainable development. The result suggests that it is necessary for OECD member nations to continue their information exchanges and dialogues based on the objectives and analyses for their balanced sustainability developments to achieve unified and stronger green growth.

We have two future tasks from this empirical application. One of these future tasks is that we need to analyze what factors have more influence on their efficiency and index measures among OECD member countries. For example, we need to consider whether the industrial composition and fuel mix may play a major role for sustainable development. The other task is that we need to measure the level of DTS (Damages to Scale) on all OECD nations and prepare policy implications on environmental protection. The two issues will be important future research agendas for the development of ESG and SDGs.

Appendix 1: Club Convergence Algorithm

Club convergence implies the performance tendency on a group of countries which converge to multiple steady states. For example, the countries form clubs (groups) in convergence. We use the factor model proposed by Phillips and Sul (2007) to test club convergence from DEA results.

To mathematically explain the club convergence, let us consider n countries with a panel of performance data y_{jt} for $j = 1, \ldots, n$ and $t = 1, \ldots, T$. Note that Sueyoshi and Wang (2020) and Goto and Sueyoshi (2022) use "i" to specify an observation, However, this chapter uses "j" to express a DMU. They use the term (i) to be consistent with the convergence algorithm proposed by Phillips and Sul (2007, 2009). Meanwhile, we use "j" to express the j th DMU as found in our previous chapters on DEA-EA.

The model adopts a time-varying latent representation for the performance (y_{jt}) of the j th DMU (e.g., country) in the t th period (e.g., year):

$$y_{jt} = \delta_{jt}\mu_t. \tag{7.6}$$

The factor (μ_t) represents the common trend of the countries and δ_{jt} captures the country-specific idiosyncratic shocks to μ_t. Here, δ_{jt} is a time-varying factor.

Using *UEM*, we may express Eq. (7.6) as follows:

$$y_{jt} = \begin{bmatrix} UEM_{11} & UEM_{12} & \ldots & UEM_{1T} \\ UEM_{21} & UEM_{22} & \cdots & UEM_{2T} \\ \vdots & \vdots & & \vdots \\ UEM_{n1} & UEM_{n2} & \cdots & UEM_{nT} \end{bmatrix}$$

$$= \begin{bmatrix} \delta_{11} & \delta_{12} & \ldots & \delta_{1T} \\ \delta_{21} & \delta_{22} & \cdots & \delta_{2T} \\ \vdots & \vdots & & \vdots \\ \delta_{n1} & \delta_{n2} & \cdots & \delta_{nT} \end{bmatrix} \begin{bmatrix} \mu_1 \\ \mu_2 \\ \vdots \\ \mu_T \end{bmatrix},$$

where Model (7.2), along with Eq. (7.3), measures *UEM*. We interpret it as the deviation of the j th country (i.e., DMU) from the trend (μ_t). It is possible for us to replace *UEM* by *UIM* that we measure by Model (7.4) along with Eq. (7.5).

Convergence for all the countries occurs if $\lim_{t\to\infty} \delta_{jt} = \delta_j$. To focus on the deviation (δ_{jt}), we can remove the common factor μ_t by scaling the performance with panel average:

$$h_{jt} = \frac{y_{jt}}{\frac{1}{n}\sum_{j=1}^{n} y_{jt}} \eta_{jt}. \tag{7.7}$$

If δ_{jt} converges to δ, then h_{jt} converges to unity by definition. Phillips and Sul (2007) have assumed that deviation δ_{it} follows the semi-parametric process:

$$\delta_{jt} = \delta_j + \frac{\sigma_j}{\log(t)t^{\alpha}} \eta_t, \tag{7.8}$$

where $\sigma_j > 0$. The η_t follows the standard normal distribution that is independent over j but may be weakly dependent over t. The model allows for a wide range of transition paths. The null hypothesis of convergence for all countries is $H_0 : \delta_j = \delta$ and $\alpha > 0$. The alternative hypothesis is $\mathrm{H}_0 : \delta_i \neq \delta$ for some j and/or $\alpha < 0$. We test the hypothesis by the following log-t regression:

$$\log\left(\frac{H_1}{H_t}\right) - 2\log L(t) = c + b\log t + \hat{u}_t, t = [wt], \ldots, T \tag{7.9}$$

where $L(t) = \log(t)$, $H(t) = \frac{1}{n}\sum_{j=1}^{n}\left(h_{jt} - 1\right)^2$, and r defines a fraction of the sample that is removed in running the regression and is recommended to be 0.3 based on extensive simulations (Phillips & Sul, 2007).[9]

To test the hypothesis, we need to check the sign of the coefficient b. If the t-statistic suggests $b \geq 0$, then the countries converge. Otherwise, we reject the null hypothesis of convergence. By convention, the critical value of t-statistic is set to -1.65.

Phillips and Sul (2007, 2009) proposed the following procedure to identify convergence clubs from the panel:

Step 1: Sort the countries based on their performance in the last observation of the sample.
Step 2: Form a core group of countries that converge. Specifically, the core convergence group can be identified by running the log-t regressions as in Eq. (7.11) for the κ ($2 \leq \kappa \leq n$) highest countries obtained in Step 1. Then choose the group size

[9] Phillips and Sul (2007) show that when T is small or moderate ($T \leq 50$), $r = 0.3$ is a preferable choice. Given that our sample spans $T = 25$ years, we use $r = 0.3$. In this analysis, we also experiment with $r = 0.2$. According to Phillips and Sul (2007), that is satisfactory for larger T. It turns out that the numbers of clubs do not change, but country classification will be different.

k^* with the highest t-statistic given that the t-statistic supports the convergence hypothesis:

$$k^* = \text{argmax}_k\{t_k \mid t_k > -1.65\}. \tag{7.10}$$

Step 3: From the remaining $n - k^*$ countries, find all countries that converge to the same steady state as the core group in Step 2, by adding a single DMU (country) each time to the core group if the t-statistic from the log-t regression exceeds the critical value. These countries and the core group consist of the first convergence club.
Step 4: Repeat the Steps 1–3 for the remaining countries if there are any to identify other clubs until all the remaining countries fail to converge.

We apply the above procedure to analyze the convergence of the countries' *UEM* and *UIM* measures. Note that *UEM* and *UIM* are relative sustainability efficiency and index measures that combine economic and environmental factors. The convergence does not necessarily translate into convergence in either economic or environmental performance. Furthermore, we need to point out that the "steady state" in club convergence means a value that the deviations (δ_{jt}) of the original data from the common trend as shown in (7.6). The deviations form a de-trended data series from the original data. The existence of club convergence means the existence of multiple steady states, which correspond to different deviations from the common trend. Within each club, the deviations from the trend converge to a common constant value.

Appendix 2: Kruskal–Wallis Rank Sum Test

To examine the null hypothesis (a group of observations distributes randomly among multiple periods), this chapter uses the Kruskal–Wallis rank sum test. We separate an entire observed period into T periods. To compute the Kruskal–Wallis statistic (H), this chapter combines all observations ($n = \sum_{t=1}^{T} n_t$) in T periods. Then, we rank them from the greatest to the least by these efficiency scores over the entire period. Let R_{jt} denote the rank of the j th plant in the t th period. The rank sum of all plants in the t th period is $R_t = \sum_{j=1}^{n_t} R_{jt}$. Then, the Kruskal–Wallis statistic (H) is determined by

$$H = \frac{12}{n(n+1)} \sum_{t=1}^{T} \frac{R_t^2}{n_t} - 3(n+1) \tag{7.11}$$

The statistic (H) follows the χ^2 distribution with a degree of freedom (df = T − 1). See Hollander and Wolfe (1999) for both a detailed description on the H statistic and a description regarding how to deal with many firms on a same rank.

References

Apergis, N., & Christou, C. (2016). Energy productivity convergence: New evidence from club converging. *Applied Economics Letters, 23*, 142–145.

Dowrick, S., & Nguyen, D. T. (1989). OECD comparative economic growth 1950–85: Catch-up and convergence. *American Economic Review, 79*, 1010–1030.

Färe, R., Grosskopf, S., Norris, M., & Zhang, Z. (1994). Productivity growth, technical progress, and efficiency change in industrialized countries. *American Economic Review, 84*, 66–93.

Goto, M., & Sueyoshi, T. (2022). Sustainable development and convergence under energy sector transition in industrial nations: An application of DEA environmental assessment. *Socio-Economic Planning Sciences, 101316*, 1–13.

Le Pen, Y., & Sevi, B. (2010). On the non-convergence of energy intensities: Evidence from a pair-wise econometric approach. *Ecological Economics, 69*, 641–650.

Liddle, B. (2010). Revisiting world energy intensity convergence for regional differences. *Applied Energy, 87*, 3218–3225.

Margaritis, D., Färe, R., & Grosskopf, S. (2002). Productivity, convergence and policy: A study of OECD countries and industries. *Journal of Productivity Analysis, 28*, 87–105.

Maudos, J., Pastor, J. M., & Serrano, l. (2010). Convergence in OECD countries: Technical change, efficiency and productivity. *Applied Economics, 32*, 757–765.

Ozbugday, F. C., Tirgil, A., & Kose, E. G. (2020). Efficiency changes in long-term care in OECD countries: A non-parametric Malmquist Index approach. *Socio-Economic Planning Sciences, 70*, 1–11.

Parker, S., & Liddle, B. (2017). Economy-wide and manufacturing energy productivity transition paths and club convergence for OECD and non-OECD countries. *Energy Economics, 62*, 338–346.

Phillips, P. C. B., & Sul, D. (2007). Transition modeling and econometric convergence tests. *Econometrica, 75*, 1771–1855.

Inklaar, R., & Timmer, M.P. (2008). GGDC productivity level database: International comparisons of output, inputs and productivity at the industry level. GGDC Research Memorandum GD-104, Groningen Growth and Development Centre, University of Groningen.

van Ark, B., O'Mahony, M., & Immer, M. P. (2008). The productivity gap between Europe and the United States: Trends and causes. *Journal of Economic Perspectives, 22*, 25–44.

Wang, Y., Sun, X., & Guo, X. (2019). Environmental regulation and green productivity growth: Empirical evidence on the Porter Hypothesis from OECD industrial sectors. *Energy Policy, 132*, 611–619.

Sueyoshi, T., & Goto, M. (2012). Data environment analysis for environmental assessment: Comparison between public and private ownership in petroleum industry. *European Journal of Operational Research, 3*, 668–678.

Sueyoshi, T., & Goto, M. (2018). *Environmental Assessment on Energy and Sustainability by Data Envelopment Analysis*. London: Wiley & Sons.

Sueyoshi, T., & Wang, D. (2020). Rank dynamics and club convergence of sustainability development in countries around the world. *Journal of Cleaner Production, 250*, 1–13.

Chapter 8
A Time Lag for Technology Shift: DEA Perspectives

Abstract While there is a plethora of literature on technology transfer (or spin-out), there is a paucity of studies on technology transition. Chapter 7 considers a technology shift among nations as an important component of OECD. This chapter reexamines the technology shift from the development of military innovations. Military industry needs very advanced technology and it needs the technology shift between a large public organization (e.g., US DoD: Department of Defense and EPA: Environmental Protection Agency) and their supporting subsidiaries. The technology transfer among subsidiaries is very important for maintaining strong military power. We may classify technology in the same category between the two chapters (Chap. 7: ESG and SDGs in OECD as well as this chapter: US military industry), but both are under different surroundings (e.g., different purposes and different industrial structures). In the end of this chapter, we compare the technology shift for ecology in OECD nations with that of military in the USA to understand the importance of technology transfer for global sustainability development. To attain the research purpose, we propose a new use of DEA which incorporates two-stage processes in the formulation. An important feature of the model is that it has "a time lag" to express a technology transfer process. The US military application on the technology transfer, compared with the ecological development in OECD nations in Chap. 7, provides us with new policy implications (e.g., strengths and limitations) for international cooperation on ESG and SGDs developments.

Keywords Technology transition · Time lag · Military industry

8.1 Introduction

A social complex (in terms of regional, industrial or national innovation system) involves many entities which are interdependent with each other (Dougherty, 2017; Katz, 2016). Generally, agencies in public sectors and non-profit organizations have a substantial amount of extramural Research and Development (R&D) budgets. They provide many opportunities to enhance knowledge generations among producers or

T. Sueyoshi and M. Goto, *Environment and Sustainability for ESG and SDGs*,
https://doi.org/10.1007/978-981-96-2464-5_8

technology developers, including military activities and ESG enhancements. Universities, national and corporate research laboratories produce knowledge or advanced technology by fully utilizing such funding opportunities. Meanwhile, the private sector capitalizes the transferred knowledge and makes revenues and profits that are sources of investment and incentives to players as found in military and ESG enhancement.

It may be true that both military and environment protection use different technologies under different surroundings. Admitting such differences, we discuss them from their technology development processes as visually summarized in Chap. 2. Figure 2.6 depicts such a technology dissemination process. This chapter understands that such different knowledge generation processes may provide us with meaningful policy/business implications to enhance the level of military advancement or that of environment protection from their different technology developments.

This chapter starts considering from the US military industry, focusing on the relationship between Department of Defense (DoD) and its military suppliers. The military industry uses the most advanced technology so that we may use it for comparison with the green industry in OECD (in Chap. 7). The US DoD develops various advanced technologies through Air Force, Army and Naval Research Laboratories as well as outsources (including high-risk, high-return R&D projects) to universities or corporations. The DoD also acquires state-of-the-art technologies from private sectors. It stresses technology transition or spin-in (e.g., a knowledge flow from businesses to DoD) as well as technology transfer or spin-out (e.g., a knowledge flow from DoD to businesses) as discussed by Lal et al. (2013). US EPA (Environment Protection Agency) and US Energy Department also help technology transfer by providing subsidiary firms with funding opportunities. When the private sector is leading in many high-tech areas such as information/communications technology and biotechnology (Sueyoshi & Ryu, 2022), we expect that the technology transfer in military industry is applicable to the area of energy and environment, so being applicable for our sustainability development. See Fig. 2.6 for a visual description on the technology transfer for ESG development.

A majority of innovation studies tend to regard a whole innovation process as a single big black box, thus making it hard to understand the specific stages of the innovation process (Chen et al., 2018). As a result, the innovation process is often oversimplified and important sub-processes over the lab course to market are skipped in the conventional studies. This aspect can be applied to ESG and SDGs, as well. The oversimplification also leads to failure to incorporate a time-consuming nature of innovation. The survey result contained in National Research Council (2009), for instance, showed that a time elapsed between R&D and actual sales (commercialization) was 5–7 years. This chapter uses five years from the survey result as discussed by Sueyoshi and Ryu (2022). Maine and Seegopaul (2016) also explored variations in the time required for development and commercialization by industry (e.g., 0–2 years for software and 5–15 years for advanced materials). Thus, the results of innovation assessment studies may change with a "time lag" between inputs and outputs (Sueyoshi & Ryu, 2022).

Here, it is important to note that outputs in this chapter are only desirable outputs while Chap. 7 deals with both desirable and undesirable outputs. Such a difference may produce different technology transfers between environmental protection and military industry. Such differences will be explored in the end of this chapter. We use only "desirable outputs" as outputs, hereafter, in this chapter.

To attain the research objective, we are methodologically interested in assessing the performance of technology transition from technology-based businesses to DoD by employing a two-stage DEA model with a time lag. We compare our findings on military technology with those of ESG and SDGs.

The remainder of this chapter has the following structure: Sect. 8.2 surveys previous studies. Section 8.3 discusses a DEA model with a time lag. Section 8.4 documents empirical results on US military industry from Sueyoshi and Ryu (2022) and reexamines them from ESG/SDGs perspectives. Section 8.5 methodologically extends the formulation for a time lag to the three-stage model from the two-stage model. Section 8.6 summaries this chapter by comparing differences on technology transfer between US military and OECD nations.

8.2 Literature Review

The previous chapters have mainly discussed DEA-EA because we need to incorporate undesirable outputs, such as CO_2 emission, to reduce them for the enhancement of ESG and SDGs. Meanwhile, this chapter discusses an extension of DEA whose use is different from the standard DEA forms. Note that the book prepared by Sueyoshi and Goto (2018) has summarized the previous standard DEA forms in past decades.

This chapter introduces some important studies that have applied DEA to the innovation process at a microscopic level. For example, Sueyoshi and Goto (2013) examined the firm-level efficiency by associating R&D expenditure with Tobin's q as an indicator for the corporate value of firms. Kuah and Wong (2011) measured the university-level R&D efficiency by using inputs (e.g., research grants and the numbers of research staff and students) and outputs (e.g., the numbers of publications, awards and intellectual property rights). Zabala-Iturriagagoitia et al. (2007) examined the performance of regional innovation systems using the European Innovation Scoreboard data. Sharma and Thomas (2008) also explored the cross-national R&D efficiency of 22 countries.

These studies offered useful information about which entities performed better in terms of innovation performance and which entities could serve as benchmarks. But, they had some limitations as described in their introduction section: (a) much fewer assessment on technology transition (when compared to technology transfer), (b) oversimplification of innovation process, (c) lack of consideration of a time lag between innovation input and output factors and (d) exclusion of important business characteristics, particularly the aspects of social capital.

To overcome these research limitations from the perspective of DEA time series, multistage and/or network DEA approaches have been recently developed and applied to measure the level of innovation efficiency. Table 8.1 summarizes most of such recent efforts in the research field. At the firm level, for instance, Chun et al. (2015) and Wang et al. (2016) used a two-stage DEA model by decomposing the innovation process into R&D and marketing/commercialization sub-processes and analyzed the innovation efficiency of Korean and Chinese companies. At the regional level, Chen and Guan (2012) and Chen et al. (2018) looked at the innovation efficiency of Chinese regions based upon two-stage network DEA models. At the national level, Carayannis et al. (2016) and Kou et al. (2016) measured the innovation efficiency of European or OECD countries. While all of these studies incorporate the systematic aspects of a complex innovation process, there are still research areas for improvement to address the remaining limitations.

8.3 Methodology

8.3.1 Formulation for a Time Lag

Before applying the proposed formulation, we need to specify the data ranges on X (inputs) and G (outputs) that are similar to Eq. (5.3). An exception is that we do not consider B (bad outputs), here. We apply the data ranges to all DMUs ($j = 1, ..., n$) in all periods ($t = 1, \ldots, T$) when applying the proposed DEA models. See Eq. (8.2). As discussed in Chap. 5, the purpose of the data ranges is that DEA results can avoid an occurrence of zero in dual variables (i.e., multipliers). Such an occurrence implies that corresponding production factors (X and G) are not fully utilized in our DEA assessment. The occurrence is problematic on ESG investment as discussed in Sect. 4.7. To avoid the difficulty, we need to incorporate the data ranges into the proposed formulations so that we can fully utilize information on the two production factors.

Here, it is important to note that the standard DEA has previously utilized the multiplier restriction approaches, such as assurance region and cone ratio analyses, to attain the status of sustainability goal as we discuss in Chap. 3. A problem of these approaches is that we must depend upon prior information (e.g., previous experience and common evidence) to restrict the multipliers to show the direction of SDGs. Acknowledging the importance of multiplier restriction, we must mention that we often cannot access the prior information (e.g., which goals are important, any priority, in terms of SDGs). The proposed data ranges avoid such a difficulty. See Sueyoshi (1991) and Sueyoshi and Goto (2018) for a detailed description on multiplier restriction from DEA practicality and applicability.

Table 8.1 Multistage DEA studies to measure innovation performance

References	Model	Level	Summary	Input variables	Intermediate variables	Output variables
Chen and Guan (2012)	Two-stage network DEA	Region	Their study measured innovation efficiency of Chinese regions based on technological development process and technological commercialization process	Expenditure on science and technology; number of science and technology personnel; foreign direct investment; expenditure on the import of technology; expenditure on the purchase of domestic technology; value of contractual inflows in domestic technical markets	Invention; utility model; external design; capital stock; labor	Gross domestic product (GDP); sale of new products; value of export; annual income in urban residents per capita
Chun et al. (2015)	Two-stage DEA	Firm	Their study looked into the R&D efficiency of 1039 Korean manufacturing firms over the innovation and commercialization stages and the impact of firm size and industry type on the efficiency	Internal R&D investments; external R&D investments; number of R&D employees	Process patent applications; product patent applications	Sales; operating income

(continued)

Table 8.1 (continued)

References	Model	Level	Summary	Input variables	Intermediate variables	Output variables
Carayannis et al. (2016)	Multistage and multilevel DEA	Country	Their study measured and compared the efficiency of innovation systems of 23 European countries and their 185 regions across two stages: knowledge production process and knowledge commercialization process	Science graduates in tertiary education; participation in lifelong learning; total R&D expenditure; R&D capital stock	Citable documents; patent applications; employment in knowledge-intensive activities; SMEs collaborating with others; venture capital investment	High tech exports; sales of new-to-market and new-to-firm innovation; license and patent revenues from abroad; trademark applications in national offices
		Region		Population with tertiary education; R&D expenditure; non-R&D innovation expenditure	SMEs innovating in-house; innovative SMEs collaborating with others; public–private co-publications; patents; employment in high-tech and knowledge-intensive services	Technological (product or process) innovators; non-technological innovators; sales of new-to-market and new-to-firm products
Kou et al. (2016)	Dynamic network DEA	Country	Their study assessed the innovation efficiency of OECD countries in the multi-period and multi-division framework	R&D personnel; R&D expenditure	Science and technology papers; EPO patents; triadic patents; technology import	Ratio of GDP to total employment; export of high-tech products
Wang et al. (2016)	Two-stage non-radial DEA	Firm	Their study analyzed the innovation efficiency of 38 Chinese energy enterprises over the R&D process and marketing process	R&D costs; staff wages; annual fixed assets	Revenues; software assets	Total profits; market value

(continued)

Table 8.1 (continued)

References	Model	Level	Summary	Input variables	Intermediate variables	Output variables
Chen et al. (2018)	Two-stage network DEA	Region	Their study explored the innovation efficiency of 29 Chinese provinces over the R&D and commercialization sub-processes	R&D personnel; intramural expenditure on R&D; invention patents stock; fixed assets	Patent applications; new product development; expenditure on new product development; expenditure for technical renovation; employed personnel	Sales revenue of new products

Note Sueyoshi and Ryu (2022) have prepared an original table. We modify their work for this study

8.3.2 Operational Efficiency Measurement

In measuring the operational performance of entities in public and private sectors, we consider each entity as a DMU (e.g., subcontractor). The DMU uses production technology which transforms an input vector with m components ($X \in R_+^m$) into a desirable output vector with s components ($G \in R_+^s$).

The axiomatic form of Production Technology (PT) on a production possibility set (P) is expressed at the specific t th period as follows:

$$P_t = \{P_t(X) : X_t \text{ can produce } G_t\} \in \mathcal{R}_+^m \tag{8.1}$$

within the framework of Eq. (8.1). The production possibility set at the t th period becomes as follows:

$$P_t^v(X_t) = \left\{ G_t \le \sum_{j=1}^{n} G_{jt}\lambda_{jt}, X_t \ge \sum_{j=1}^{n} X_{jt}\lambda_{jt}, \sum_{j=1}^{n} \lambda_{jt} = 1 \text{ and } \lambda_{jt} \ge 0\,(j = 1, \ldots, n) \right\} \tag{8.2}$$

The expression on P incorporates the assumption on variable RTS because Eq. (8.2) has the side constraint (i.e., $\sum_{j=1}^{n} \lambda_{jt} = 1$). See Sueyoshi and Goto (2018) for a detailed description on the type of RTS. See also Sueyoshi and Sekitani (2005) for RTS in a network DEA model.

Figure 8.1 depicts a projection from inefficiency to efficiency in a framework of OE measurement. It has been long considered that DEA can provide such a holistic measure (e.g., Sueyoshi & Sekitani, 2009; Yu et al, 2021). However, the straightforward use of the standard DEA may be insufficient to provide such a methodological capability. For example, an input-oriented DEA can measure the level of input-based efficiency (θ^*) of the specific k th DMU. The superscript symbol (*) denotes the optimal solution(s) obtained from a DEA model. The level of efficiency is referred to as "*OE* (θ^*: Operational Efficiency)", along with its related slacks (d_i^{x*} and d^{g*}) on optimality. This type of efficiency measure originates from reducing the amount of input(s). See Model (3.1) that incorporates constraints in addition to the objective function (8.3). The reduction is the input-oriented measure to improve the level of *OE* measures. The projection of $\{a\}$ to $\{f\}$ is the input-oriented *OE* enhancement ($=$ {f}/{a}) in Fig. 8.1. We measure the level of the input-based *OE* (θ^*) on optimality in the following manner:

$$OE(\text{input})^* = \theta^* - \varepsilon_s \left(\sum_{i=1}^{m} d_i^{x*} + d_r^{g*} \right). \tag{8.3}$$

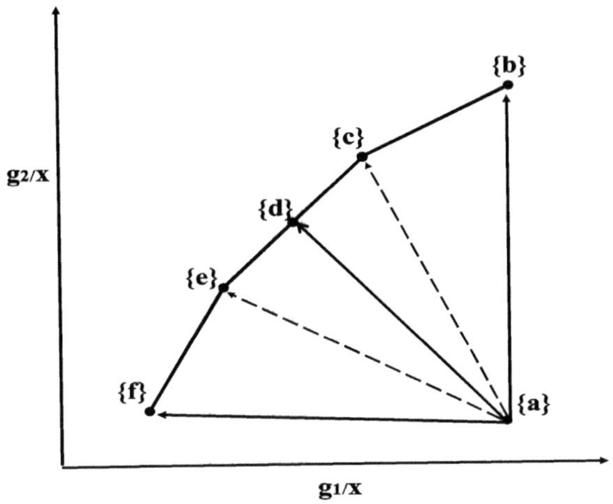

Fig. 8.1 Possible multiple projections. *Note* (a) An efficiency frontier consists of observed DMUs {f}–{e}–{d}–{c}–{b}. The input-oriented model projects from DMU {a} to DMU {f}, while the output-oriented model projects from DMU {a} to DMU {b}. Different projections produce different *OE* measures. Any multiple projections occur onto the frontier (f)–{e}–{c}–{b}. The DEA model in this chapter produces a projection from (a) to {d} (a projected point) so that it is unique, not depending upon input/output orientation as found in the standard DMU model. (b) The projection onto DMU {d} may suffer from an occurrence of multiple solutions between DMUs ({c} and {e}) due to the nature of linear programming. See Sueyoshi and Goto (2018). A computational benefit of DEA is that we can solve DEA by linear programming but it suffers from an occurrence of multiple solutions. Computational tractability is indeed a benefit of DEA

Meanwhile, we measure the output-oriented *OE* by an inefficiency measure ($\tau *$) as follows:

$$OE(\text{output})^{*} = 1/\left[\tau^{*} + \varepsilon_s\left(\sum_{i=1}^{m} d_i^{x*} + d_r^{g*}\right)\right]. \tag{8.4}$$

This type of efficiency measure originates from output enhancement. The output increase leads to the enhancement of the *OE* measure, for instance, a projection from {a} to {b}. The output-oriented *OE* measures the ratio ($= \{a\}/\{b\}$) in Fig. 8.1.

We compute both Eqs. (8.3) and (8.4) by the standard (radial) DEA models. See Chap. 3 for a description on the radial models. An important feature of the two standard models is that they produce different efficiency measures in the manner that $OE(\text{input})^{*} \neq OE(\text{output})^{*}$. As a result, we encounter a difficulty in evaluating the performance of many entities. Here, we may wonder which one we use for our assessment? To handle the difficulty, we need to unify the input-oriented and output-oriented measures to identify a single measure as an *OE* measures. The projection from {a} to {d} is such a visual example, as found in Fig. 8.1. We use such a unified DEA model for this research.

After unifying the input-based and output-based measures, we measure the level of *OE* of the specific *k* th DMU by the following formulation:

$$\begin{aligned}
&Maximize\ \xi_k + \varepsilon_s\left(\sum_{i=1}^{m} R_i^x d_i^x + \sum_{r=1}^{s} R_r^g d_r^g\right) \\
&s.t. \quad \sum_{j=1}^{n} x_{ij}\lambda_j + d_i^x + \xi_k x_{ik} = x_{ik}\ (i = 1, \ldots, m), \\
&\qquad \sum_{j=1}^{n} g_{rj}\lambda_j - d_r^g - \xi_k g_{rk} = g_{rk}\ (r = 1, \ldots, s), \\
&\qquad \sum_{j=1}^{n} \lambda_j = 1, \lambda_j \geq 0\ (j = 1, \ldots, n), \\
&\qquad \xi_k : URS, d_i^x \geq 0\ (i = 1, \ldots, m)\ \& \\
&\qquad d_r^g \geq 0\ (r = 1, \ldots, s).
\end{aligned} \tag{8.5}$$

The left-hand side of Model (8.5) indicates an efficiency frontier of DMUs. The right-hand side indicates the performance of the specific *k* th DMU to be examined. The observation (x_i and g_r) serves as a directional vector in which Model (8.5) maximizes the level of inefficiency for calculation. Since standard DEA models do not have such a directional vector, their efficiency measures depend upon input-oriented or output-oriented. Meanwhile, Model (8.5) incorporates the directional vector to produce an efficiency measure, not depending upon the input/output orientation.

The distance measures ($+d_i^x + \xi_k x_{ik}$ and $-d_r^g - \xi_k g_{rk}$) indicate differences between the observed performance of each DMU and the efficiency frontier in multiple dimensional factors (e.g., inputs and outputs). The unified inefficiency (ξ_k) indicates the degree of a directional vector, which should be arranged toward the efficiency frontier. The slacks (d_i^x and d_r^g) express the remaining parts of the difference, which we cannot specify in measuring the level of inefficiency. The small number (ε_s), expressing the relationship between inefficiency and total slacks, indicates a number that we need to prescribe for the operation of Model (8.5).

Strengths. Model (8.5) has an important feature, in which an efficiency score does not depend upon input or output orientation, as found in the standard DEA models. This feature is different from them which depend upon the orientation. As discussed previously, input-oriented efficiency is different from output-oriented efficiency under variable RTS. Model (8.5) does not have such difficulty because all factors (inputs and outputs) are unified in a single inefficiency measure and there is no difference between them.

We measure the degree of OE_k of the *k* th DMU by

$$OE_k = 1 - \left[\xi_k + \varepsilon_s\left(\sum_{i=1}^{m} R_i^x d_i^x + \sum_{r=1}^{s} R_r^g d_r^g\right)\right] \tag{8.6}$$

Here, Model (8.6) is under "variable" RTS. The optimality (*) of Model (8.6) determines the inefficiency measure (ξ_k) and all slack variables. We determine the degree by subtracting the level from unity, as specified in Eq. (8.6). The important feature of Model (8.5) is that it puts an inefficiency measure (ξ_k) before inputs and outputs. The optimization attempts to minimize the level of inefficiency. As mentioned previously, such a feature does not exist in the previous DEA studies.

8.3.3 Measurement by a Time Lag Model

Nomenclature used for the DEA time lag model are summarized as follows.

x_{ijt} is the observed i th input of the j th DMU at the t th stage, g_{rjt+1} is the observed r th output of the j th DMU at the $t+1$ th stage, y_{hjt} is the observed h th intermediate output of the j th DMU at the t th stage, y_{rjt+1} is the observed h th intermediate input of the j th DMU at the $t+1$ th stage, ξ is an inefficiency measure, d_{it}^{x} is an unknown slack variable of the i th input at the t th stage, d_{rt}^{g} is an unknown slack variable of the r th output at the t th stage, d_{ht}^{y} is an unknown slack variable of the h th intermediate output/input at the t and $t+1$ th stages, λ_{jt} is an unknown intensity (or structural) variable of the j th DMU at the t th stage, ε_s is a prescribed very small number and J_t is a set of all DMUs at the t th stage. This study considers the first and second stages, so setting $t = 1$ and 2.

Figure 8.2 visually specifies the contract assessment with a time lag. This section discusses how to analytically incorporate the time lag into Model (8.5). As visually specified in Fig. 8.2, the contract consists of two stage processes to express the time lag. There is an intermediate stage that connects between them by considering the time lag. The first stage uses the first input (e.g., this amount of funding from a large organization), the second input (e.g., the number of employees) and the third input (e.g., the level of technology distance). There are two outputs: the first output/input (e.g., the number of patents) and the second output/input (e.g., the number of social connections) at the intermediate stage. After five years, the two outputs from the first stage serve as inputs at the second stage (Sueyoshi & Ryu, 2022). This is just an assumption that the final output is the amount of contract (e.g., procurement) from the large organization such as US DoD.

Figure 8.2 has the following production factors: x_{1t} is the amount of funding from a public agent, x_{2t} is the number of employees, x_{3t} is a technology distance from the expectation by the public agency at the first stage, $y_{1t} = y_{1t+1}$ is the number of patents and $y_{2t} = y_{2t+1}$ is the number of social connections at the intermediate stage and g_{t+1} is the amount of contracts from the public agency to businesses (including universities) at the second stage. The subscript (t) indicates the starting stage. We assume five annual periods for the final contracts for the second ($t + 1$) period.

Here, it is worth noting two concerns. First, as depicted in Fig. 8.2, we assume that the intermediate factors ($y_{1t} = y_{1t+1}$ and $y_{2t} = y_{2t+1}$) occur between the first and second stages. We cannot specify an exact period, but it occurs between the two stages. There is some level of social connection between the two stages. To measure

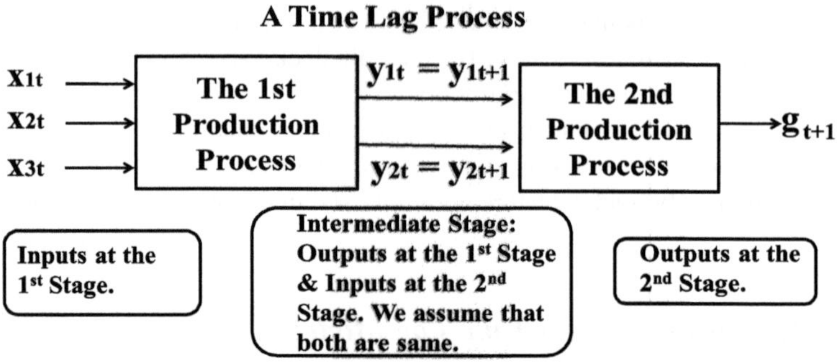

Fig. 8.2 Framework for time lag (two stages) assessment. *Note* The 1st is the first stage and the 2nd is the second stage. The time lag exists between the two periods (processes)

the level of connection, we may incorporate a technology distance and the number of connections that represent social capital, which may be fuzzy on the specification. Hence, Sueyoshi and Ryu (2022) made the assumption to prepare DEA formulation at the intermediate stage. Second, to analyze the procurement process specified in Figs. 8.1 and 8.2, we use a DEA-based approach (not standard) to determine the level of *OE* on the specific *k* th DMU in the whole innovation process.

Given production factors at the two stages, we evaluate the performance of the *k* th DMU to be examined. From the framework of Fig. 8.2, we propose the following formulation to measure the level of OE_{kt}^{t+1} on the *k* th DMU at the two stages:

$$
\begin{aligned}
&Maximize\ \xi_{kt}^{t+1} + \varepsilon_s\left(\sum_{i=1}^{m} R_i^x d_{it}^x + \sum_{r=1}^{s} R_r^g d_{rt+1}^g\right) - \sum_{h=1}^{z}\left(d_{ht}^y + d_{ht+1}^y\right)\\
&s.t.\quad \sum_{j=1}^{n} x_{ijt}\lambda_{jt} + d_{it}^x + \xi_{kt}^{t+1} x_{ikt} = x_{ikt} \quad (i = 1, \ldots, m),\\
&\qquad \sum_{j=1}^{n} y_{hjt}\lambda_{jt} - d_{ht}^y = y_{hkt} \quad (h = 1, \ldots, z),\\
&\qquad \sum_{j=1}^{n} y_{hjt+1}\lambda_{jt+1} + d_{ht+1}^y = y_{hkt+1} \quad (h = 1, \ldots, z),\\
&\qquad \sum_{j=1}^{n} g_{rjt+1}\lambda_{jt+1} - d_{rt+1}^g - \xi_{kt}^{t+1} g_{rkt+1} = g_{rkt+1} \quad (r = 1, \ldots, s),\\
&\qquad \sum_{j=1}^{n} \lambda_{jt} = 1\,(j = 1, \ldots, n),\ \sum_{j=1}^{n} \lambda_{jt+1} = 1 \quad (j = 1, \ldots, n),\\
&\qquad \lambda_{jt} \geq 0\,(j = 1, \ldots, n),\ \lambda_{jt+1} \geq 0\,(j = 1, \ldots, n),\\
&\qquad \xi_{kt}^{t+1} : URS,\ d_{it}^x \geq 0\ (i = 1, \ldots, m),\\
&\qquad d_{ht}^y \geq 0\,(h = 1, \ldots, z),\ d_{ht+1}^y \geq 0\,(h = 1, \ldots, z)\&\\
&\qquad d_{rt+1}^g \geq 0\,(r = 1, \ldots, s).
\end{aligned}
\tag{8.7}
$$

Here, the first and second constraints ($\sum_{j=1}^{n} x_{ij1}\lambda_{jt} + d_{it}^{x} + \xi_{kt}^{t+1} x_{ikt} = x_{ikt}$ and $\sum_{j=1}^{n} y_{hjt}\lambda_{jt} - d_{ht}^{y} = y_{hkt}$) indicate a production process for the first stage. The second stage is specified by the third and fourth constraints ($\sum_{j=1}^{n} y_{hjt+1}\lambda_{jt+1} + d_{ht+1}^{y} = y_{hkt+1}$ and $\sum_{j=1}^{n} g_{rjt+1}\lambda_{jt+1} - d_{rt+1}^{g} - \xi_{kt}^{t+1} g_{rkt+1} = g_{rkt+1}$). We structure Model (8.7) under variable RTS by incorporating both $\sum_{j=1}^{n} \lambda_{jt} = 1$ and $\sum_{j=1}^{n} \lambda_{jt+1} = 1$. It is possible for us to the side constraints under the assumption of constant RTS. An important feature of Model (8.7) is that we may separate the production process into the 1st and 2nd stages. A time lag is implicitly expressed by intermediate variables (outputs for the first stage and inputs for the second stage). Both have the same amount on the variables. This is a major assumption in formulating Model (8.7).

For the two stages (t and $t+1$), we determine the degree of Operational Efficiency (OE_{kt}^{t+1}) of the k th DMU as follows;

$$OE_{kt}^{t+1} = 1 - \left[\xi_{kt}^{t+1*} + \varepsilon_s \left(\sum_{i=1}^{m} R_i^x d_{it}^{x*} + \sum_{r=1}^{s} R_r^g d_{rt+1}^{g*} \right) \right], \tag{8.8}$$

where the inefficiency score and all slack variables exist on the optimality (*) of Model (8.7). We drop $\sum_{h=1}^{z} (d_{ht}^{y*} + d_{ht+1}^{y*})$ from Eq. (8.8) because they are slacks for intermediate variables, indicating a time lag for technology transition between the two periods (t and $t+1$). We consider that OE_{kt}^{t+1} should be measured by inputs at the t th period and outputs at the $t+1$ th period. The equation within the parenthesis is obtained from the optimality of the objective value of Model (8.7). We obtain the degree of OE_{kt}^{t+1} by subtracting the level of inefficiency from unity. If the degree of OE_{kt}^{t+1} is unity, then it indicates the status of "full efficiency". On the other hand, if the degree is less than unity; it includes some level of "inefficiency". If the degree is zero, it indicates "full inefficiency".

Returning to Fig. 8.1, we add the analytical structure of Model (8.7). The figure consists of the horizontal axis (g_1/x) and the vertical axis (g_2/x). The DMU {a} is inefficient and the other DMUs {b, c, d, e and f} are efficient. An efficient frontier is a piece-wise linear line {b–c–d–e–f}. The inefficient DMU {a} needs to project itself to {d} on the frontier to attain the status of full efficiency. The proposed formulation uses a single projection from {a} to {d} because the directional vector (x_{ikt}, g_{rkt+1}) is incorporated in Model (8.7). Thus, Model (8.3) has a single projection from {a} to {d}. Meanwhile, the standard DEA does not incorporate such a projection vector so that it may suffer from an occurrence of multiple projections, depending upon input and output orientations. Such projections occur on the range between {b} and {f} on the frontier.

Methodological originality: The single projection is important in connecting between the two stages as listed in Fig. 8.1. The standard DEA models, including network ones, did not have such an analytical capability. Sueyoshi and Ryu (2022) have first proposed the new formulation for (8.3) in the two-stage approach. The book prepared by Sueyoshi and Goto (2018) has summarized previous DEA works, but not listing the formulation of Model (8.7). We have reminded that standard DEA models have different efficiency measures [i.e., $OE(\text{input})^* \neq OE(\text{output})^*$], depending upon the type of factors (i.e., input-oriented model or output-oriented model), so that we always wonder which result becomes the type of efficiency to evaluate the performance of each DMU. Model (8.7) does not have such a problem (i.e., different efficiency measures). See Chap. 3 for a description on the standard models.

The dual formulation of (8.7) becomes as follows:

$$\begin{aligned}
&\textit{Minimize} \sum_{i=1}^{m} v_i^t x_{ikt} - \sum_{h=1}^{z} w_h^t y_{hkt} + \sum_{h=1}^{z} w_h^{t+1} y_{hkt+1} - \sum_{r=1}^{s} u_r^{t+1} g_{rkt+1} + \sigma_t + \sigma_{t+1} \\
&s.t. \quad \sum_{i=1}^{m} v_i^t x_{ijt} - \sum_{h=1}^{z} w_h^t y_{hjt} + \sigma_t \geq 0 \quad (j = 1, \ldots, n), \\
&\qquad \sum_{h=1}^{z} w_h^{t+1} y_{hjt+1} - \sum_{r=1}^{s} u_r^{t+1} g_{rjt+1} + \sigma_{t+1} \geq 0 \quad (j = 1, \ldots, n), \\
&\qquad \sum_{i=1}^{m} v_i^t x_{ikt} + \sum_{r=1}^{s} u_r^{t+1} g_{rkt+1} = 1, \\
&\qquad v_i^t \geq \varepsilon_s R_i^x \ (i = 1, \ldots, m),\ w_h^t \geq \varepsilon_s R_r^g \ (h = 1, \ldots, z), \\
&\qquad w_h^t \geq -1 \ (h = 1, \ldots, z),\ u_r^{t+1} \geq -1 \ (r = 1, \ldots, s), \\
&\qquad \sigma_t: URS \ \& \ \sigma_{t+1}: URS,
\end{aligned} \tag{8.9}$$

where v_i^t $(i = 1, \ldots, m)$, w_h^t $(h = 1, \ldots, z)$, w_h^{t+1} $(h = 1, \ldots, z)$, u_r^{t+1} $(r = 1, \ldots, s)$, σ_t and σ_{t+1} are dual variables related to the first, second, third, fourth, fifth and sixth constraints of Model (8.7). The input at the t th period is non-negative because $v_i^t \geq \varepsilon_s R_i^x$. Similarly, the intermediate variable (as an output) at the t th period is non-negative because $w_h^t \geq \varepsilon_s R_r^g$. The data range is important to avoid an occurrence of zero in multipliers (dual variables). Without the range, they may become zero, implying that we cannot fully use the corresponding factor(s) in determining the degree of OE.

We measure the degree of OE_{kt}^{t+1} by

$$OE_{kt}^{t+1} = 1 - \left[\sum_{i=1}^{m} v_i^{t*} x_{ikt} - \sum_{r=1}^{s} u_r^{t+1*} g_{rkt+1} + \sigma_t^* + \sigma_{t+1}^* \right], \tag{8.10}$$

where the inefficiency score and all slack variables exist on the optimality of Model (8.10).

Following Eq. (8.10), we may drop the dual variables (w_h^{t*} and w_h^{t+1*}) from Model (8.9), both are from intermediate variables to express a time lag of technology shift. Equation (8.9) implies that each dual variable indicates how much the degree of inefficiency increases or decreases due to a unit increase in factors. For example, v_i^{t*} implies the amount of OE decrease due to a unit increase in the i th input at the t th period. Conversely, u_r^{t+1*} implies the amount of OE increase due to a unit increase in the r th output at the $t + 1$ th period. The intercept of a supporting hyperplane is expressed by $\sigma_t^* + \sigma_{t+1}^*$. See Sueyoshi and Goto (2018) on the relationship between the dual formulation and the supporting hyperplane(s).

It is important to note six additional concerns on Models (8.7) and (8.9). First, as formulated in Model (8.7), we measure the degree of OE_{kt}^{t+1} by the first group of constraints (i.e., $\sum_{j=1}^{n} x_{ijt}\lambda_{jt} + d_{it}^{x} + \xi x_{ikt} = x_{ikt}$) on inputs at the t th period and the fourth group of constraints (i.e., $\sum_{j=1}^{n} g_{rjt+1}\lambda_{jt+1} - d_{rt+1}^{g} - \xi g_{rkt+1} = g_{rkt+1}$) on outputs at the $t+1$ th period. Both are used to determine a degree of the inefficiency measure between the two (t and $t+1$) periods.

Next, the second group of constraints (i.e., $\sum_{j=1}^{n} y_{hjt}\lambda_{jt} - d_{ht}^{y} = y_{hkt}$) indicates that intermediate factors function as outputs at the t th period so that the frontier (i.e., $\sum_{j=1}^{n} y_{hjt}\lambda_{jt}$) is located above or on their observed values (y_{hkt}) because of $y_{hkt} + d_{ht}^{y}$. . Model (8.3) minimizes the slacks (d_{ht}^{y}). Meanwhile, the third group of constraints (i.e., $\sum_{j=1}^{n} y_{hjt+1}\lambda_{jt+1} + d_{ht+1}^{y} = y_{hkt+1}$) indicates that intermediate factors may function as inputs at the $t+1$ th period so that the frontier (i.e., $\sum_{j=1}^{n} y_{hjt+1}\lambda_{jt+1}$) locates below or on their observed values (y_{hkt+1}) because of $y_{hkt+1} - d_{ht+1}^{y}$. Model (8.7) minimizes the slacks (d_{ht+1}^{y}).

Third, the fifth and sixth constraints ($\sum_{j=1}^{n} \lambda_{jt} = 1$ and $\sum_{j=1}^{n} \lambda_{jt+1} = 1$) indicate that the sum of these intensities (weights) is unit at the t th and $t+1$ th periods, respectively. Such constraints imply that the degree of OE_{kt}^{t+1} is under variable RTS.

Fourth, we are interested in the performance between initial inputs (X_t) and final outputs (G_{t+1}) at the t+1 th period. Therefore, Eq. (8.9) measures $OE_{kt}^{t+1} = 1 - \left[\xi_{kt}^{t+1*} + \varepsilon_s\left(\sum_{i=1}^{m} R_i^x d_{it}^{x*} + \sum_{r=1}^{s} R_{rt}^g d_{rt}^{g*}\right)\right]$, The intermediate factors (Y_t and Y_{t+1}) make a linkage between the two stages. Figure 8.2 visually describes such relationship among the three groups of factors. Here, Model (8.7) for two periods is different from the standard DEA network approach. First, the standard approach looks for the level of "efficiency" (Sueyoshi & Sekitani, 2005), but Model (8.7) first attempts to identify that of "inefficiency". Then, it measures the level of efficiency by subtracting it from unity. Second, the two-stage approach has a connection by the two different types of intermediate variables. The proposed approach considers only the connection (to express a time lag for technology transition) between two periods, so being not the optimization for whole periods as found in the standard network models (e.g., Kao, 2018). Finally, the standard network approach does not incorporate a directional vector for optimization, but the proposed approach incorporates the vector in the formulation.

Fifth, before computing Model (8.7), we have divided each observed factor by the factor average. The rationale is that this study needs to avoid a case in which a large data set dominates the small one in the computation process. The data adjustment makes Model (8.7) to maintain the property of "unit invariance". See Sueyoshi and Sekitani (2009) for a mathematical definition on the property.

Finally, it is possible for us to separate Model (8.7) into two formulations related to the t th and $t+1$ th periods. However, such a separation does not produce any useful implications to this study because the linkage between two periods is the gist of Model (8.7) to understand the influence of a time lag for technology transition.

8.4 Application

Readers may find an application of the DEA time lag model in the following article:

T. Sueyoshi and Y. Ryu (2022) "Performance Assessment on Technology Transition from Small Businesses to the U.S. Department of Defense" Socio-Economic Planning Sciences. Vol. 80. No. 101177, pp. 1–13.

The research has used x_{1t} that is the amount of funding from a public agent, x_{2t} that is the number of employees, x_{3t} that is a technology distance from the expectation by the public agency at the first stage. Intermediate variables include $y_{1t} = y_{1t+1}$ that is the number of patents and $y_{2t} = y_{2+1}$ that is the number of social connections. The (desirable) output is g_{t+1} that is the amount of contracts from the public agency to businesses at the second stage.

This chapter does not document the practicality of the proposed approach, rather summarizing their empirical results prepared by Sueyoshi and Ryu (2022). We connect their work to the principles of ESG. The empirical importance of their study is summarized by the following three hypotheses.

Their first hypothesis examined the distribution of firms' *OE* scores and their skewness and kurtosis. Their study found that 60 companies out of 252 (or about 24% of study subjects) were efficient. While other companies were inefficient, there were 100 companies whose *OE* scores were more than 0.5. In total, 160 companies out of 252 (or about 63% of study subjects) had *OE* scores above 50%. The average *OE* score was 0.63. They could not find the assessment of technology transition performance. However, they enumerated some results of overall innovation performance assessments. Any technology development for ESG, including the military industry, depends upon technology shift under the policy change of a public agency (e.g., EPA). Such a regulation change often needs a time lag.

The second hypothesis assumed that Eigenvector Centrality in the funding network (EC) was positively related to *OE* scores, implying that firms' more connections to funders and/or stronger connections to big-sized DoD components enhanced their operational performance. However, they noted that the relationship was not linear but curvilinear with a U shape, suggesting that technology transition performance was not monotonically increasing as EC increased. Like the military industry, the EC on *OE* is important in enhancing ESG because the social connection (knowledge dissemination among members) is important in technological transfer even in environment protection as discussed in Fig. 2.6.

The result on social connection seems very strange to us in comparison with Chap. 7. The chapter has considered that the membership (connection) within OECD is not so important as we expect even though OECD indicates the importance of connection among members. Such a difference for technology transfer may be explained by a membership structure among many OECD countries and a business structure between DoD and subsidiaries in the USA. In other words, US military subsidiaries may easily attain the social connection under the control of DOD. However, nations with different economic and historical conditions cannot attain such social connection under the leadership of an international organization, such as OECD, that coordinates its member nations for technology transfer.

Third, they showed that small firms with the most central network position (top 25%) performed the best but they were followed by those with the least central network position (bottom 25%), not by those between them. This indicated firms with fewer connections to funders and/or weaker connections to them were also successful in transitioning their technologies. It implies that firms with specialized technology can stick to one or a few small or medium-sized DoD components and sustain the relationships as a specialized supplier. It verifies that not only connectedness (the number of connections) but also cohesion or conciseness (strong connections or low redundancy) may be effective for the growth of DoD awardees. They also suggest that technology specialization (targeting one agency with depth) as well as technology diversification (targeting multiple agencies with breadth) may be a useful strategy for firms in the federal procurement market. This result implies that the size of firms may be impotent in terms of technology transfer in both military industry and ESG development.

They found that the technological dissimilarity was important to the operational performance of DoD. Their result also shows that technological similarity may be better for small firms' technology transition, rather than technological dissimilarity. It implies that (a) high similarity may hinder small firms from developing networks with DoD and (b) the DoD may use its program as an avenue to acquire outcomes of incremental innovation rather than radical innovation. This finding may be applicable to the innovation for ESG development. For example, countries with similar economies may easily transfer ESG technology among them. Such a transfer may not occur if nations do not have a similar size of economy.

Table 8.2 summarizes differences between Chaps. 7 and this chapter. First, Chap. 7 has discussed a convergence of *UEM* and that of *UEI* in a long run. Meanwhile, this chapter has discussed *OE* that we measured by a time lag with five years. Second, Chap. 7 measured both *UEM* and *UEI* of OECD along with their convergence. Meanwhile, this chapter has measured *OE* of US DoD. We discuss the *OE* measurement from technology development. Both chapters are interested in technology shift and development even if the context has different forms and applications for green technology (in Chap. 7) and military technology (in this Chapter). Third, Chap. 7 has discussed the international dissemination of environmental technology among OECD nations, while this chapter has considered technology dissemination within the US military industry. We have obtained an opposite result. Chapter 7 indicates a difficulty in disseminating environmental technology among member nations in OECD. Why? All nations pay attention to their benefits, not the other countries. Meanwhile, Chapter 8 considers the dissemination within a single nation (USA) so that all firms can easily coordinate among subsidiary firms on military technology under the coordination of DoD. This may imply that OECD, or more globally UN, may plan and discuss international coordination among member nations in order to promote green technology transfer and dissemination as found in ESG and SDGs. However, it is not successful, very difficult, for them to attain such an international effort and coordination.

Table 8.2 Implementation differences between Chap. 7 and this chapter

Analytical features	Chap. 7	This chapter
Type of transfer	A convergence of UEM and UIM in a long run	A shift of OE in military technology
Research target	Environmental improvement in 37 OECD nations. UEM and UEI measure an annual change not only technology and management where environment is the first priority and economy is the second priority	Relationship between US DoD and its subsidiary firms in terms of technology development
Country	OECD nations (difficult in technology dissemination among member nations)	USA (not difficult for technology dissemination within the nation)
Implication	OECD membership has been not useful to reduce CO_2 emission because each nation has its own benefit first, not the whole nations	Social connections are important for developing military technology within the same nation (USA) Easy to obtain consensus among subsidiary firms

8.5 Extension

In the previous discussion, we assume that the intermediate factors ($y_{1t} = y_{1t+1}$ and $y_{2t} = y_{2t+1}$) occur between the first and second stages. However, there is a learning effect between the two stages so that the intermediate process may increase the number of patents (y_{1t}) and the number of social connections (y_{2t}). As a result, we cannot maintain the assumption in a practical perspective. In the case of $y_{1t} \neq y_{1t+1}$ and $y_{2t} \neq y_{2t+1}$, the whole computational framework may change as depicted in Fig. 8.3.

The formulation, corresponding to Fig. 8.3, becomes Model (8.11) where the intermediate process incorporates an organizational learning process so that it has $y_{1t} \neq y_{1t+1}$ and $y_{2t} \neq y_{2t+1}$. Of course, we can access the additional data set on the number of patents and the number of social connections. See Fig. 2.6 about an organizational learning. Mathematically, Fig. 8.3 has the three-stage process as follows:

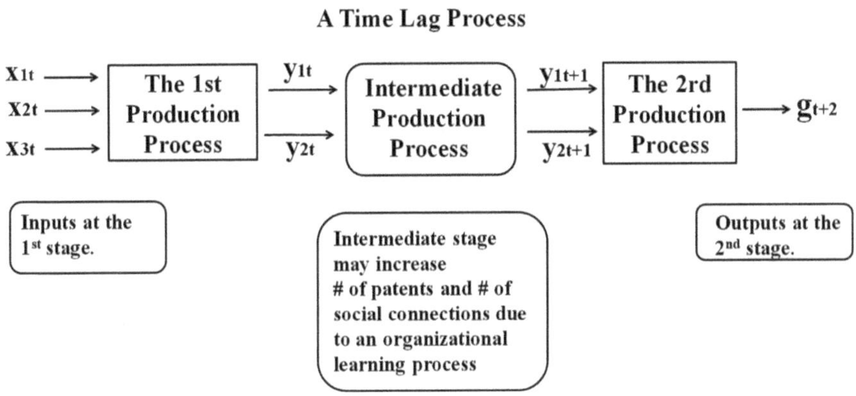

Fig. 8.3 Framework for time lag (three stages) assessment. *Note*: (a) Fig. 2.6 in Chap. 2 visually describes an organizational learning process that produces the increase (exactly speaking, non-decreasing) in social connections. We gradually establish "organizational learning" by communication and connection among members. (b) We can easily extend this type of formulation more than the three stages. The problem is data accessibility on the learning process in our research scope

$$
\begin{aligned}
&\textit{Maximize}\ \xi_{kt}^{t+2} + \varepsilon_s\left(\sum_{i=1}^{m} R_i^x d_{it}^x + \sum_{r=1}^{s} R_r^g d_{rt+2}^g\right) - \sum_{h=1}^{z}\left(d_{ht}^y + d_{ht+1}^y + d_{rt+2}^g\right) \\
&s.t.\quad \sum_{j=1}^{n} x_{ijt}\lambda_{jt} + d_{it}^x + \xi_{kt}^{t+2} x_{ikt} = x_{ikt} \quad (i = 1, \ldots, m), \\
&\qquad \sum_{j=1}^{n} y_{hjt}\lambda_{jt} - d_{ht}^y = y_{hkt} \quad (h = 1, \ldots, z), \\
&\qquad \sum_{j=1}^{n} y_{hjt}\lambda_{jt} + d_{ht}^y = y_{hkt} \quad (h = 1, \ldots, z), \\
&\qquad \sum_{j=1}^{n} y_{hjt}\lambda_{jt+1} - d_{ht+1}^y = y_{hkt+1} \quad (h = 1, \ldots, z), \\
&\qquad \sum_{j=1}^{n} y_{hjt+1}\lambda_{jt+1} + d_{ht+1}^y = y_{hkt+1} \quad (h = 1, \ldots, z), \\
&\qquad \sum_{j=1}^{n} g_{rjt+2}\lambda_{jt+2} - d_{rt+2}^g - \xi_{kt}^{t+2} g_{rkt+2} = g_{rkt+2} \quad (r = 1, \ldots, s), \\
&\qquad \sum_{j=1}^{n} \lambda_{jt} = 1\ (j = 1, \ldots, n),\ \sum_{j=1}^{n} \lambda_{jt+1} = 1\ (j = 1, \ldots, n),\ \sum_{j=1}^{n} \lambda_{jt+2} \geq 0\ (j = 1, \ldots, n), \\
&\qquad \lambda_{jt} \geq 0\ (j = 1, \ldots, n),\ \lambda_{jt+1} \geq 0\ (j = 1, \ldots, n),\ \lambda_{jt+2} \geq 0\ (j = 1, \ldots, n), \\
&\qquad \xi_{kt}^{t+2} : URS,\ d_{it}^x \geq 0 \quad (i = 1, \ldots, m), \\
&\qquad d_{ht}^y \geq 0\ (h = 1, \ldots, z),\ d_{ht+1}^y \geq 0 \quad (h = 1, \ldots, z)\ \& \\
&\qquad d_{rt+2}^g \geq 0\ (r = 1, \ldots, s).
\end{aligned}
\tag{8.11}
$$

For the three stages (t, $t + 1$, and $t + 2$), we determine the degree of Operational Efficiency (OE_{kt}^{t+2}) of the k th DMU as follows:

$$
OE_{kt}^{t+2} = 1 - \left[\xi_{kt}^{t+2*} + \varepsilon_s\left(\sum_{i=1}^{m} R_i^x d_{it}^{x*} + \sum_{r=1}^{s} R_r^g d_{rt+2}^{g*}\right)\right], \tag{8.12}
$$

where the inefficiency score and all slack variables exist on the optimality (*) of Model (8.11).

Here, it is necessary to make two comments on the methodological extension. One of the two concerns is that we can easily extend the learning process more than the three stages. The difficulty for the extension is our data accessibility. The other is that researchers who have been working on DEA network believe that the relationship between inputs and outputs is a "black box" so that we need to study DEA by using network models. A problem is that they have not demonstrated any computational feasibility on their network models. More importantly, such a black box feature may be a drawback, indeed, but it is simultaneously a methodological strength because it simplifies some complicated business phenomena by only inputs and outputs (so, a black box). That is an original rationale on why we have been long developed various DEA approaches. See Sueyoshi and Goto (2018) for the history of DEA.

8.6 Discussion

This chapter summarized the innovation performance of 252 firms which worked with US DoD in the context of technology transition. We followed the empirical results of Sueyoshi and Ryu (2022). According to the results of the two-stage DEA model with a time lag, more than a quarter of companies turned out efficient and the distribution of *OE* scores was left-skewed. We compared the technology innovation process for military applications with the technology dissemination for the development of ESG and SDGs.

Methodologically, this chapter utilized a new type of DEA, incorporating a time lag, which consisted of two-stage production processes. The proposed DEA formulation considered a time lag model to understand the technology transfer for military technology and the knowledge dissemination of environmental technology. We also discussed the models and implications in terms of technology transfer. The implications obtained in this chapter on military application may be useful for the development of ESG and SDGs.

It is trivial that ESG and SDGs discussed in Chap. 7 need international cooperation and technology dissemination. However, it is not easily to implement technology transfer for global sustainability development because it needs the cooperation of many nations which do not have an enough financial support for sustainability development. Meanwhile, in this chapter, we have discussed that the USA may relatively easily implement the technology transfer within the military industry because all members (military firms) are controlled by the US military admiration.

Finally, as a global policy, we can easily imagine that ESG and SDGs need to establish the worldwide international cooperation under the control of organizations such as UN and OECD. However, they do not function as we expect at the level that we expect to attain a high level of sustainability. The UN and OECD must reorganize their current decision making processes in the manner that the UN reorganizes the current Permanent Security Council member countries. Furthermore, the OECD allocates the number of employees based upon the amount of financial supports from member nations. The suggestion is due to the fact that technology development depends upon economic prosperity of each nation. The governance efforts on UN and OECD will be the first step to enhance the level of global ESG and SDGs, as we have discussed in Chap. 2.

References

Carayannis, E. G., Grigoroudis, E., & Goletsis, Y. (2016). A multilevel and multistage efficiency evaluation of innovation systems: A multi-objective DEA approach. *Expert Systems with Applications, 62*, 63–80.

Chen, K., & Guan, J. (2012). Measuring the efficiency of China's regional innovation systems: Application of network data envelopment analysis (DEA). *Regional Studies, 46*, 355–377.

Chen, X., Liu, Z., & Zhu, Q. (2018). Performance evaluation of China's high-tech innovation process: Analysis based on the innovation value chain. *Technovation, 74–75*, 42–53.

Chun, D., Chung, Y., & Bang, S. (2015). Impact of firm size and industry type on R&D efficiency throughout innovation and commercialization stages: Evidence from Korean manufacturing firms. *Technology Analysis and Strategic Management, 27*, 895–909.

Dougherty, D. (2017). Organizing for innovation in complex innovation systems. *Innovation, 19*, 11–15.

Katz, J. S. (2016). What is a complex innovation system? *PloS One, 11*(6), e0156150.

Kou, M., Chen, K., Wang, S., & Shao, Y. (2016). Measuring efficiencies of multi-period and multi-division systems associated with DEA: An application to OECD countries' national innovation systems. *Expert Systems with Applications, 46*, 494–510.

Kuah, C. T., & Wong, K. Y. (2011). Efficiency assessment of universities through data envelopment analysis. *Procedia Computer Science, 3*, 499–506.

Lal, B., Holloman, S. S., Mahoney, R., Martin, C. A., Koopman, K. A., Hallion, R. P., & Rood, S. A. (2013). *Expediting the transfer of technology from government laboratories into the aeronautics industry*. Institute for Defense Analyses.

Maine, E., & Seegopaul, P. (2016). Accelerating advanced-materials commercialization. *Nature Materials, 15*, 487–491.

Sharma, S., & Thomas, V. (2008). Inter-country R&D efficiency analysis: An application of data envelopment analysis. *Scientometrics, 76*, 483–501.

Sueyoshi, T. (1991). Algorithmic strategy for assurance region analysis in DEA. *Journal of the Operations Research Society of Japan, 35*, 62–76.

Sueyoshi, T., & Goto, M. (2013). A use of DEA–DA to measure importance of R&D expenditure in Japanese information technology industry. *Decision Support Systems, 54*, 941–952.

Sueyoshi, T., & Goto, M. (2018). *Environmental assessment on energy and sustainability by data envelopment analysis*. Wiley.

Sueyoshi, T., & Sekitani, K. (2005). Return to scale in dynamic DEA. *European Journal of Operational Research, 161*, 536–544.

Sueyoshi, T., & Sekitani, K. (2009). An occurrence of multiple projections in DEA-based measurement of technical efficiency: Theoretical comparison among DEA models from desirable properties. *European Journal of Operational Research, 196*, 764–794.

Sueyoshi, T., & Ryu, T. (2022). Performance assessment on technology transition from small businesses to the U.S. Department of Defense. *Socio-Economic Planning Sciences, 80*, 1–13.

Wang, Q., Hang, Y., Sun, L., & Zhao, Z. (2016). Two-stage innovation efficiency of new energy enterprises in China: A non-radial DEA approach. *Technological Forecasting and Social Change, 112*, 254–261.

Yu, A., Shi, Y., You, J., & Zhu, J. (2021). Innovation performance evaluation for high-tech companies using a dynamic network data envelopment analysis approach. *European Journal of Operational Research, 292*, 199–212.

Zabala-Iturriagagoitia, J. M., Voigt, P., Gutiérrez-Gracia, A., & Jiménez-Sáez, F. (2007). Regional innovation systems: How to assess performance. *Regional Studies, 41*, 661–672.

MIX
Papier aus verantwortungsvollen Quellen
Paper from responsible sources
FSC® C105338

If you have any concerns about our products,
you can contact us on
ProductSafety@springernature.com

In case Publisher is established outside the EU,
the EU authorized representative is:
Springer Nature Customer Service Center GmbH
Europaplatz 3, 69115 Heidelberg, Germany

Printed by Libri Plureos GmbH
in Hamburg, Germany